Men of Mark in Georgia

A Complete and Elaborate History of the State from its settlement
to the present time, chiefly told in biographies and auto-
biographies of the most eminent men of each
period of Georgia's progress and
development

Edited by
William J. Northen, LL.D.
Ex-Governor of Georgia

Advisory Board

HON. J. C. C. BLACK	HON. G. GUNBY JORDAN
HON. W. G. BRANTLEY	HON. P. W. MELDRIM
HON. ALLEN FORT	HON. W. J. NORTHEN
HON. DUPONT GUERRY	HON. HOKE SMITH
HON. W. M. HAMMOND	HON. J. M. TERRELL
HON. WALTER B. HILL	HON. MOSES WRIGHT

Illustrated

Historical Introductory by John Temple Graves, Editor

Southern Historical Press, Inc.
Greenville, South Carolina

Please direct all correspondence and book orders to:
SOUTHERN HISTORICAL PRESS, Inc.
PO Box 1267
Greenville, SC   29602-1267

Originally printed: Atlanta, GA. 1907
Copyright 1906 by: A.B. Caldwell
ISBN #978-1-63914-111-1
Printed in the United States of America

Table of Contents.

A consolidated index of all the volumes of this work will be found at the end of each volume.

Pubisher's Preface.

THE scope and character of this work are indicated by the title page.

From the earliest times biography has been one of the leading departments of literature. It has long been regarded as one of the great foundations of history. Emerson says, "There is no history, only biography." Carlyle puts the same thought in different form when he says, "History is but the essence of innumerable biographies."

The most attractive history of any movement which can be written is the story of the successes, the failures, the life-struggles of its leaders. So, in the production of this elaborate History of Georgia, the work has been built around the lives of those men who, by their intelligence, energy, and capacity, have, in every period of her history and in every department of her activities, made themselves potent factors in the progress and development of our great commonwealth.

The work comprises six volumes and is, in a general way, chronological.

The first volume contains the biographies of nearly a hundred of the leaders prior to 1800, covering the colonial, revolutionary, and formative periods of our history. No other single publication contains so much valuable biographical matter relating to the early men of Georgia.

In this volume we have drawn freely from McCall, Stevens, White, and Jones. *Biographical Sketches of Delegates from Georgia to the Continental Congress,* by the latter, has been especially helpful; and several of his sketches have been included, by permission, without modification. A few sketches from *White's Collections* have also been inserted unchanged.

The second volume presents the lives of those sturdy men, who, from 1800 till the War between the States, raised Georgia from a condition of struggling poverty to a position of great material wealth and prosperity and of civic greatness; men who took and held rank with the nation's leaders; men who pushed Georgia's frontier back from a narrow strip along the Atlantic coast to her present western limits.

Volume three is the war volume and contains sketches of the most brilliant galaxy of men that graces our annals. What a priceless heritage to any State is the story of such popular heroes as the Cobbs, Stephens, Toombs, Hill, Brown, Gordon, and scores of others, whose deeds will live in song and story! Their biographies will appear in the third volume.

The last three volumes tell the story of Georgia since the war, as illustrated by the men who have been, and are, the leaders of the State's political, professional, and industrial life.

In every period of the State's history, men have struggled up from obscurity to lives of broad usefulness and deserved success and have left the youth of the State, in their examples, a source of helpful inspiration. The record of these lives belongs to the State and should be placed within the reach of all.

As frequent references are made in these sketches to parishes, districts, counties, and other sub-divisions of the commonwealth which have frequently been changed, it has been thought wise to include in the first volume a chapter giving the political and judicial divisions of Georgia. For the careful compilation of this we are largely indebted to Mr. Charles Edgeworth Jones, of Augusta.

A list of all Georgia's representatives in the National Congress, from the organization of the government to the present time is also appended, as well as a list of her governors.

It was to be expected that matter, being brought together from various sources, would require some editing to make it harmonize with the general plan of the publication. This work has been carefully supervised by Hon. W. J. Northen, LL.D., whose patient co-operation has made "Men of Mark in Georgia" possible. Each sketch is signed by the writer.

Grateful acknowledgment is made to members of the Advisory Board for their co-operation and for valuable suggestions. They do not endorse a man's individual views or personal traits by awarding him a place in the work. Admission is based on merit and achievement.

Some of the best historical collections of the State have been freely put at our service; the leading educators have not only applauded our efforts, but have helped in the most substantial way; the press has given us hearty endorsement and co-operation; the public libraries have done their part. For all these we are deeply grateful.

The portraiture is an especially valuable feature of the publication. The numerous splendid steel engravings of Georgia's leaders with which its pages are embellished, make it a portrait gallery of Georgia's great men.   THE PUBLISHER.

Historical Introductory.

THE STATE OF GEORGIA is the first and most successful altruistic colony in the history of the world.

It was established upon the largest and loftiest principles of philanthropy that have moved an enterprise among men.

It was founded by as gallant and knightly a gentleman, as broad and noble a statesman, as ever gave his time and talents to the service of his fellow-men.

Originally a part of the vast domain of the Creek and Cherokee Indians, themselves the successors of a superior race, the territory which is now Georgia was first explored and conquered by Ferdinand DeSoto, of the Spaniards, and by Ribault, of the enterprising French. Though included in the grant to the Carolina proprietors the English did not occupy the region until the latter had fought the French and Spanish from its soil.

In 1732 the territory was ceded to a body of trustees organized for the purpose of establishing the colony of Georgia in America. Chief among these trustees was General James Oglethorpe, a nobleman and gentleman of England.

In the history of this country from the landing of Columbus to the times in which we live there has been no nobler gentleman, no braver soldier, no more generous citizen, no more unselfish pioneer, no better leader and no broader lover of the human race than this gentleman of England, first an ensign of the English army then a lieutenant of the first troop of the Queen's lifeguard; a soldier and aide-de-camp in the martial camp of Prince Eugene, and finally commander-in-chief of all the armies of imperial England herself.

There is much in James Oglethorpe to rank him in fame, in

character, and in service, with George Washington and Robert E. Lee. His unselfish courage, his lofty spirit, his stainless honor, his gentle courtesy, and his heroic loyalty to the causes he espoused, link him in character and in quality to the two immortal names in all our southern history.

It is something extraordinary in human nature that a gentleman of rank and fortune, with fame and high station looking him in the eyes, should give himself to a distant and uncultivated country with no other society but the unhappy people whom he went to assist, exposing himself freely to hardships, when he might have lived in the luxuries of a palace, and consecrating his prime of life to the heroic work of an altruistic pioneer when he might have worn the martial uniform of England in the dress parades of the greatest and most advanced civilization in the world.

But to the heart of this great and consecrated knight and gentleman there came the appeal of the unfortunate poor in England—many of them in prison for debt, some for political offenses, and many the victims of cruelty and injustice by the factions of the time.

The suffering and injustice dealt to this unhappy class attracted the attention of the British Parliament, and James Oglethorpe, a member of that Parliament, was chairman of a committee to look into their affairs. He visited the prisons, he saw that the poor men could not possibly earn money to pay their debts while they were shut up in confinement. He saw that under the industrial conditions of England it was not probable that they could prosper if they were set free. The land in England belonged then, as much of it belongs now in America, to the rich, and a poor man, although willing to work, had no right to plant this land and raise food for his family. The great Englishman, looking across the sea to the vast acres lying idle on the shores of America, saw there an opportunity for his unfortunate countrymen, and into his great heart and great mind there came the scheme to better them. Several of the noblemen about him were persuaded by him to unite their names and their influences in a petition to the King, and these gentlemen asked of George II. a grant of land in his Majesty's province of America where they could colonize the worthy and honest poor suffering in and near the city of London.

It has been thought and claimed in flippant and envious quarters that Georgia was settled by convicts and criminals from the debtor prisons of England. There is no better time than this to refute the charge.

When James Oglethorpe made public the announcement of his colony there were hundreds of people who came to join him. Many of these were rejected. No debtor was taken without the consent of the creditor. No criminals or wicked persons were accepted. No man was received who would leave a wife or little children dependent upon him for support. The debtor prisons were carefully examined and only the worthiest of these unhappy people were given an opportunity in this new land of hope and promise.

So that Georgia, named for the second English King who bore the name of George, was settled only by the best people among the needy population of the English from whom they came.

"Non sibi sed aliis," "Not for ourselves, but for others," was the motto of the colony because it was the motto of the man who made it, and this brave and generous commonwealth was settled by noble and unselfish gentlemen who, without one throb of selfish ambition, or without a tinge of prospective graft, simply builded out of their munificence and their philanthropy a state where the unfortunate could be free and could in time grow great and prosperous.

The altruistic spirit of our original Georgia had another expression in the fact that the English King and the English noblemen, who counseled him, saw that it was wise to plant in this territory of Georgia another colony of citizens who would be a bulwark between the Carolinas and the Spaniards and Indians in Florida and the territory to the west of them.

The motto set upon the seal has preserved to history and the future the principle upon which this great commonwealth was founded, and if Georgia, in the 173 years of her life, has done great things for the republic, for humanity and for history, who can doubt that the great original motto of unselfishness and service which gave it birth has rolled like an inspiration through its annals and through the hearts of its splendid people?

One other name deserves to be linked with that of Oglethorpe in these early and heroic times. Tomochichi, a savage, stood shoulder to shoulder in character and in service with the flower of England in this heroic work.

Tomochichi was the noble and aged chief of the tribe of the Yamacraws. He had been banished for political reasons from the tribe of the Lower Creeks, to whom he belonged, and had been chosen among the Yamacraws for his heroic virtues as their chief. Ninety-one years old the day Oglethorpe met him— tall, vigorous, dignified and manly, he was from that day to the day of his death the true, honored, loyal, noble and helpful friend of the colonists. He aided them in making treaties with the other tribes of Indians. He gave the protection of himself and his own tribe to the defense of the colony from outside depredations, and never, in summer or in winter, in success or in failure, did this noble and loyal savage fail to keep the faith of his friendship or the sanctity of his obligations to the founder of Georgia and his friends. Oglethorpe loved and honored him as long as he lived.

The first settlers of Georgia were from the class whom we have mentioned in our opening paragraph. The next ship from England brought over 250 emigrants of the same race and class of people. A later ship landed forty Israelites, who asked permission to join the colony and were received. Eight months later came that heroic band of Salzburgers who had been cast out of Germany on account of their religion. Two years later Oglethorpe brought over a colony of Swiss and Moravian emigrants, who settled near Ft. Argyle on the Ogeechee River.

And later still a number of Scotch Highlanders who settled at the town of New Inverness in the district of Darien, on the Altamaha.

These Salzburgers and Moravians especially brought to the colony an influx of courage, character, piety and industry which stiffened the colony and all of its descendants through all the years that followed until the present day. There is nothing nobler in the early composition of Georgia than these Salzburgers and Moravians who settled in Ebeneezer, in what is now Effingham County. The faith and the fidelity of them never wavered throughout all the storms which came to the colonists. Upon the ship that brought them came John Wesley, the great first Methodist of his times, and on the voyage there rose a storm so violent that the sea broke over the vessel and burst through the windows of the state cabin, drenching the inmates. The storm was so violent that a panic seized all on board except the Salzburgers and Moravians, who were so calm and so unterrified that John Wesley said that the example of these people had such an influence upon him as to make him doubt if he were really converted before he met them.

From this beginning and from this heroic and composite band of pioneers began the commonwealth which is known and honored throughout the republic and throughout the world to-day, and the individuality of its statesmen, the fidelity of its people, the salubrity of its climate, the heroic qualities of its people are the splendid possibilities of its moral and material future.

We have not time in this brief sketch to follow the brave battles of James Oglethorpe and his heroic companions against the Spaniards of that earlier time. He fought them in Florida and he fought them all over Georgia, with a courage and a dash and a brilliant series of successes which has scarcely been surpassed in the history of war. Always and everywhere James Oglethorpe was an aggressive soldier. He carried the battle to his enemies. He invaded Florida and went to the walls of St. Augustine, which he would have captured but for the disobedience of a subordinate who robbed him of his strength in the critical moment. He fought always with inferior forces against overwhelming odds, and he nearly always won.

Where the courage of the lion could not avail, he eked it out with the cunning of the fox. At Frederica in St. Simon's Island, where, with Spaniards in overwhelming force and with himself almost in their power, a deserter from his ranks fired his gun and fled to the Spanish camp. Whereupon Oglethorpe, with the strategy of the great general that he was, allowed a Spanish prisoner to escape, carrying a letter to the deserter, urging the Spaniards to attack him that night as he was in position to destroy them, or at least to remain over for two days when overwhelming re-inforcements would come to his aid. Upon receipt of the letter the Spaniards hoisted sail and fled without waiting to give battle, and Oglethorpe remained in possession of Frederica and the island.

The spirit of Oglethorpe and the earlier founders has run with a distinctly moral current through the history of the state. For a long series of years the spirit of temperance dominated the policies of the colony. One of its earliest laws prevented the sale of rum or whiskey, and the prohibition battle was one of the earliest fought in the colony, and in the province of Georgia was, as it is to-day, a large and vital issue among the people of this time. Negro slavery was upon high grounds prohibited in the colony, whose leaders encouraged the employment of white servants. These white servants bound themselves to work for their employers for seven years, and at the end of that time each received a portion of land for himself. This was a wholesome form of peonage which might very well be considered practical at the present day. Petition after petition for permission to use negro slaves in the colony was presented to the trustees, and was promptly and persistently refused. There was one in 1735, another in 1738. Several years later the colonists sent the son of their president to England to secure an appeal of the regulation. George Whitfield, perhaps the greatest preacher whose voice ever thundered in America, old or new, exerted his whole influence in favor of these petitions, but they were persistently refused. Public sentiment, however, continued to grow, and in a convention of the colonists, under the suggestions of the trustees, negro slaves, under certain rigid regulations, were by law admitted into Georgia on the 26th of October, 1794.

Georgia was first a colony, then a royal province, and finally, a state. After the passage of the trustees its first colonial governor was John Reynolds, and among the last of these governors was Archibald Bulloch, ancestor of President Roosevelt, himself one of the first and most forceful characters of these earlier times. John A. Treutlen was the first of the state governors, and was followed by a long line of splendid men, including John Houstoun, John Martin, Lyman Hall, Saml. Elbert, Ed. Telfair and George Handley. The first governor under the Federal

Constitution was George Walton, from whose administration, to the present day, there have been 42 governors of Georgia. Hoke Smith will be the 43d governor of Georgia under the Federal Constitution. Georgia has had five capitals. Savannah, Augusta, Louisville, Milledgeville and Atlanta. Georgia is the largest state east of the Mississippi River. Its area being 59,475 square miles, of which 495 square miles is water. It is 320 miles in length from north to south, and its greatest breadth is 250 miles. The state lies in both the Appalachian and coast plain regions, so that its climate is happily divided between the highlands and lowlands, affording almost every range of temperature desired for the changes demanded by the human system from time to time. It is one of the best drained states in the republic by the multitude of rivers and small streams which it contains. The Savannah is the largest river, while the Altamaha, the Oconee, the Ocmulgee, the Flynt, the Chattahoochee, the Ogeechee the Satilla and the Willacoochee are a joy to its agriculture and to its sportsmen.

In the Revolutionary War, Georgia ranked with Massachusetts in its sturdy stand for liberty and in its early defiance of the aggressions of the mother country. There were no patriots in all those times whose courage was higher and whose love of liberty was stronger than the sons of the heroic pioneers who had wrought out their liberty and their right to be free. The ringing words of Patrick Henry in the Virginia House of Burgesses were answered by a procession in Savannah, which denounced the Stamp Act and burned in effigy those persons who had favored submission to it. In the latter part of January, 1766, a body of 600 men arranged to assemble in Savannah to coerce the royal governor to destroy the stamps in his possession, so that not even the "Boston Tea Party" was more emphatic or more pioneer in its spirit of liberty than the sons of Georgia. The county of Liberty received its name because of the stalwart spirit of its people in opposition to any trespass upon their rights from the mother country. And Noble W. Jones, one of its sons, has been called one of the Morning Stars of Liberty in Georgia.

George Walton, Button Gwinnett and Lyman Hall were the Georgia signers of the American Declaration of Independence. Archibald Bulloch, ancestor of President Roosevelt, the distinguished patriot who had been president of both provincial congresses, had the honor of being elected the first president of the first republican government organized on Georgia soil. It was only because his official duties as president of Georgia imperatively held him and John Houstoun at home that they too were not among the Georgia signers of the Declaration of Independence. All through the long years of the Revolution such dauntless soldiers as the McIntoshes, Twiggs, Baker, Jackson, Elbert, Glascock, John White, Sergeant Jasper and Elijah Clark fought with heroic courage for the independence of the commonwealth, and their names have been embalmed in the memories of their descendants, and most of them given to the various counties of the state.

In all the noble list only John Adam Truetlen, the first governor of Georgia, lies with his grave unmarked, without a monument, and with not a Georgia county named in his honor. Some day when Georgia is at her best and highest she will erect a monument to this first governor of the independent state, and in the same hour she will unveil her tallest and stateliest shaft to her incomparable hero and founder, James Edward Oglethorpe.

Out of the Revolution, Georgia came crippled and impoverished to a large degree, but with undaunted spirit, for the building of the great commonwealth which we have to-day. In the establishment of her constitution, and in the early writing of her laws, there are great names which cannot be forgotten by the

Georgians to-day.   There were Abraham Baldwin and William Few, from Georgia, who signed the Constitution of the United States which Gladstone declared to be the most wonderful work ever struck off at a given time by the brain and purpose of man. There were James Gunn and James Jackson and George Matthews and Edward Telfair and Noble Jones, Button Gwinnett, Lyman Hall, John Hamby, Archibald Bulloch and Joseph Habersham and General James Jackson upon whose tomb is written, "A soldier of the Revolution. He deserved and enjoyed the confidence of a grateful country."   These are to be remembered by those who look with reverence to our earlier annals.

The sternest and most stirring period of politics that Georgia ever knew was in the battles between Troup and Clark.   One of the great men in these days was William H. Crawford, counted by many as the most majestic personality in our history. While he was Minister to France he was presented to Napoleon, and the great Corsican was so struck by the firm step, lofty bearing, manly vigor and magnificent blue eyes of the American that he bowed twice, a tribute never paid by Napoleon to any other man.   Crawford was at first the strong center of this period of politics.   He was the leader of one personal faction; on the other side was General John Clark, as fearless and as forceful as himself.   They fought a duel once over some charges which Crawford preferred against a friend of Clarke's, and Crawford was wounded in the wrist.   Their bitter enmity lasted through life, and their personal quarrel made, as long as they lived, two factions in the state of Georgia.   George M. Troup was an ardent admirer and supporter of Crawford, and became the leader of that party when ill health retired Crawford from politics.   Then began the fierce faction between Troup and Clark which lasted for so many years.   Clark defeated Troup for governor in 1819 by a majority of 13 votes; and in 1821, after another fierce contest, Clark defeated Troup again by a majority of two votes. In 1823 Troup did not have Clark to oppose him but Matthew Talbot, one of the leaders of the party, and Troup defeated Talbot by a majority of four votes. Troup was the last governor of Georgia elected by the Legislature, and in his next election was the first governor elected by the people. He was a man of splendid courage, great originality and uncompromising integrity. In his administration Georgia defied the Federal government in the matter of authority to make a treaty ceding to the Creek Indians a large area of valuable lands in Georgia, and the military forces of Georgia were actually assembled to put into execution their defiance of the United States. At this point the wisdom of the national government asserted itself and the contention of Troup and of Georgia was maintained.

The Whig party was always strong in Georgia, and when the secession movement broke out in 1860 there was a powerful unionist element in the state. The radical party, however, prevailed, and on January 18, 1861, the convention passed an ordinance of secession from the Federal government by 208 votes against 89 votes in opposition.

Georgia bore her share of sorrow and misfortune in the Civil War. In 1863 there was great want in North Georgia, and in 1864 the northwestern part of the state was laid waste and scores of thousands were living on government bounty. Georgia's soldiers fought with heroic courage in this civil strife. The gallant Gordon, the dashing Bartow and Bee, Clement A. Evans, Robert Toombs and a host of heroes won enduring fame and many scars in this battle between the states.

At the end of the war it was estimated that four-fifths of the public wealth of Georgia had been destroyed. On October the 30th, 1865, a convention of delegates · at Milledgeville repealed the ordinance of secession. On November the

7th the war debt was repudiated, and on December the 5th the Legislature ratified the 13th amendment. In 1866 the Legislature refused to ratify the 14th amendment, and by the reconstruction act of 1867 Georgia came once more under military rule. The Constitutional Convention, however, of 1867 and 1868 formed and accepted the new constitution which complied with the demands of the reconstruction act, and elected United States Senators; but when the Legislature afterwards expelled its colored members on the ground of inability and failed to ratify the 15th amendment, Georgia was for the third time excluded from Congress and subjected to military rule, under which the expelled negroes were re-instated and the 14th and 15th amendments were ratified. Georgia Representatives were not finally admitted to Congress until January, 1871.

Since the war between the States, Georgia has kept pace with her sister commonwealths in a splendid miracle of recuperation. Under Governor Bulloch, the public debt was increased from 5,000,000 to 16,000,000 dollars. After 1880 economic development became especially marked, and the growing of cotton, the manufacturing of iron, steel and oil, and mining of coal grew to large proportions. The Cotton Exposition in 1881, and the Cotton States International Exposition of 1895, both held in Atlanta, testify to the magnificent resources and to the future prosperity of the state. While outranked by the Carolinas in the manufacture of cotton, and by Alabama in the matter of iron, Georgia has a great variety of manufacturing interests and excels these two states in the sum total of manufactured products.

There is something perhaps in the earlier history of this commonwealth which stamps a peculiar individuality upon the public men of Georgia. In all forums, state, national and international, in which they have had a voice, they have received a recognition to talent and to conviction such as has been accorded to few of the representatives of other states. When we look back upon a long line of our splendid sons, to John Forsyth, John McPherson Berrien, and William H. Crawford, to General James Jackson, to Troup and Clark, to Toombs, Stevens, Hill, Herschell V. Johnson, to Charles J. Jenkins, Joseph E. Brown, Gordon, Colquitt, and to Henry Grady, and to the impression which they made upon the times in which they lived and the men among whom they moved, we must believe there is something in the inheritance of Oglethorpe; something in the unselfishness of the earlier colonists, something in the heroic purposefulness of the pioneers of this commonwealth which has pulsed in the veins of all their descendants and made the public men of Georgia resolute, definite, sweepingly eloquent, and profoundly impressive upon the outside world.

In this year of grace in which we are giving to the public, to our country, and to the leading citizens of the state "MEN OF MARK IN GEORGIA," we cannot but feel that there are a thousand traditions in the past and a thousand heroic memories behind them whose force has not expired in the creation of our former statesmen and heroes, but that in the bosoms of the present vigorous and high-minded group of men, who are making history in the state, the Georgia of the present, in its superb and thrilling commercial life, in its wonderful industrial development, is not to forget the lofty and the heroic spirit of the pioneers who lived for something better than gain, and who have sent down the aisles of the century the message of patriotism and integrity and statesmanship to the MEN OF MARK who are here to-day, and who will surely answer to the roll-call of to-morrow.

JOHN TEMPLE GRAVES.

Benjamin Andrew.

BORN in Dorchester, South Carolina, about 1730, Mr. Andrew led the life of a planter. He came of that sturdy Puritan congregation which, abandoning England in 1630, after a residence of some sixty-five years in Massachusetts, removed to South Carolina and formed a settlement on the northeast bank of the Ashley River about eighteen miles above Charles Town. In 1754 Mr. Andrew, bringing his family with him, left Dorchester in South Carolina, and made a new home in the Midway District, subsequently constituting a part of St. John's Parish in the Colony of Georgia. Here he became the owner of a swamp plantation and engaged in the cultivation of rice.

In the preliminary discussions and demonstrations which eventuated in a declaration of independence on the part of the parish of St. John and afterwards of the Colony of Georgia, Mr. Andrew allied himself with the revolutionists, and, in company with Lyman Hall, Button Gwinnett, Daniel Roberts, Samuel Stevens, Joseph Wood, Daniel Baker, and other local patriots, was earnest in the support of the rights of the American provinces in their struggle with Great Britain for liberation from kingly rule.

In the spring of 1773 William Bartram, the naturalist, who, at the request of Dr. Fothergill, of London, had undertaken a visit to the Floridas "for the discovery of rare and useful productions of nature, chiefly in the vegetable kingdom," gives us this glimpse of the home of Mr. Andrew, then not many miles distant from Midway Meeting House in St. John's Parish. "In the evening," writes Mr. Bartram, "I arrived at the seat of the Hon. B. Andrew, Esq., who received and entertained me in every respect as a worthy gentleman would a stranger, that is, with hearty welcome, plain but plentiful board, free conversation, and liberality of sentiment. I spent the evening very agreeably, and the day following (for I was not permitted to depart sooner) I viewed with pleasure this gentleman's exemplary improvements in agriculture, particularly in the growth of rice, and in his machines for shelling that valuable grain, which stands in the water almost from the time it is sown until within a few days before it is reaped, when they draw off the water by sluices, which ripens it all at once; and when the heads, or panicles, are dry ripe, it is reaped and left standing in the field in small ricks until the straw is quite dry, when it is hauled and stacked in the barnyard. The machines for cleaning the rice are worked by the force of water. They stand on the great reservoir which contains the waters that flood the rice-fields below.

"Towards the evening we made a little party at fishing. We chose a shaded retreat in a beautiful grove of magnolias, myrtles, and sweet bay trees, which were left standing on the bank of a fine creek, that from this place took a slow serpentine course through the plantation. We presently took some fish, one kind of which is very beautiful; they call it the red-belly. It is as large as a man's hand, nearly oval and thin, being compressed on each side; the tail is beautifully formed; the top of the head and back of an olive green, besprinkled with russet specks; the sides of a sea-green, inclining to azure, insensibly blended with the olive above, and beneath lightens to a silvery white or pearl color, elegantly powdered with specks of the finest green, russet and gold; the belly is of a bright scarlet red or vermilion, darting up rays or fiery streaks into the pearl on each side; the ultimate angle of the branchiostega extends backwards with a long spatula, ending with a round or oval particoloured spot representing the eye in the long feathers of a peacock's train, verged round with a thin flame-coloured membrane, and appears like a brilliant ruby fixed on the side of the fish; the eyes are large, encircled with a fiery iris; they are a voracious fish, and are easily caught with a suitable bait.

"The next morning I took leave of this worthy family, and sat off for the settlements on the Alatamaha, still pursuing the high road for Fort Barrington, till towards noon, when I turned off to the left, following the road to Darian, a settlement on the river twenty miles lower down and near the coast."

We offer no apology for making this quotation, because it conveys a pleasant impression of person and place. Of the first Executive Council convened upon the election of John Adam Treutlen as Governor of Georgia in 1777, Benjamin Andrew was chosen President, with Samuel Stirk as clerk. Three years afterwards Mr. Andrew was elected a member of the Continental Congress. His associates were Edward Telfair, George Walton, Lyman Hall, and William Few. Upon the conclusion of the war of the Revolution Mr. Andrew became an Associate Justice for the county of Liberty, and in that capacity sat for several terms with Chief Justice Walton.

One of his sons bore arms in the primal contest for freedom, and subsequently removed from Liberty County to Washington, Wilkes County, where, on the 3d of May, 1794, a son was born unto him—James Osgood Andrew by name—who acquired some prominence as a Bishop of the Methodist Episcopal church, South. The honorable Benjamin Andrew died in Liberty County, Georgia, toward the close of the last century.

C. C. JONES, JR.

John Baker.

THE State of Georgia honored herself when, in 1825, she named one of her greatest agricultural counties for that affluent farmer, partisan soldier, and useful citizen, Colonel John Baker. He was a son of Benjamin Baker, who was a soldier under the illustrious Oglethorpe in his expedition against St. Augustine in 1740, and who was very active in securing a proper constitution for the Province of Georgia. He was also clerk of Midway Church for twenty-seven years, and his manuscripts are valuable historical documents. Colonel John Baker served the colony of Georgia as a Lieutenant in the King's Troops.

Our subject was elected a delegate to the Georgia Provincial Congress, which met in the Long Room at Tondee's Tavern in Savannah on the 4th of July, 1775. He was also a member of the Georgia Council of Safety. In January, 1776, he was elected by a company of St. John's parish as their captain, and on January 8, 1776, was commissioned as "Captain of the Saint John's Riflemen." Being assigned to the fort at Sunbury, he took charge and repaired the entrenchment around the fort and assisted in putting this important work in first-class condition with the materials that could be procured. He marched with seventy-five militiamen and made an attack on Fort Wright on the St. Mary's River; but, owing to the treachery of the McGirths and other members of his company who deserted and carried off nearly all his horses, he was obliged to retreat. The McGirths left a record of cruelty and bloodshed during the war that would cause the most savage to blush.

McCall says: "At the White House in Liberty County, 1779, at the head of a few militia, he defeated the enemy. Among those of the enemy killed was Lieutenant Gray; his head was almost severed from his body by one blow from the sabre of that relentless and fearless hard fighter, Robert Sallette."

A short time after this, Colonels Baker and Twiggs, commanding the Georgia Militia, made an attack upon McGirth's men at Midway Meeting House, where they captured some prisoners. Colonel Baker, learning that some Continental officers and prisoners on parole were going from Savannah to Sunbury, went in search of them and overtook them at Mrs. Arthur's house. Captains Mosby, Nash, Booker, Hicks, and Templeton and Lieutenants Mosely, Davenport, and Mitchel were captured and with the other prisoners were sent up to Cannouchee. On March 3, 1776, we find Colonel Baker in Savannah with Captain James Screven, demanding the release of Captain Rice and his crew who had fallen into the hands of the British while attempting to dismantle some vessels at Savannah wharf. Meeting with disappointment, Colonel McIntosh with three hundred men marched to Yamacraw Bluff and threw up some breastworks. The space between Montgomery and Williamson streets is thought to be the exact location where the fortifications stood. Here he mounted three four-pounders. Lieutenant Daniel Roberts and Mr. Raymond Demere were sent with a flag of truce to demand the release of Rice, and were themselves taken prisoners. A demand from shore being made for the prisoners, and an insulting reply being given, two shots from the battery were fired at the vessels. When the signal from the British read that if two others of proper rank were sent they would treat with them, Colonel John Baker and Captain James Screven were sent. Upon arriving close to the vessels the British returned insulting replies to their demands, and Colonel Baker fired upon the speaker, and he and Captain Screven beat a hasty retreat to the shore. Fortunately no one in the boat was killed.

Our battery opened fire and kept it up for four hours, during which time Commodore Bowen and others fired the rigging of the Inverness, when she drifted upon the Nelly, setting her and other vessels on fire. The British officers and men fled and crossed Hutchinson's Island, but many were killed; three vessels were destroyed, six dismantled and two escaped. Colonel Baker was wounded at Bull Town Swamp, where he fought General Prescott with a few militiamen.

Colonel Baker and Maj. John Jones, having had a disagreement, were about to fight a duel. They were both to fight in full uniform on horseback and with their broadswords; the hour arrived, when, unexpectedly, General James Screven appeared on the ground. He knew the determined courage of these men, and, approaching them, he said: "My friends and companions in arms! Can it be, when your country is bleeding at every pore and needs the support of her sons in her defence, that you are about to sacrifice your lives to feelings of personal hostility and revenge? If you cannot extend to each other the hand of confidence and friendship, for your country's sake, do not destroy each others lives." The appeal was heard; the drawn swords were returned to their scabbards; and the spirit of patriotism in these great heroes triumphed over the desire for private revenge. To live and war for dear ones and country was more noble than to die for themselves. After the Revolution Colonel Baker served against the Indians with General James Jackson.

Colonel Baker died June 3, 1792, in Liberty county, the place of his birth, and his sacred ashes rest at Sunbury. Among his honored descendants are Wm. Harden, member of the Georgia Legislature and librarian of the Georgia Historical Society for the last thirty years, and Hon. Marcus S. Baker, tax receiver of Chatham county.

WM. BERRIEN BURROUGHS, M.D.

Engraved by J.B. Forrest from a drawing by E. G. Leutze after an original sketch by R. Fulton.

ABRAHAM BALDWIN.

Abraham Baldwin.

A MONG the notable men who helped to mould the character of the State of Georgia as well as fix the destiny of the government of the United States, Abraham Baldwin played a conspicuous part. He seemed to have been one of those "providential men" who are set apart in the scheme of human development to fill a large place in public affairs. No thoughtful student of history can contemplate his career nor measure his achievements without saying "for these things was this man come to the kingdom."

He was born November 6, 1754, at Guilford, Connecticut. Of his early life we know little. We have hints that he was a dreamy, thoughtful lad, asking questions often that his elders could not answer. The loss of his mother at an early age put a shadow over his boyhood life that made him even more reserved and determined to honor her memory by developing his powers as best he could and filling a useful career. Longfellow described a boy in his case when he says:

> " A boy's will is the wind's will,
> But thoughts of my youth are long, long thoughts."

His father must have given him exceptionally good advantages for he graduated from Yale College in 1772 at eighteen years of age. He was regarded as one of the best mathematical and classical students of his day and was immediately employed as tutor in his *alma mater*. He filled a professorship in this institution until 1779, when he began the study of Theology. He then served as chaplain in the Continental Army until the close of the war.

Upon the termination of hostilities between this country and England he began the study of law. With unflagging industry the intense grasp of his powers soon mastered the science, and under the advice of General Nathanael Greene he moved to Savannah, Georgia, in 1784, and began the practice of his profession. At Savannah his commanding personal bearing and his magnetic intellectual force brought him into immediate notice. It may sound strange to readers of our own time, but within three months from the date of his arrival in Savannah he had been elected a member of the Georgia Legislature. When he took his seat in the Legislature the providence of his coming to Georgia began to be revealed. His first dream of a great commonwealth was a commonwealth of educated constituents. He drew a charter for a complete system of State education, supported by taxation of all property in the State, with a great university at the head and common schools at the base. The charter, born in the brain of this militant educationist, lawyer, and statesman, adopted by the State before the Federal Constitution had been ratified, has come down to us practically unaltered to this day. His provisions have been, one after another, put into execution by successive legislation until now the system, as outlined by Baldwin in 1784, is well nigh complete. Only one provision indeed remains to be added, viz.: the provision for secondary schools in each county in the State.

From the preamble to this charter, which as a whole has evoked encomiums from the learned and the virtuous, we make the following extract as illustrating the wisdom and patriotism of Mr. Baldwin:

"As it is the distinguishing happiness of free governments that civil order should be the result of choice and not of necessity, and the common wishes of the people become the laws of the land, their public prosperity and even existence very much depend upon suitably forming the minds and morals of their citizens. When the minds of the people in general are viciously disposed and unprincipled, and their conduct disorderly, a free government will be attended with greater confusions and evils more horrid than the wild, uncultivated state of nature. It can only be happy when the public principles and opinions are properly directed and their manners regulated. This is an influence beyond the reach of laws and punishments, and can be reclaimed only by religion and education. It should therefore be among the first objects of those who wish well to the national prosperity to encourage and support the principles of religion and morality, and early to place the youth under the forming hand of society, that by instruction they may be moulded to the love of virtue and good order. Sending them abroad to other countries for their education will not answer these purposes, is too humiliating an acknowledgment of the ignorance or inferiority of our own, and will always be the cause of so great foreign attachments that upon the principles of policy it is inadmissible."

The State of Georgia was then in a most impoverished condition. The losses and distractions experienced during the war just ended had been immense. In the face of every retarding circumstance Mr. Baldwin compassed this important measure; and the University of Georgia to-day is a living monument of his wisdom, prescience and patriotism. The munificence of the Hon. John Milledge and the co-operative aid of Governor John Houstoun and the Honorables James Habersham, William Few, Joseph Clay, William Houstoun, and Nathan Brownson, were potent factors in the consummation of this educational scheme, which for a century has proven of incalculable benefit to the commonwealth of Georgia. Had he performed no other public duty than this, Mr. Baldwin's title to the gratitude of succeeding generations would have been unquestioned.

His political advancement was rapid. In 1785 he was elected by the Legislature to a seat in the Continental Congress, and from that time until the day of his death he remained in the public service. When he died, four years of his second term as United States Senator from Georgia had not expired.

Of the convention, which in 1787 framed the Constitution of the United States, he was a very active member. It is stated on good authority that some of the essential clauses of that memorable instrument were formulated by him.

"His manner of conducting business" says the author of the sketch which appears in the fourth volume of *The National Portrait Gallery of Distinguished Americans* "was worthy of the highest commendation; he may have wanted ambition to make himself brilliant, but he never wanted industry to make himself useful. His oratory was simple, forcible, convincing. His maxim of never asserting anything but what he believed to be true could not fail to be useful in carrying convictions to others. Patient of contradiction, and tolerant to the wildest opinions, he could be as indulgent to the errors of judgment as if he had stood the most in need of such indulgence for himself."

Mr. Baldwin was a Federalist. So manly was his course in Congress and in the Senate of the United States, so conservative were his views, so conscientious was his conduct in the discussion of all constitutional questions, and so steadfast his adherence to what he conceived to be the cardinal principles of government, that he acquired and retained in a wonderful degree the confidence of the party to which he was attached, the respect of those who held different notions, with regard to the political questions which then agitated the country, and the approbation of his constituents. Of him it has been truthfully said he "died with the consciousness of having faithfully and fearlessly filled the measure of his public duties."

Col. C. C. Jones, in *Biographical Sketches of Delegates to the Continental Congress,* says:

"In private life he was correct in all of his habits and given to benevolent deeds. Never having married he expended his accumulations in assisting worthy young men in acquiring an education and in establishing them in business. In this regard his charities were akin to those which so beautified the life of Alexander Stephens. Upon the death of his father in 1787 he assumed in large measure the payment of his debts and the maintenance and education of his six orphan children. So far as the record stands the reputation of Mr. Baldwin for purity of character, honesty of purpose and act, fidelity to trusts reposed, and genuine benevolence, is most admirable."

To Connecticut is Georgia greatly indebted for Lyman Hall and Abraham Baldwin. Of their adopted citizenship she is justly proud, and in token of her appreciation of their virtuous lives and useful services she perpetuates their names in two of her counties.

Mr. Baldwin died in harness as a senator from Georgia at the national capital, on the 4th of March, 1807. His last illness was so short and his death so unexpected that none of his relatives, except his brother-in-law, were able to be present at his funeral. But it seemed as if the public in general were his near relatives. There have rarely been witnessed more general and genuine marks of regret at the loss of any of the great benefactors of our country, particularly among the members of Congress from Georgia. In this State his loss was most deeply felt, though very sensibly perceived in the councils of the Union. Though his funeral was two days after Congress dissolved, many members stayed expressly to attend it. His remains were deposited by the side of his old friend, General James Jackson, his former colleague, whom he had followed to the grave just one year before. G. R. GLENN.

John Berrien.

THIS soldier of the Revolution was born at Rocky Ford, four miles from Princeton College, New Jersey, in the historic "Judge Berrien Mansion" which his father owned and occupied, and from which General Washington wrote and delivered his farewell address to his army, November 2, 1783. It was while General Washington was the guest of the Berrien family at this house that he signed, on September 3, 1783, the Treaty of Peace with Great Brittain. The sloping green in front of this historic house still held the camps of the American soldiers who had won the independence of the colonies.

John Berrien's father was Judge John Berrien, one of the Justices of Nova Cæsarea; his mother was Margarette (Eaton) Berrien. He received an excellent school education and, at an early age, became an officer in the King's army. When the colonies rebelled against the King he resigned his office, and was shortly after commissioned Second Lieutenant in the First Battalion of Continental troops, Company B., commanded by Captain Oliver Bowen. He was at this time only fifteen years old.

Georgia was slow to rebel against the King, but quick to raise troops for her defence after she had thrown off allegiance to the Crown. From General Lachlan McIntosh's order book we find that on the 16th of April, 1777, with headquarters at Sunbury, he commanded "all the Continental troops to parade at three o'clock, when the officers are to take the oath of fidelity to the United States of America, before a civil Magistrate. Lieutenant Berrien is appointed to act as Aide-de-Camp to the General, with the rank of Captain."

When General McIntosh was appointed by General Washington to a command in the Northern Army, Captain Berrien was selected by him as Brigade-Major, and in that capacity he joined the army at Valley Forge. He was very conspicuous in the battle of Monmouth, where he was wounded in the head. He was in several other engagements, and continued in service until the close of the Revolution. On the return of peace, being qualified by an active and well-cultivated mind and correct judgment for public usefulness, the greater part of his life was occupied in offices of honor and trust, the duties of which he performed with integrity and diligence.

He was decorated by the hands of the illustrious Washington with the "Eagle," the emblem of the Society of the Cincinnati. This "Eagle" is known as the "Washington-Berrien Eagle." A die, made from it by Tiffany, has been adopted by the Georgia Society as its "Eagle." This relic is now owned by the writer of this sketch, a great-grandson of Major Berrien, having descended to him through his mother, who was the oldest daughter of Senator John Macpherson Berrien.

> " The flag of the ' Eagle ' will never be furled,
> Though battle skies scowl with the wrath of a world;
> Like the brave bird, its emblem, the wilder the blast
> The broader its storm-scorning folds will be cast."

Major Berrien went through all the chairs of the Society of the Cincinnati, and while holding the office of President held also the office of State Treasurer.

In 1784, he was commissioned Captain of the first Cavalry Company raised after the war, and this company, "The Liberty Independent Troops," is one of the oldest in America, having passed its one hundred and twenty-second year.

Major Berrien died in Savannah, and is buried in the old

Savannah cemetery. Upon his marble shaft is the following inscription:

"Major John Berrien, died 1815. In early youth he drew his sword in defence of his country, and served with reputation in the war of the Revolution."

WM. BERRIEN BURROUGHS, M.D.

Oliver Bowen.

FEW Georgians did more for the cause of America's independence in the Revolutionary War and received less recognition than this gallant patriot, soldier, sailor and privateer. No other Georgian rose to the rank of Commodore in the Navy.

On the fourth of July, 1775, we find him a delegate to the provincial Congress of Georgia. In December, 1775, he was a member of the "Council of Safety" and took an active part in its deliberations. In January, 1776, his name appears as Captain of Second Company of First Battalion of Georgia Continental troops. Georgia was so thinly settled that she was required to raise only one battalion of 750 men. This was commanded by Colonel Lachlan McIntosh, "Battalions being substituted for regiments to get rid of the rank of Colonel, which had occasioned difficulty about exchanges." The same orders required Massachusetts to raise fifteen battalions.

As early as July 10, 1775, Captain Bowen, commanding a Georgia armed schooner carrying ten carriage guns and many swivels, and manned by a detachment of fifty picked men from Savannah, captured a British armed schooner direct from London, at the mouth of the Savannah River. This ship was commanded by Captain Maitland and had, besides other military stores, 14,000 pounds of gunpowder; 5,000 pounds were shipped to Philadelphia, a part of which was used by the American army at Bunker Hill; 9,000 pounds were kept for Georgia and South Carolina military forces. This was the first provincial vessel commissioned for naval purposes in the Revolution, and this was the first capture made by any order of any congress in America.

On August 28, 1776, the Committee of the Council of Safety recommended that Captain Bowen be sent to Cape Francois and letters be given him to the Governor; that he be given power to open commercial relations with her capital merchants; that he be allowed to contract for armed vessels to the amount of 3,000 pounds; also to purchase arms, ammunition and warlike stores to the amount of 5,000 pounds, and to charter vessels, etc.; to enlist men in the service of this colony, giving them bounty and monthly salaries, and pledge the faith of this province for the same. Also that he be furnished with a copy of the Declaration of the Independent States of America and the Proclamation of our President, offering French subjects free trade.

In the spring of 1776, when the British had captured by treachery eleven rice-laden ships at Savannah wharf, Captain Bowen, at the head of several prominent citizens, set fire to the schooner Inverness and cut her cable. She drifted down the river and set fire to the Nelly, and in this novel way of battle many officers and men of the British Navy were killed and wounded, three vessels were destroyed, six were dismantled, and only two escaped to sea.

The following record will be of interest:

"State of Georgia: This day, January 30, 1777, in Convention, ordered that the House do proceed immediately to ballot for a Commodore. The House proceeded to ballot accordingly, when on closing the polls it appeared that Oliver Bowen, Esquire, was elected Commodore or Commander of our Naval Department. A true extract from minutes of Convention. Jas. Wood, Jr., Clerk, House of Assembly."

He appears to have had much trouble in getting his land warrant issued. Dr. Geo. G. Smith in his *Georgia History* says: "To those who served in the Navy only nine land warrants were issued."

These records are to be found in the office of the Secretary of State:

"SAVANNAH, GA., October 28, 1783.

Whereas, some doubts have arisen with the Governor and Council respecting the rank of the appointment of Oliver Bowen to the command of the gallies, and the Journals of the Assembly of that time being lost, we do certify that we were members of the Assembly for the county of Chatham in the year 1777, and Oliver Bowen was to our certain knowledge at the time appointed to the command of the gallies, with the rank, pay and emoluments of a Colonel in the land army.

JAS. HABERSHAM.

THOS. STONE.

This was allowed.

D. REES,

Secretary of Executive Council."

"Georgia: These are to certify that Oliver Bowen, Esq., as Commodore, is entitled to 1,000 acres of land as a bounty agreeable to an act and resolution of the General Assembly passed at Augusta, August 19, 1781, and the resolution of Congress 16th of September, 1776.

Given under my hand, Savannah, 27th day of January, seventeen hundred and eighty-four. JNO. HOUSTOUN.

Attest: *D. Rees,* Secretary.

Bounty from Congress 500 acres. Bounty from State 500 acres."

Commodore Bowen owned his own vessel, and made many captures of parties along the Georgia coast, who were carrying

2

away provisions for the British. He was a native of the State of Rhode Island. He died on the 11th of July, 1800, at the age of 59, and was buried in St. Paul's churchyard, Augusta, where a stone was placed to his memory by fraternal affection.

The inscription on this stone reads as follows:

"This stone is placed by the Fraternal affection, to the memory of Commodore OLIVER BOWEN a native of the State of Rhode Island where he sprang from an honourable Stock. He departed this Life July the 11th A. D. 1800 in the 59th year of his Age.

A Patriot of 1775—he was among the first in this State who steped forth in Vindication of our Rights. His life equally with his property were often risqued in the Cause.

His Widow, his Relations, and his many Friends will ever regret the departure of the Benevolent and Honest Man."

WM. BERRIEN BURROUGHS, M.D.

Nathan Brownson.

G EORGIA is indebted to New England for Dr. Nathan Brownson. He was born in Woodbury, Connecticut, on May 14, 1742, the sixth child and the fifth son of Timothy Brownson. His grandfather was Cornelius Brownson. His mother was Abigail (Jenner) Brownson, youngest daughter of Samuel and Hannah Jenner, also of Woodbury.

He was graduated from Yale College in 1761. He studied medicine and probably began the practice in his native town, where he married and had one or two children.

About 1764, Dr. Brownson, at the suggestion of Dr. John Dunwody, removed to Georgia and purchased a plantation of some five hundred acres in St. John's parish, in what is now Liberty county, about two miles from the present village of Riceboro, and a little more than thirty from Savannah. He owned a few slaves and cultivated rice. He also followed his profession, being the first physician to practice south of the Ogeechee.

He soon acquired a reputation in the community for honesty, intelligence, and patriotism as well as professional skill, and when the cause of liberty was agitated he was put forward as the spokesman for the community. Accordingly when the Provincial Congress was convoked in Savannah on July 4, 1775, we find Dr. Brownson with eleven other prominent citizens representing St. John's parish.

The following year, 1776, he served with Jonathan Bryan on a commission appointed by the Council to report on the advisability of an "irruption into East Florida." They reported that "an irruption into the province of East Florida will be attended with the most salutary consequences to this province, and, of course, render service to the whole continent."

He was a delegate from Georgia to the Continental Congress from 1776 to 1778 and is credited with faithful and efficient services. At one time during the war he served in the capacity of surgeon of a Georgia brigade in the Continental Army. On March 28, 1781, Congress appointed him as Deputy-Purveyor of the hospitals.

At that time the Governor of Georgia was elected by the Legislature, and received a salary of five hundred pounds per annum. Dr. Brownson was Speaker of the Legislature at the session of 1781, and on August 16th was by that body made Governor to succeed Stephen Heard. The address of the House to him upon his election was highly complimentary to his character. After his election he issued the following proclamation: "Since the present crisis demands the most vigorous exertions on the part of each individual to finish the glorious contest in which we are engaged, and justice requires that the weight of the difficulties still to be surmounted before we can reach that happy period should be equally divided; and since the present situation of Georgia claims the assistance of all her citizens, in consequence of a resolution of the Honorable House of Assembly of this State, I publish the present proclamation, by which it is decreed that all who consider themselves as citizens shall return hither, within the different spaces of time hereafter prescribed; that is to say, if they are in South Carolina within thirty days, if in North Carolina in sixty days, if in Virginia ninety, and if further northward four months; and we assure by these presents, all who neglect or refuse to conform to them, that in consequence of the aforesaid resolution their landed property will be charged with a treble tax, commencing from the expiration of the time fixed for their return.

Signed by my hand, and sealed with this great seal of the State at Augusta, 24th of August, 1781, in the sixt.. year of the Independence of America.

NATHAN BROWNSON."

On January 8, 1782, he was succeeded as Governor by John Martin, and on the 6th of the following June was re-appointed by Congress to the care of the Southern hospitals.

After the war he still kept in touch with public affairs and his interest in public education is evidenced by the fact that in 1784 he was appointed one of the Trustees of the State College which later became the University of Georgia. He was a member of the State Convention in 1788 which ratified the Constitution of the United States and also of the Georgia Constitutional Convention of 1789.

Under the new Constitution he was chosen first President of the Senate which met in Augusta on the 3d of November, 1789. He served in this capacity at the sessions of 1790 and 1791. He was also a Commissioner on behalf of the State to superintend the erection of the public buildings at Louisville in Jefferson county, whence the seat of government was removed from Augusta.

Thus it will be seen that there was scarcely any time when this conscientious and efficient public servant was not entrusted with the performance of some important duty by his fellow-citizens.

Dr. Brownson died on his plantation in Liberty county on October 18, 1796, in the 55th year of his age. His last words were, "The scene is now closing; the business of life is nearly over. I have, like the rest of my fellow-creatures, been guilty of foibles, but I trust to the mercy of God to pardon them, and to His justice to reward my good deeds."

His wife died on April 4, 1775, and he is said to have married for the second time a Southern lady who survived him many years. In the Records of the Midway church is the birth of a son to Nathan and Elizabeth Brownson in October, 1778; the death of another son is recorded in September, 1777.

The venerable Andrew Maybank, who was personally acquainted with Dr. Brownson, related this anecdote: "Mrs. Brownson, while a good and faithful wife, was not always pliable or prompt in responding to the requests of her husband. On occasions the Doctor has been known, in a playful way, to say to her, 'Have a care; if you do not acquiesce in my wish, when I am dead I will come back and plague you.' Years after the Doctor's demise the old lady—his widow—as she would brush from her nose some vexatious fly or annoying insect, has been heard to exclaim: 'Go away, Doctor Brownson,' and as the persistent fly or pertinacious gnat would return she would, with emphatic gesture and in decided tone, repeat the injunction, 'Go away, I tell you, Doctor Brownson, and stop bothering me.'"

A. B. CALDWELL.

Jonathan Bryan.

JONATHAN BRYAN was born in South Carolina on September 12, 1708. His father was Joseph Bryan. His mother was Janet (Cochran) Bryan, and died when Jonathan was but three weeks old.

The first grant of land to Joseph Bryan, dated at "Charles Towne, the eighth day of November, Anno Dom., 1697," was a "plantation containing two hundred acres of land, English measure, and lying in Colleton County." His son, Hugh Bryan, was captured in the Indian War of 1715 and was held a captive for one year, and his life was saved on more than one occasion by an Indian chief, "for the kindness he had shown the savages in former years."

Jonathan Bryan is first referred to in Georgia history by McCall as one of those citizens of Carolina who accompanied Oglethorpe on January 19, 1733, when the site of Savannah, in Georgia, was chosen for the colonists from England, who were to be the pioneers in the creation of the present great State of Georgia.

Francis Moore's "Voyage to Georgia," published in London 1744, states that at last, in March, 1736, "Mr. Jonathan Brian brought down a new Scout Boat with ten oars."

On March 30, 1736, Mr. Bryan, of St. Helena's, Berkeley county, in the province of Carolina, made a deposition before Mr. Francis Moore, Recorder of Frederica, St. Simon's Island, touching the Spanish settlements. This deposition was read June 16, 1736, before the Trustees for Georgia in London.

Francis Moore records in April, 1736: "The 30th Mr. Oglethorpe agreed with Mr. Jonathan Brian to furnish him with eighteen hands to assist him in cutting roads through that part of Georgia which is from the River Savannah to the River Ogeechee, and for that purpose to begin by making a road passable from his own house in Carolina to the River Savannah, and thereby carry all things along with him that were necessary for the support of the men. In the evening Mr. Bryan and Mr. Barnwell set out for Carolina, of their own accord, Mr. Bryan promising if we should be attacked they would come down with a large number of volunteers from thence." The house referred to was either at "Good Hope," near Port Royal, or at "Walnut Hill." Mr. Bryan began to settle this latter in 1734. It is located on the eastern bank of the Pocotaligo River, not far from its head-waters.

On May 27, 1740, Jonathan Bryan, as a Lieutenant of a company of "Gentlemen Volunteers" from South Carolina, accompanied General Oglethorpe in his unsuccessful expedition against St. Augustine. On his return he made a sworn report to the committee of South Carolinians appointed to inquire into the merits of this expedition.

Mr. Bryan recorded in his Bible:

" John 3:5, 6. My conversion from corruption to Christianity the time whereof (I bless God) I well remember was October 24, 1740." The Rev. George Whitefield, the creator and benefactor of the Bethesda Orphans' Home in Georgia, had reached the mind and heart of this sturdy man, who with his nephew, Stephen Bull, in 1742, when the Spaniards invaded Georgia, entertained these orphans at their plantations in South Carolina. He recorded in his Bible that the "Meeting House at Stono Creek was built in the year 1742;" and, according to Howe's History of the Presbyterian Church, on May 20, 1743, he was one of seven who invited the Rev. Wm. Hutson to be their pastor. "A covenant and articles of faith were adopted" and signed on June 8, 1743 by the pastor and "Hugh Bryan and Jonathan Bryan, deacons." This church, "The Stoney Creek Independent Presbyterian Church," was established in what was called the "Indian Land," near Pocotaligo." It is believed that Mr. Bryan had been prior to this of the Church of England, for in 1736 "he was appointed a Commissioner with Hugh Bryan, Joseph Izard, and John Mulverin to build a chapel near Hoospa Neck, St. Helena's Parish."

Mr. Bryan also records that he began to settle his new plantation in Georgia the first day of January, 1751, and removed to Georgia from Carolina with his family December 27, 1752.

On the 6th of August, 1754, Mr. Bryan was confirmed one of the ten members of His Majesty's Council for Georgia, and with Noble Jones was commissioned a Justice of a "Court of Session of Oyer and Terminer and General Goal Delivery." On the 12th of December, 1754, Messrs. Jones and Bryan were commissioned Justices of the "General Court."

"At a council held in the Council Chambers at Savannah 16th January, 1756, a grant was issued to Jonathan Bryan and others, their heirs and assigns, of a public lot in Savannah, known by the letter K, in Decker Ward, yielding and paying therefor annually one pepper corn if demanded, to be held in trust that a Meeting House or place of public worship be erected thereon for the use and benefit of professors of the doctrine of the Church of Scotland agreeable to the Westminister Confession of Faith." This grant was the inception, the ultimate fruition of which was the Independent Presbyterian church, which has adorned Savannah for so many years.

On April 2, 1757, Mr. Bryan was commissioned Captain of "First Troop of Horse Militia," and Colonel Jones speaks of "Captain Bryan and a cavalcade of citizens" assisting in the reception, by Governor Ellis, of the Chiefs and Headmen of the Upper and Lower Creek Nations.

In 1766 the names of Governor Wright and the Council of which Mr. Bryan was a member, and the names of many others, appeared on what has been called the "Georgia Roll," being a form of abjuration adopted in the sixth year of the reign of King George the Third.

Mr. Bryan recorded in his Bible: "The year 1766 memorable for the most detestable act of paramount will, the Stamp Act." This was the almost universal impression of the colonists from Boston to Georgia.

A meeting of merchants was held in Savannah September 16, 1769. Mr. Bryan presided. Certain resolutions were agreed upon in consequence of the acts of the British Parliament. Mr. Bryan was still a member of His Majesty's Council. When informed, the King was indignant and, on December 9, 1769, directed that Mr. Bryan "should be immediately suspended from his seat at the Council Board, and removed from any office he might hold in Georgia."

"Thus," says Jones in his History of Georgia, Vol. II, p. 115, "in the person of the Honorable Jonathan Bryan, a pure patriot, an influential citizen and a brave man, do we record the first instance of political martyrdom in Georgia. But his deposition did not intimidate the "Liberty Boys." It caused their number to multiply and their hearts to grow stronger."

Learning through Mr. Lloyd, of London, that Rev. John Wesley was inclined to visit America, Mr. Bryan wrote to him from New York April 1, 1772. After detailing the "deplorable ignorance of the Gospel among those who lived at a distance from the seaport towns and the populous parts of the provinces and the unhappy condition of our negroes, kept as they are from the key of knowledge," he added these words, "If, therefore, you are not too advanced in years, I say to you, in the name of God, come and help us. In doing which you will oblige many thousands and, among the rest, your friend and brother."

On July 27, 1774, Mr. Bryan, being one of a committee of citizens appointed "to prepare resolutions, similar to those adopted by the Northern Colonies in consequence of the late acts of the British Parliament towards Boston, as well as the existing acts to raise a perpetual revenue without the consent of the Provinces or their representatives," and Governor Wright, becoming alarmed at the proceedings, convened the Council. Whereupon, "a motion was made to expel Mr. Bryan from the Council, because his name appeared among the committeemen." With patriotic indignation he informed them in a style peculiar to himself for its candor and energy, that he would "save them the trouble" and handed his resignation to the Governor. Soon after this occurrence a handsome silver vase was presented to Mr. Bryan, upon one side of which was inscribed, "To Jonathan Bryan, Esq., who for publicly appearing in favor of the rights and liberties of the people was excluded from His Majesty's Council of this Province, this piece of plate as a mark of their esteem is presented by the Union Society of Georgia." On the obverse is, "Union, Frendship and Love," and "Ita cuique eveniat de Republica Meruit." Mr. Bryan was a member of this society, which is among the oldest societies in the United States.

On October 28, 1774, twenty-two headmen, warriors and chiefs of the Upper and Lower Creek Nations, for themselves and the rest of the Creek Nations, agreed to and signed their names to a lease for ninety-nine years of "all that plantation, tract or parcel of land known by the name of the Locheway and Appalache Old Fields," in Florida, to Mr. Bryan, his heirs and assigns, "in consideration of the great regard they bear to the said Jonathan Bryan and the payment of one thousand pounds of the lawful money of the Province of Georgia, at or before the sealing and delivery of these presents," and the annual payment thereafter of "one hundred bushels of Indian corn." This lease does not appear complete, but is on record in the Department of State at Atlanta. The Governor and Council made strenuous objections to this transaction and incited the indignation and opposition of the Indians then assembled at Savannah. Colonel Jones, the Georgia Historian, says, "Had Mr. Bryan carried his intention into effect and withdrawn from Christ Church Parish into the wilds of Florida, Georgia would have lost one of her purest, best and most influential citizens, and the 'Liberty Boys' a strong friend, a trusted adviser and a brave leader."

Mr. Bryan represented the town and district of Savannah in the Provincial Congress, which met at Savannah July 4, 1775, and on December 11, 1775. He was appointed a member of the Council of Safety, and at a meeting of this Council, May 16, 1776, he took the oath as one of the Justices of the "Quorum."

On June 18, 1776, the Council of Safety appointed Mr. Bryan and John Houstoun, his son-in-law, as members of the Council, and Colonel Lachlan McIntosh a committee to proceed to Charleston for the purpose of conferring with General Lee. On July 5, 1776, this committee reported to the Council what they represented to General Lee relative to the state of the provinces.

It appears from documentary evidence that Mr. Bryan acted as Vice-President and Commander-in-Chief of the State of Georgia and Ordinary of the same on March 26, 1777, and April 14, 1777, in the period of Governor Gwinnett's administration. He was elected a member of the "Executive Council" by the Legislature which met on May 8, 1777. He was present at the last meeting of the Council of Safety held February 22, 1777.

In December, 1778, in consequence of the then threatened

attack upon Savannah by the British, Governor John Houstoun directed Captain John Milton, the Secretary of State, to pack and move by boats the State records to Purysburg, and thence to the residence of Mr. Bryan, at his Union plantation, which was situated about twelve miles above Savannah and on the Carolina shore of the Savannah River.

It will be remembered that an attempt was made to capture Governor Houstoun at the Union plantation. Major-General Prevost writes January 18, 1779: "On the first of January Lieutenant Clark, of the Phœnix, was detached with row-boats seventeen miles up the River Savannah, above Savannah, upon the information that the late rebel Governor of Georgia was at a plantation on the Carolina shore. He did not get the Governor but returned with one Bryan, a notorious ringleader of Rebellion." This capture occurred at the "Union" plantation, already mentioned. James Bryan, the son of Jonathan Bryan was captured at the same time and place.

The General Assembly of the Royalists met at Savannah in May, 1780, and passed an act disqualifying the parties involved and rendering them ever afterwards incapable of holding or exercising any office of trust, honor or profit within the limits of Georgia. Among those mentioned was "Jonathan Bryan, Rebel Counselor."

Mr. Bryan and his son were held prisoners on Long Island for two years or more. Almost immediately after his return to Georgia, early in 1781, he was appointed by the Executive Council of Georgia a member of that body, and on August 30, 1781, his son, James Bryan, was elected Treasurer of the State. There are extant two letters of Mr. Bryan to Mrs. Bryan at "Brampton," dated Long Island, January 2, 1780, and June 3, 1780, and one from Mrs. Bryan dated June 11, 1780, directed "To Jonathan Bryan, Esq., Prisoner of War at Long Island, and to the particular care of the Commissary of Prisoners."

Their son, James Bryan, was born in South Carolina, September 22, 1752. He volunteered with Captain Bowen, Lieutenant James Jackson and Thomas Hamilton to burn several vessels at Savannah, which were loaded with rice, to prevent their capture by the British naval vessels. His name appears as Lieutenant on a roll of officers of the Continental Line of the Georgia Brigade.

On the 21st of May, 1782, says Ramsay, "Colonel Brown at the head of a considerable party marched out of the garrison of Savannah with the apparent intention of attacking the Americans, when General Wayne met him and routed the whole party. Mr. Jonathan Bryan, a respectable citizen of Georgia, though nearly eighty years of age, was among the foremost on this occasion and showed as much fire and spirit as could be exhibited by a young soldier in the pursuit of military fame."

The "First Bryan Baptist Church" in Savannah has a history which originated through the interest which Mr. Bryan had in the welfare of the negroes. One of his servants, Andrew by name, then Andrew Bryan and finally the Rev. Andrew Bryan had been baptized by the Rev. George Liele. The Rev. Andrew Bryan preached first at "Brampton" plantation and then in Savannah until his death in October, 1812. At his burial eulogies were delivered by the Rev. Mr. Johnson, of the Baptist church, and by the Rev. Mr. Kollock, D.D., of the Independent Presbyterian church, and by Mr. Thos. F. Williams.

The *Georgia Gazette* of Thursday, March 13, 1788, gave notice of Mr. Jonathan Bryan's death, which occurred March 9, 1788, at his "Brampton" plantation and where his remains were interred. In the language of the *Gazette*: "He may be justly styled one of the principal founders and fathers of Georgia. Zealous in the cause of Christianity, he considered modes of worship as secondary, whilst a great first principle with him in all true religion was universal charity."

"Being in the late war taken prisoner he was made to undergo a series of persecutions and hardships scarcely to be paralleled and never to be justified, but the strength of his constitution and the unshaken firmness of his mind, even at the advanced age of seventy years, rose superior to all difficulties, and at length brought him to die in the arms of peace."

White, in his Statistics of Georgia, described Mr. Bryan as "a tall and large man, of wonderful strength and of imposing appearance."

A new county was laid out in 1793 south of the Great Ogeechee River in Georgia, and named Bryan, in honor of Jonathan Bryan, "One of the men of mark in Georgia."

T. F. SCREVEN.

Archibald Bulloch.

ARCHIBALD BULLOCH, one of the most distinguished of Georgia's Revolutionary patriots, was born in Charles Town, South Carolina, in 1730. His father was the Rev. James Bulloch, of Wilton, Colleton Parish, South Carolina, a well known clergyman and planter, who came from Scotland to Carolina about 1729. His mother, who was also of Scotch descent, was Jean Stobo, daughter of the Rev. Archibald Stobo, of South Carolina.

Much care was bestowed upon his early education, and in youth he chose the legal profession, for which he was carefully prepared.

In 1750 the family moved to Georgia and settled upon a plantation on the Savannah River, where he lived till about the beginning of the Revolution, when he moved to Savannah, Georgia. Here he applied himself with energy and success to the practice of law.

Mr. Bulloch married Miss Mary DeVeaux, a daughter of Judge James DeVeaux, of Savannah. Of this union there were four children—James, Archibald Stobo, Jane, and William Bellinger. Among his descendants many distinguished men have appeared, of whom President Theodore Roosevelt is one, being descended in a direct line through James, the eldest son of Archibald Bulloch.

In 1768 Mr. Bulloch became a member of the Commons House of Assembly in the Province of Georgia, and in that body he served with much ability and success. He was appointed on a committee to correspond with Dr. Benjamin

Franklin, Georgia's Provincial agent at the time, and to give him such instruction as might be necessary in transacting the affairs of Georgia in Great Brittain.

When the Commons House of Assembly met in Savannah in April, 1772, the name of Dr. Noble Wymberley Jones, who was regarded as very jealous in maintaining the rights of the colonists, was twice presented to acting Governor Habersham for his approval, and twice was the Governor's negative put upon it. Dr. Jones was chosen the third time by the House, but he declined under the circumstances to serve. Whereupon Archibald Bulloch was chosen Speaker, and the entry on the minutes of the House stated that Mr. Bulloch's election was only in consequence of Dr. Jones' declining the chair. Governor Habersham then addressed a communication to the House stating that if this minute was to stand upon the journals he would have no other choice than to dissolve the Assembly. The House declined to change the minutes, and Governor Habersham, having summoned the members before him in the Council Chamber, peremptorily dissolved the Assembly.

In 1773 Mr. Bulloch was appointed commissioner of "Public Roads," and in many of the patriotic movements of those stirring times he took a prominent part. His name was signed to a call made in the *Georgia Gazette* of July 14, 1774, to the inhabitants of Savannah to take into consideration the propriety of resisting the oppressions of Great Brittain, and he was placed upon a committee to confer with a committee from the other parishes.

In July, 1775, Archibald Bulloch was unanimously chosen President of the Provincial Congress, called at that time to take into their own hands the reins of power which were rapidly slipping from the grasp of England.

The deliberations of this Congress, which was one of the most important ever convened in Georgia, were conducted with marked ability, at a time when the crisis of revolution hung on every act.

It was by this Congress that Mr. Bulloch, John Houstoun, the Rev. Dr. Zubly, Noble W. Jones and Dr. Lyman Hall were selected and commissioned as representatives from Georgia to the Continental Congress.

Mr. Bulloch, together with Mr. Houstoun and Dr. Zubly, in response to the trust imposed in them, attended an adjourned session of the Continental Congress, held in Philadelphia on the 13th of September, 1775, and took part in its deliberations.

When the Provincial Congress assembled in Savannah, January 20, 1776, it elected Archibald Bulloch again as "President and Commander-in-Chief of Georgia." John Glen was elected Chief Justice, William Stephens Attorney-General, and James Jackson Clerk of Court.

January, 1776, Archibald Bulloch, John Houstoun, Dr. Lyman Hall, Button Gwinnett and George Walton were delegates to the Continental Congress. Bulloch, being President of Georgia, could not leave; and Houstoun, being detained at home, they thus lost the honor of being among the signers of the Declaration of Independence.

The Council of Safety, organized in these critical times from the best men in the Province, trusted Mr. Bulloch implicitly, and the minutes of this body show that he sat with its members in their important deliberations. He was indeed a tower of strength at this time. The high personal character of the man himself, his official integrity and ability, and his lofty conceptions of patriotic duty powerfully contributed to the force and direction of public sentiment in all matters affecting the welfare of the people. The simplicity of his character and his confidence in the people are illustrated by the following incident: When Mr. Bulloch was elected President, Colonel McIntosh, commanding the Provincial troops in Savannah, in accordance with previous custom, caused a sentinel to be posted at the door of his residence. To this Mr. Bulloch objected with the remark: "I act for a free people in whom I have the most entire confidence, and I wish to avoid on all occasions the appearance of ostentation."

Mr. Bulloch was a man of courage as well as a wise counsellor. When the British took possession of Tybee Island, he led an expedition against them, and in the face of great danger he succeeded in burning every house on the island except one in which a sick woman and several children were lying.

By reason of the slow communication in that day the news of the Declaration of Independence, sanctioned in Philadelphia July 4, 1776, did not reach Savannah till August 10th. A copy of the declaration and a letter from John Hancock were delivered to Mr. Bulloch, who at once assembled the Provincial Congress, and read aloud to them the famous document. He then repaired to the public square, where the Declaration of Independence was again read to the assembled people. Twice again during the same day it was publicly read, amid the applause of the people and the booming of cannon. At a public dinner under the cedar trees, President Bulloch, the members of Council, Colonel McIntosh, many gentlemen and the militia, cordially drank to the "prosperity and perpetuity of the United, Free, and Independent States of America."

At night the town was illuminated and with solemn ceremonies George the Third was buried in effigy.

With the swelling tide of the Revolution, the dramatic events of this critical period followed so precipitately that the Council of Safety, unable itself to convene at all times with sufficient promptness for the dispatch of urgent business, requested President Bulloch "to take upon himself the whole executive powers of government, calling to his assistance not less than five persons of his own choosing to consult and advise with him on every occasion when a sufficient number of councilors could not be convened to make a board."

The delegation of this unusual power shows how much he was trusted by the people. But this patriotic man did not live to see the issue of the struggle for liberty, for on February 22, 1777, he died suddenly at his home in Savannah. His remains were interred in the family vault in the Old Colonial cemetery in that city, where they still repose.

Mr. Bulloch was a man of commanding presence, and of great firmness and force of character. His good name and brave deeds are indissolubly associated with the proudest triumphs of the early history of the State, and his memory should be an inspiration to the generations to come. Of him it may be truly said:

> " His life was gentle; and the elements
> So mixed in him that Nature might stand up,
> And say to all the world, This was a man."

OTIS ASHMORE.

Thomas P. Carnes.

HON. THOMAS P. CARNES descended directly from pure English ancestry. His foreparents came to Maryland at the beginning of the eighteenth century. Here Thomas P. Carnes was born in 1762. After receiving a liberal education, at the age of nineteen, he chose the profession of law. As soon as he was licensed to practice he removed to Georgia, and settled at Augusta. The Carnes Road was named for him. He removed to the town of Milledgeville as soon as it was located and continued to reside there until he died in 1822.

His talents were of such marked character that he was soon appointed Solicitor-General of the Northern Circuit of Georgia. At the expiration of the term of this office he was promoted to the judgeship of the same circuit. Here he became a personal friend to one of Georgia's greatest men, Hon. William H. Crawford.

In the early days of Georgia there was no Supreme Court or last court of appeals. In conclusion, the ruling decisions of the judges presiding in the different circuits often conflicted. To obviate this the judges met in convention once or twice a year. Their functions were purely advisory and revisory, but their opinions were generally accepted by the balance of the judges. Judge Crawford was for a number of years Chairman of this Convention and Judge Carnes a warm supporter. To the personal efforts of these two leading spirits, and others who succeeded them, as, for instance, Governor Gilmer, is due the existence and great efficiency of the present Supreme Court of Georgia.

With Abraham Baldwin and George Matthews, each of whom afterwards became Governor of Georgia, Judge Carnes represented Georgia in the United States Congress from 1793 to 1795. As an evidence of his popularity the people settling Franklin County named their county site Carnesville in his honor.

In May, 1798, Georgia had only twenty-one counties. From these fifty-six of her best men were selected as delegates to a convention held for the purpose of revising the Constitution of the State so as to adapt it to the changed condition of affairs. Among the notable men of the State who were members of the convention may be mentioned James Jackson, Jared Irwin, Thomas Glascock, and Jesse Mercer. Judge Carnes was also a member of the convention.

After a short session the Constitution was drawn up, engrossed on parchment and signed by the different members. As the last man signed the document a salute of sixteen guns was fired by the military company, stationed and in waiting, as soon as the signal was given. It was then and there deposited in the office of the Secretary of State, where it remains to this date. Of this convention the late Chief Justice Joseph Henry Lumpkin wrote in 1860: "The expiration of sixty or more years has demonstrated the wisdom of this Constitution of '98. It has undergone but few changes, and these were rendered necessary by the changes in the condition of the country."

At the November session of the Legislature of 1806, the President and members of the Senate being seated in the Representative Chamber, both branches proceeded by joint ballot to elect Thomas P. Carnes, Thomas Flourney and William Barnett Commissioners to ascertain the location of the 35th degree of north latitude, and to run and mark the dividing line between the State of Georgia and the States of North Carolina and Tennessee.

In executing this commission, a slight error was made which caused a divergence of about four miles at the western terminus of the line where the State line falls that distance south of the 35th parallel. In this strip of land between the State line, as surveyed, and the 35th parallel was Ross' Landing, known to-day as the city of Chattanooga. Thus, by this small divergence, Georgia was made to lose one of the most flourishing cities of the South. This mistake was detected about twenty years ago.

Judge Carnes died at Milledgeville in May, 1822, at the age of sixty.   R. J. MASSEY.

General Elijah Clarke.

ELIJAH CLARKE was born in Edgecombe County, North Carolina, in 1733. There is no well authenticated record of his ancestry nor is anything definite known of his youth. He married Hannah Arrington in North Carolina. About the year 1774 the Clarke family, together with a number of other North Carolinians from the same section, came to Georgia. They settled on what was then known as the "ceded lands," which had been purchased from the Indians in 1773. As there were no grants made to lands in this section till after the Revolution, the newcomers simply chose their homes and settled upon them. They had few comforts and no luxuries. They had brought with them cattle and horses and a scant supply of such furniture and household utensils as could be transported so far in carts.

The Indians were not pleased with this encroachment on their hunting grounds, so that these frontiersmen had to be constantly on their guard and to depend largely on themselves to preserve their lives and property. It was in such a school as this that Elijah Clarke was trained for leadership.

The first we hear of him is as Captain of a body of horsemen whose duty it was to guard some wagons loaded with provisions for the little army which was gathering at Savannah. On the way, while crossing a little stream, they were attacked by Indians; but, after a severe contest, the Indians were put to flight. He and his troops joined General Howe in the unfortunate expedition against St. Augustine, and he was wounded in the only skirmish in which they were engaged.

ELIJAH CLARKE

After General Howe's return to Savannah he repaired to his home in the up-country, and there is no record of further military service on his part till the invasion of Georgia by General Prevost in 1778. The British overran the struggling commonwealth and marched through the country as far as Petersburg on the Savannah. This detachment returned to Augusta, and a separate body of Tories, under Colonel Boyd, crossed the Savannah to take possession of the forts on the frontier. Clarke and his troopers, who were in South Georgia, joined Colonel Pickens and pursued Colonel Boyd. The armies met at Kettle Creek. Clarke, with foresight and courage, seized a strategic point in the rear of the enemy and turned the tide of the battle in favor of the Americans. Colonel Boyd fell, mortally wounded, and his force was almost annihilated.

The country was again free but was soon invaded by Colonel Innes, a Scotch loyalist. To Colonel Clarke fell the task of combating him and his followers. There were several contests in which he took part and in none of which was he worsted. They met at Wofford's Iron Works where Clarke awaited the attack and bravely defended his post. They clashed again at Musgrove's Mill in Oglethorpe County and Clarke was twice wounded on the back of his head and neck, his stock-buckle saving his life.

The enemy having been driven from the frontier, Clarke gathered a body of three hundred and fifty men and pounced down on Augusta so suddenly that he succeeded in capturing it, but, the British rallying, he was forced to abandon it. With upper South Carolina overrun and Augusta occupied by the British and the hostile Indians on the north and west, he saw the impossibility of holding the ceded land and decided on a general exodus.

He gathered all the families then left, and, with his body

of troops for a guard, he, together with Colonel Candler from the adjoining county, conveyed the women and children over the mountains to the valley of the Watauga in upper Tennessee. As soon as they were in a place of safety he returned South and, uniting with the South Carolina forces and the refugee Georgians, again actively took the field. At Blackstocks, at the head of his Wilkes riflemen, Clarke charged and drove the British light infantry in on an open field, where, although he did not command, he might be said to have insured the day by turning the enemy's right flank. At Long Cane he was again wounded and was carried off the field. He soon recovered, went into the army again, and after a short campaign contracted small-pox, but was out again in time to take command at Augusta, and was in the siege before General Lee arrived to take charge of the movement. Of his action at this time it has been said, "In the American army there was one man who would seem to have sworn a vow on the altar of American independence that Augusta should not remain under the flag of the King. That man was Colonel Elijah Clarke. Cato was not more insistent that Carthage must be destroyed than was Colonel Clarke that Augusta's fort must be taken. From the day that Browne took possession of it and hoisted the British flag Clarke went everywhere, gathering recruits to drive him out. It was Clarke who planned the attack upon the White House, which deserved success, but failed at the moment of impending victory. It was he who gathered the forces which under Pickens and Williamson and McCall came and sat down before the town here for two months, resolved never to go away until that flag came down." Later he joined General Wayne and was with him when the victorious entry was made into Savannah. He had marched from Savannah at the beginning of the war six years before, and he was now among those who marched triumphantly into the capital of the State delivered from its foes.

The Legislature recognized his distinguished services and gave him a commission as Major-General and voted him a very liberal grant of confiscated property. His sound judgment and his devotion to Georgia led to his being chosen one of the treaty-makers with the Indians.. He and his fellow-commissioners gained from them large and valuable concessions. And when the Indians made their last effort to recover their hunting grounds and invaded upper Georgia, reaching as far as Greensboro, General Clarke and his son, Major John or Jack, as he was called, marched against them and defeated them in a battle known as the battle of Jack's Creek.

As will be seen from the above account General Clarke had never been where it was necessary to cultivate the grace of submission to authority. He was generally in independent command and it was not unnatural that he should have been somewhat impatient of restraint. In those days the people were of much the same spirit. Governor Gilmer tells of how General Clarke at one time prosecuted a man before the courts for horsestealing. The jury decided he was not guilty and discharged him; but the General summarily reversed their verdict and was about to hang him when Colonel Pendleton persuaded them to let the man go free.

His course when the land office was opened in Augusta was, as described by Stevens, the historian, more vigorous than conventional. But the General made the sad mistake of his great career, when revolting against the laws he disliked, he incurred the displeasure of his own State and of the general government by invading the Indian country. The whole story is too long to be related here. He accepted a commission from the French Republic as a Major-General, organized a small army and built some forts on the Indian lands across the Oconee. He also crossed the St. Mary's into Florida and drove in some of the

Spanish posts. Colonel Absalom Chappell makes a masterly defence of him, and this generation will hardly question the fact that he did not really design any rebellion against the State or the general government, for which he had no special affection, but was organizing for an invasion of Florida in the interest of France. The old friends and comrades of General Clarke were forced to oppose him, and the militia was ordered out, when he quietly retired to his estate in Wilkes County, where he died in 1799 at the age of sixty-six.

In estimating the character of this remarkable man we must take into consideration the circumstances of his early life, his own fiery nature and the state of things during and just after the Revolution. It would be absurd to claim that this sturdy old soldier was a man of culture or polish. He was a frontier man from the first, and as a fighter takes rank with Marion, Sumter and Pickens. It is said that the women always felt safe when it was known that Clarke was leading the fight. He had nothing of the holiday soldier about him, as he had lived on the border of civilization all his life, and had lacked the advantages of classical training. He is said, however, to have been very courtly in manner and commanding in person. His portraits show a bold, striking face and figure suggesting strength, courage and ambition. He scorned hardship, loved danger and appeared at his best in a fight. He resented bitterly what he thought was injustice to the poor whites and undue favor to the Indians on the part of the United States government, and was not diplomatic enough to conceal his feelings.

His good wife was one of the heroines of the Revolution. Her house was burned by the Tories while her husband was in the field. She was at the siege of Augusta and at its final capitulation. Once when she was on her way to nurse her wounded husband her horse was taken from her and at another time her horse was shot under her while trying to reach a place of safety. She survived the General for more than thirty years, and died at the ripe old age of ninety in 1829, and was buried at their home in Wilkes County, known as Woburn.

His children were John, Governor of Georgia; Gibson, one of the first graduates of the University of Georgia; Elijah, Jr., a lawyer and at one time candidate for Congress; Mrs. Thompson; Mrs. Walton and Mrs. Benajah Smith. All his children, except John, were given the advantages of the schools. He was deprived of an education by the Revolution. The daughters married into the leading families of their section and their descendants have been among the best people of the land.

Georgia has recognized the great debt she owes to General Clarke by naming one of her counties Clarke for him. Athens is the county site of Clarke County, and on one of its principal streets the Daughters of the Revolution have erected a beautiful marble shaft to his memory.

The following obituary of General Clarke was written by General James Jackson, his companion in arms:

"Died at his seat in Wilkes County on the 15th inst., Jan., 1799, General Elijah Clarke, late a Major-General of the militia of this State, and one of the most distinguished militia officers in the Union. When Georgia and South Carolina were evacuated by their governments, and the forces of the United States were withdrawn from them, Clarke alone kept the field, and his name spread terror through the whole line of British posts, from the Catawba to the Creek Nation. The first action in which the militia were taught to disregard the bayonets of the British was gained by him over a British detachment at the Enoree in South Carolina, though with a far inferior force, of this he was robbed by the historians, and the credit given to Col. Williams, of South Carolina. To check Clarke, Lord Cornwallis detached the celebrated partisan, Ferguson, which produced the decisive battle of King's Mountain, which ended in the death of Ferguson and the destruction of his whole corps. At Blackstocks at the head of his Wilkes riflemen he charged and drove the British light infantry in an open field, where altho' he did not command he might be said to have insured the day by turning the enemy's right flank. This also as well as the merits of his compatriot, General Twiggs, who commanded during two-thirds of that action and gained it after General Sumpter was wounded, Dr. Ramsey has ascribed to South Carolina. The Iron Works of Pacolet and a variety of other places in the north parts of that State bear witness by the British skeletons on them, of Clarke's prowess. And on his return to Georgia he attacked, defeated, killed and took prisoners the British Major Dunlap with his whole detachment of dragoons and Tories, sent purposely to fall in with him. The British Colonels Brown and Cruger, though gallant officers, the one commanding at Augusta, the other at Ninety-six, dreaded his approach towards either of those posts, and the former will remember the White House, now Harrisburg, as long as he exists. He was present when Augusta surrendered to the American arms, and had gallantly confined the British garrison to their works for weeks before Colonel Lee arrived, although his name, with that of some other Georgia officers, without whose exertions Augusta would not have fallen, were never noticed as being even present on the occasion. His last opposition to the British arms in the field was under General Wayne before Savannah, which city he had the satisfaction to see evacuated, and by that event his country altogether relieved from the British yoke. He has since fought some decisive actions with the Creek Indians, who will by his death feel themselves freed from dread of this once formidable enemy.

To say that General Clarke was perfect is to advance more than is allotted to human nature. He incurred the displeasure of the United States in an attempt some years since to settle on the Indian side of the Oconee River, and by a more recent action of crossing the St. Mary's to the Florida side and driving in the Spanish posts. His merits as a soldier may easily be ascertained by the solicitations of the two great European nations to engage him in their service. That he had a commission of Major-General in that of France is generally believed, but the noble disdain with which he resisted the importunities of the British to take side with their nation is in everybody's mouth and on record, and proves him to have been actuated by an uniform principle.

The writer hereof, one of the companions of the heroic Clarke in most of the trying scenes he was engaged in during the Revolutionary War, has thought it his duty to Clarke and his country to give this little sketch of his character, and although he always disapproved of his intended settlement over the Oconee River, engaging in foreign service and his subsequent expedition into Florida, yet from his knowledge of the man he will be bold to assert that the United States by the death of Clarke has lost a brave and meritorious officer, and that the State of Georgia in gratitude to her departed hero ought to perpetuate his name by some public act.

General Clarke was in his private life as open, candid and sincere a friend as he was in war a generous, brave and determinded enemy, a kind husband and an affectionate parent."

GEORGE G. SMITH.

Joseph Clay.

RALPH CLAY, the father of the subject of this sketch, married Elizabeth, a sister of the Honorable James Habersham, intimate friend of the Rev. George Whitefield, and, during the absence of Sir James Wright in 1771-72, the royal Governor of Georgia. Joseph Clay, the only son of this marriage, was born at Beverley, Yorkshire, England, on the 16th of October, 1741. At the suggestion of his distinguished uncle, supplemented by the persuasions of the Rev. Mr. Whitefield, young Clay came to Georgia in 1760. A few years afterwards, responding to the wish of Governor Habersham, who furnished the means requisite for the adventure, his son, James Habersham, Jr., and his nephew, Joseph Clay, associated themselves in a general commission business in Savannah. The partnership thus formed lasted about five years. With the exception of the period covered by the war of the Revolution Mr. Clay remained actively engaged in commercial pursuits. He and Colonel Joseph Habersham were at one time associated under the firm name of Joseph Clay & Company. He was also a partner in the house of Seth John Cuthbert & Company; at another time he was the senior member of the firm of Clay, Telfair & Company, and again was interested as a co-partner in the house of William Fox & Company, of Newport, Rhode Island. His home was always in Savannah, where, on the 2d of January, 1763, he married Ann Legardere. Soon after establishing himself in business in Savannah Mr. Clay became interested, in connection with his relatives, the Habershams, in the cultivation of rice, which was then the principal market crop produced upon the marish lands of Southern Georgia. Both as a merchant and as a planter he prospered. In conducting his business affairs he was prompt, energetic, and competent.

By the meeting of patriotic citizens assembled at the Liberty Pole at Tondee's Tavern in Savannah on the 27th of July, 1774, he was chosen a member of the committee then raised and charged with the preparation of resolutions expressive of the rebel sentiments of the community, and of the determination of Georgia, at an early day, to associate herself with her sister American colonies in opposition to the enforcement of the unjustifiable and arbitrary acts of the British Parliament.

On the 10th of the following August he appeared with this committee and united in submitting a report which, unanimously adopted, proclaimed in brave language the rights claimed by the protesting provinces, condemned in emphatic terms the policy inaugurated by England, and promised co-operation on the part of Georgia in all constitutional measures devised to obtain a redress of existing grievances and to maintain the inestimable blessings granted by God and guaranteed by a constitution founded upon reason and justice. He was also of the committee then appointed to solicit and forward supplies for the relief of the suffering poor of Boston. In the rape of six hundred pounds of powder from the King's magazine in Savannah during the night of the 11th of May, 1775, and in its subsequent distribution among parties intent upon rebellion, Mr. Clay personally participated. By the Assembly, which convened on the 22d of June in the same year, he was complimented with a place in the Council of Safety. To the famous Provincial Congress which met in Savannah twelve days afterwards, he was a delegate accredited from the town and district of Savannah. By that Congress he was placed upon a committee to frame an address to his Excellency Governor Wright. He was also desig-

4

nated as a member of the important "Committee of Intelligence," and commissioned as one of another committee to present the "Article of Association," then adopted, to the inhabitants of the town and district of Savannah for signature.

Deeming it essential to the success of the liberty cause that no officer of the militia should be retained in commission who refused or neglected to sign this "Article of Association," and yet exhibiting a show of respect for Sir James Wright, the royal Governor, George Walton, William Le Conte, Francis Harris, William Young, George Houstoun, William Ewen, John Glen, Samuel Elbert, Basil Cowper, and Joseph Clay, acting in behalf of the Council of Safety, on the 8th of August, 1775, addressed a communication to his Excellency the Governor, asking permission that the several militia companies of the province should be permitted to elect their own officers. It was suggested that some of them were distasteful to those whom they were appointed to command. Deeming it an extraordinary application, dangerous in its tendency and calculated to wrest the control of the military from the crown officers, Sir James sought the advice of his Council. An answer was returned, "that for many very substantial reasons the Governor would not comply with the request." Nothing daunted, the members of the Council of Safety, who really cared but little for the mind of the Governor on the subject, took the matter in their own hands, and proceeded to purge the militia of any loyal element which lurked in the ranks of its commissioned officers. The revolutionists were in earnest. With rapid strides they marched forward, overcoming in succession every obstacle which retarded their progress towards the consummation of the complete overthrow of kingly dominion in Georgia. In this rebel procession Joseph Clay was an active and efficient Lieutenant.

When, early in March, 1776, Barclay and Grant threatened

Savannah, the Council of Safety resolved to defend that town and the rice-laden vessels lying at its wharves, to the last extremity. Mr. Clay was then named as chairman of a committee to inventory and value the shipping in port, and all houses in Savannah and its hamlets belonging to the friends of America who were prepared to participate in the common defence. In that inventory and appraisement were to be included the homes and property of widows and orphans. So firm was the resolution of the patriots that they were determined to commit everything to the flames rather than have their town and shipping pass into the hands of British soldiers.

The inventory and appraisement were made with a view to future indemnification at the hands of the general government. Fortunately the contemplated sacrifice was not demanded at the hands of these gallant defenders.

On the 6th of August, 1777, Mr. Clay was recognized by the Continental Congress as Deputy Paymaster-General in Georgia, with the rank of Colonel. This position was subsequently enlarged so as to embrace the Southern Department. When General Greene assumed command of this department, Colonel Clay was brought into personal association with him, and secured his confidence and esteem. Large sums of money were disbursed by him in the execution of his office, and there remains no suggestion of default or misappropriation. During the years 1778, 1779, and 1780 Georgia named him as one of her delegates to the Continental Congress.

By the first General Assembly which convened in Savannah after its evacuation by General Alured Clarke and the King's forces in July, 1782, Colonel Clay was elected Treasurer of the State of Georgia, and his salary was fixed at £300 per annum.

In 1785 he was named as one of the trustees for establishing the college or seminary of learning which subsequently developed into the present University of Georgia; and during the following year he became one of the Justices of Chatham County. In May, 1791, he was a member of the committee which welcomed President Washington on the occasion of his visit to Savannah. He died in that city on·the 15th of November, 1804.

His son Joseph was a prominent lawyer, and for several years occupied the bench as United States Judge for the District of Georgia. Resigning this position he entered the sacred ministry, and was regarded as one of the most eloquent pulpit orators of his day. In later generations the descendants of Colonel Clay have been noted in the church, at the Bar, in the domain of politics, and in social life.

C. C. JONES, JR.

Myrick Davies.

MYRICK DAVIES was President of the Executive Council during the darkest days of the Revolution, and as such was, for a time, *de facto* Governor of Georgia. Stephen Heard had succeeded George Wells early in 1780 and from Heard's Fort (now Washington) had administered the affairs of the State. Late in that year he found it necessary to retreat into North Carolina, and the subject of this sketch was elevated to the Presidency of the Council.

Georgia was almost entirely overrun by the British at this time and there was hardly a semblance of civil authority exercised in the State. Mr. Davies was officially displaced by the election of a new Council and a new Governor. Nothing is known of his personal history prior to his election to office. He fell a victim to the Tories towards the close of the year 1781.

A. B. CALDWELL.

Colonel John Dooly.

OF the many heroic men who illustrated that stormy period of the Revolution in Georgia that "tried men's souls" none deserves a more grateful remembrance by posterity than Col. John Dooly.

The ancestors of this sterling patriot came from Ireland originally, and settled in North Carolina. About the beginning of the Revolution, John Dooly, together with other members of his family, and with many of his neighbors, moved to Georgia and settled in what is now the northeastern part of Lincoln County, not far from the Savannah River. The country was new, and exposed to all the difficulties and dangers incident to frontier life in those troublous times. Between the invasions of British soldiers and the attacks of savage Indians, these early settlers lived in constant peril, and often bloody conflicts occurred. On July 22, 1776, Captain Thomas Dooly, a brother of Colonel John Dooly, and a gallant officer, was murdered by the Indians near the Oconee River in a skirmish, under circumstances of great aggravation. Captain Thomas Dooly had received a severe wound, but indifferent to his sufferings he continued to encourage his men, and he himself fired two shots at the enemy after he was wounded. The officer next in command, thinking more of his own safety than of his duty, was among the first to leave the field and the helpless Dooly in the power of his enemies. He bravely defended himself to the last with the end of his gun, but he was finally overcome and murdered by the foe.

This cruel and cowardly act Colonel John Dooly, his brother, determined to avenge. Fired by resentment at his brother's death, as well as by a lofty feeling of patriotism, he became a terror to the Indians throughout Georgia. So eager was he to carry out his purposes that he planned an attack upon the Indians at Galphinton, after propositions of peace had been made by the constituted authorities. The plan was discovered, and Dooly was arrested. General Elbert was ordered to try him by a court-martial. Dooly requested to resign his commission, which was granted. He was shortly afterwards appointed Colonel of militia in Wilkes County.

During the Revolution Colonel John Dooly was a prominent figure in the various skirmishes which took place on both sides of the Savannah River above Augusta.

When the British took possession of Augusta many of the inhabitants of what is now known as Wilkes and Lincoln counties hastily collected their household effects and cattle, and fled into Carolina, where they placed themselves under the protection of Colonel John Dooly just across the river.

McGirth with three hundred loyalists was occupying a position lower down on Kiokee Creek, watching the ferries and collecting boats. Dooly now returned to the Georgia side of the river with a part of his command, but being quickly pursued by Lieutenant-Colonel Hamilton he re-crossed the Savannah just below the mouth of Broad River barely in time to escape. Dooly was now joined by Colonel Andrew Pickens, of South Carolina, with two hundred and fifty men. Although senior in rank, Dooly yielded the command to Pickens, for the reason that Pickens had furnished more than two-thirds of the troops constituting their little army. Hamilton with one hundred men was encamped on Water's plantation just across the river on the Georgia side, three miles below the mouth of Broad River.

With their united forces Pickens and Dooly crossed the river on the night of February 10th at Cowen's ferry, three miles above Hamilton's encampment, and prepared for a surprise assault upon the enemy the next morning. Much to their astonishment and regret they found that Hamilton, in entire ignorance of the planned attack, had left for Carr's Fort. Pickens and Dooly pursued Hamilton, and after capturing nearly all of his horses and baggage, laid siege to Carr's Fort, whither the enemy had fled just in time to escape capture. Unfortunately, just as the fort was on the point of capitulation, a message announced that Colonel Boyd, with eight hundred loyalists, was moving through Carolina towards Georgia, destroying by fire and sword whatever lay in their path. The siege was at once abandoned, and Pickens and Dooly turned their forces to the new enemy. After considerable difficulty Colonel Boyd succeeded in crossing the Savannah River, and he shaped his course westward with the purpose of joining McGirth on Little River. Pickens and Dooly, reinforced by Captain Anderson and Colonel Clark, pursued Boyd to Kettle Creek in Wilkes County, where a decisive battle was fought on February 14, 1779, resulting in a complete victory for the American arms. In this battle, which must be regarded as one of the decisive conflicts of the war, Colonel John Dooly commanded the right wing, and to his bravery and skill must be credited much of the honor and success of the day.

In these stirring times much of Colonel Dooly's life was spent in the camp. His home and his neighbors, who looked to him for leadership in these days of peril, lay between the contending forces of relentless war. Bands of Tories, Indians and marauders were scouring the country, leaving death and desolation in their track. The name of Dooly was a terror to these parties, and in 1780 a band of Tories, headed by Captain Corker, who had been dispatched by the British commander at Augusta into the adjacent country with authority to grant protection and exact oaths of allegiance to the British Crown, forced an entrance into the dwelling house of Colonel John Dooly, and in the most barbarous manner murdered him in the presence of his wife and children. There is a well authenticated tradition that at least three of these Tories were caught and hanged to a red-oak tree near what is still known as Tory Pond on the Egypt plantation in Lincoln County. Five of the party crossed Broad River and paid a visit to the famous Nancy Hart, whose daring act, which led to the capture and execution of the whole number, forms one of the most thrilling episodes in the history of the Revolution.

That Colonel Dooly was a man of rare natural ability and great force of character the records and traditions of his time, though scant, abundantly show.

When the first court was held in Wilkes County on August 25, 1779, the record shows that John Dooly was appointed to act as attorney for the State. At this court nine persons were sentenced to be hanged, principally for treason "under indictments," as Judge Andrews says in "The Bench and Bar of Georgia," "about as long as your finger. The records are interesting and curious."

The celebrated Judge John M. Dooly, one of the most extraordinary men that Georgia ever produced, was the son of Col. John Dooly.

The State of Georgia has honored the memory and services of Colonel Dooly by naming one of its counties for him.

OTIS ASHMORE.

Samuel Elbert.

FEW men connected with Georgia's revolutionary history can claim pre-eminence over the subject of this sketch.

He was born of English parents in the Parish of Prince William, South Carolina, in 1740, and was early left an orphan. He made his way to Savannah, seeking work, and soon identified himself with the commercial life of the city. His honest-minded and industrious qualities attracted attention, and, in course of time, he became one of Savannah's leading and prosperous merchants. He married Miss Elizabeth Rae, who bore him six children.

His love of military life led him to become one of the King's soldiers, and, as early as June 4, 1774, we find him the captain of a company of grenadiers.

He was a member of Georgia's first Council of Safety, organized on the 22d of June, 1775. On the 4th of July of the same year he was sent as a delegate to the Provincial Congress and was by that body assigned to an important committee, along with Edward Telfair and Joseph Habersham, and specially charged with the task of placing Georgia on a military basis. When the Georgia Assembly passed resolutions on the 4th of February, 1776, to raise a battalion of Continental troops for the protection of the Commonwealth, he was honored with the commission of Lieutenant-Colonel; Lachlan McIntosh was commissioned Colonel, and Joseph Habersham Major.

Early in March, 1776, when the British undertook to capture the rice-laden vessels at the Savannah wharves, Colonel Elbert took part in the first clash of arms in Georgia between the

British and the soldiers of the Commonwealth. From this time till the close of the Revolution his attitude was one of courageous and unswerving loyalty to the patriot government, and no sword brighter or truer than his was drawn in the cause of American independence. On the 16th of September, 1776, he was promoted to the rank of Colonel and, in May of the following year, was designated by President Gwinnett over his own General, Lachlan McIntosh, to command the expedition against St. Augustine, by which it was hoped to reduce East Florida, with a view to its annexation to Georgia. The sickness of his men and other causes rendered the expedition a fruitless one and he returned to Savannah. Upon the departure of General McIntosh from Georgia on account of his duel with Button Gwinnett, Colonel Elbert succeeded him to the command of the Continental forces in Georgia.

In the spring of 1778, while commanding at Fort Howe, and learning that the British were at Frederica, he achieved a victory which is best told in his letter to General Howe, dated Frederica, 19th of April, 1778:

"DEAR GENERAL:—It gives me pleasure to tell you that at 10 A. M. to-day the brigantine Hinchinbrooke, the sloop Rebecca and a prize brig all struck the British tyrant's colors and surrendered to the American arms. Having heard that these vessels were at this place I put 300 of my troops on board the three little gallies, "The Washington," Captain Hardy; "The Lee," Captain Braddock; and "The Bulloch," Captain Hutcher; and Captain Young with a detachment of artillery and two field pieces I put on board a boat. With this little army we embarked to Darien and landed at a bluff a mile below the town. I immediately dispatched Lieut.-Colonel Ray and Major Roberts with 100 men to march to town, who captured three marines and two sailors. The next day our three little men-of-war made an attack on these three British vessels, who have spread terror on our coast, and who were drawn up in the order of battle; but the weight of our metal soon dampened their courage, for they took to their boats and abandoned everything on board, of which we immediately took possession. Captain Ellis, of the Hinchinbrooke, was drowned and Captain Mowbray, of the Rebecca, made his escape."

Toward the close of December, 1778, Colonel Elbert engaged in that memorable battle of Savannah, which culminated in the disastrous defeat of the Americans and the loss of Savannah to the patriot government. The British under Colonel Archibald Campbell out-generaled the Americans under Howe and drove them through the streets of Savannah at the point of the bayonet, although they made a brave resistance and fought the enemy at every corner.

Colonel Elbert, with that part of his forces which was not lost in the battle, retreated up the Savannah, and we next hear from him at Brier Creek near Augusta, where General Ashe, of North Carolina, was in command. His center, which was thrown a little forward, soon broke and fled in wild confusion before the British. The right flank followed the example of the center, while the left, under Colonel Elbert, stubbornly held its ground until every man of his command was either killed, wounded or captured. The brave Colonel was himself struck down and was about to be dispatched by a bayonet thrust, when he gave the Masonic sign of distress. An officer saw it and instantly responded and Colonel Elbert's life was saved by the benevolent principle of brotherly love. While a prisoner on parole in the British camp every courtesy was shown him. Offers of promotion, honors, rewards and other inducements were tendered him with the hope of winning him to the British cause; and when all these failed, an attempt was made by two

Indians to take his life. He fortunately discovered them in time and gave them a signal which he had formerly been accustomed to use among them. Their guns were immediately lowered and they came forward to shake his hands. This signal had probably been agreed upon and used when, with his company, by order of Governor Wright, he guarded the Indian Chiefs back to the Creek Nation. In former years, in his mercantile relations with the Indians, he had been a great favorite among them.

Colonel Elbert was held a prisoner until after the fall of Charleston, when having been exchanged, he went North and offered his services to General Washington as his own State was now almost completely overrun by the enemy. That great chieftain gladly accepted his services, and at the siege of York Town he was honored with the command of the Grand Deposit of Arms and Military Stores, a post of great trust and distinction. In this position he won the approbation of the Commander-in-Chief and the friendship of our distinguished ally, General LaFayette, with whom he kept up a correspondence for several years, and for whom he named one of his sons. In recognition of his gallant and patriotic services his own State honored him with the rank of Major-General, the highest military honor that Georgia could confer. In the Continental Army he was a full Colonel and was brevetted Brigadier-General.

After the close of the Revolution he returned to Savannah and resumed his commercial pursuits. He was not allowed to remain in private life, for in January, 1785, he was elevated to the Governorship of Georgia. His administration was clean, energetic and business-like and was marked by the passage of the bill creating the State University. Upon the conclusion of his term as Governor he was made Sheriff of Chatham County.

When he died on November 2, 1788, at the age of forty-eight, all the military of Savannah, the Masonic Lodge and the Society of the Cincinnati attended the funeral. Rev. Philip Lindsay, D.D., preached the sermon and the remains were carried to the private cemetery of the Rae family, four miles from the city of Savannah. The papers of the day extolled his honor, his courage and his patriotism.

Six of his most valuable letters have been preserved by Mr. I. K. Tefft, of Savannah, the pioneer autograph collector of Georgia. They were addressed to Dr. Noble Wymberly Jones, Brigadier-General James Jackson, Colonel William Maxwell, Baron de Steuben, Andrew McLean, Major-General Lachlan McIntosh. The State has honored his memory by naming for him one of her most prosperous counties.

WM. BERRIEN BURROUGHS.

Henry Ellis.

WHEN John Reynolds resigned his position as Governor of Georgia he was succeeded by Henry Ellis, a man by temperament and training admirably fitted for the difficult task to which he was assigned.

He was born in England about 1720, and was educated to the law at Temple Court. In early life he devoted himself to the study of scientific subjects, and became specially interested in geographical discovery.

In 1746 a committee of Parliament placed him in charge of an expedition to find a new passage to the Pacific Ocean. After twelve months spent in persevering but fruitless efforts to find the desired passage, he returned to England and published such an interesting narrative of his voyage that he was elected a Fellow of the Royal Society, and appointed Deputy Commissary General.

One of these publications, entitled "Voyages made to Hudson's Bay in 1746-47 by the Dobbs Galley and the California to discover a Northwest Passage," was presented in 1748, and another in 1750, entitled "Considerations Relating to the Northwest Passage."

Through the influence of the Earl of Halifax he received his appointment as Governor of Georgia on August 3, 1756, but it was not until February 16, 1757, that he reached Savannah, having first landed in Charlestown, where he was the recipient of many honors from the Carolina officials. The people of Georgia hailed his arrival with delight, for the administration of Governor Reynolds had been very unpopular, and they longed for a change in the position of Chief Magistrate. Immediately upon his arrival he repaired to the residence of Governor Reynolds, to whom he paid his formal respects, and then appeared before the Council where he was duly inducted into office.

Before leaving England he had familiarized himself with the distracting state of affairs in Georgia, and he at once set himself to the task of remedying these evils. He had sent over five hundred muskets with which to arm the militia, a ship of war to protect the coast, and presents for the Indians. In the midst of dissensions growing out of the previous administration, his conduct was calm, conservative, tactful, and statesman-like, and his integrity and impartiality were soon recognized by the people.

Governor Ellis took important steps to strengthen and improve the judiciary system of the Province, and to establish friendly relations with the Indians. He visited the southern parts of the Province to acquaint himself more thoroughly with the people, and to inspect the settlements more remote from Savannah. He was much impressed with the advantageous location of Hardwicke on the Great Ogeechee, and sympathized fully with the suggestion of Governor Reynolds to make that town the capital of the Province instead of Savannah.

It was during the administration of Governor Ellis that the town of Sunbury was laid out, and the Province of Georgia divided into eight parishes, with laws for holding public worship in each of these parishes, for supporting the churches at public expense, and for the relief of the poor.

The employment of negro slaves in the industrial arts was forbidden, unless white artisans refused to work at fair wages to be determined by Commissioners appointed for that purpose.

Nearly fifty acts of the administration of Governor Ellis received the royal sanction, and under his wise and conservative management Georgia was rapidly recovering from the effects of her recent political dissensions under Governor Reynolds. For the purpose of providing against attack from the Spaniards and the Indians Governor Ellis made a personal inspection of the forts in the Province and took steps to strengthen them.

At this time the Indians were a constant menace to the peace of the Province, but by the tact and wisdom of Governor Ellis the savages were conciliated, and a treaty between them and the whites resulted.

Of the Conference held in Savannah on October 25, 1757, with the Upper and Lower Creeks, Colonel Jones thus speaks: "Anxious to impress these savages with the highest possible conception of the military strength of the town, Governor Ellis ordered that they should be received by the first regiment of militia, commanded by Colonel Noble Jones, that sixteen cannon should be mounted in the different batteries around Savannah, and that seven field pieces should be placed in position in front of his dwelling. As the Indians approached, escorted by Captain Milledge and the Rangers, they were met beyond the lines by Captain Bryan and a cavalcade of the principal inhabitants, who welcomed them in the name of the Governor and regaled them in a tent pitched for that purpose. This preliminary reception concluded, preceded by the citizens on horseback, the Rangers bringing up the rear, the procession of Indians advanced to the town gate where salutation was made with three cannon from the King's battery, three from the Prince's, five from Fort Halifax, and five from Loudoun's bastions. Pausing at the gate the citizens opened to the right and left, facing inwards, and the Indians, marching between them, entered the town, where they were received by Colonel Jones at the head of the regiment and conducted with drums beating and colors flying to the council chamber. While passing the Governor's residence the column was saluted by the battery there stationed, and this compliment was repeated by the guns in the water battery and by cannon on vessels in the river.

"At the council house the regiment filed to the right and left and, in parallel lines facing the chiefs and warriors as they advanced, presented arms. At the steps of the council chamber they were saluted by the Virginia Blues; and, upon entering the house, they were met by the Governor, who with outstretched arms, welcomed them thus: 'My friends and brothers, behold my hands and my arms. Our common enemies, the French, have told you they are red to the elbows. View them. Do they speak the truth? Let your own eyes witness. You see they are white, and could you see my heart you would find it as pure, but very warm and true to you, my friends. The French tell you whoever shakes my hands will immediately be struck with disease and die. If you believe this lying, foolish talk, don't touch me. If you do not, I am ready to embrace you.'

This speech, so well adapted to the comprehension of the natives, and so much in unison with their favorite style of utterance, completely captivated their hearts. Approaching the Governor they shook his hand warmly, and declared that the French had often sought to deceive them. Friendly greetings followed, and the ceremonies of the day were concluded by a dinner at which the head men of the twenty-one towns represented were kindly and pleasantly entertained. During their stay in Savannah these red men were complimented with many presents, and were bountifully feasted. On the following Thursday, having been honored with another military parade and by martial salutes, they assembled in the council chamber, which was thronged to its utmost capacity by the citizens. There they were again addressed by Governor Ellis. 'Observe, my friends,' said he, 'how serene and cloudless this day appears. I cannot but consider it as a good omen of the success of this interview; and I hope that you are all come with hearts resembling it, unclouded by jealousies and with dispositions suitable to the good work of tightening the chain and making the path straight forever between us.' He then read in their hearing, with great solemnity, a communication which he had prepared, entitled 'A letter from the Great King to his Beloved Children of the Creek Nation.' Its conciliatory terms were pleasing to the Indians, and their response promised peace and amity.

"The result of this convention was all that could have been desired. It was shown in the treaty of the 3d of November following, by which friendly relations between the Province of Georgia and the Creek confederacy were firmly pledged."

The peaceful removal of outlaws and fugitives from justice who had settled on the Satilla River, and the final settlement of the vexatious claims of Mary Bosomworth were wisely and tactfully brought about through the good judgment and skill of Governor Ellis.

At this time the health of Governor Ellis became seriously impaired, and as he believed a change of climate would benefit him he requested the Crown of England to relieve him from his official duties in Georgia. The request was reluctantly granted, and the people of the entire Province were deeply moved at the retirement of a man who had contributed so much to their happiness and prosperity. Having turned over the affairs of state to the Hon. James Wright, his successor in office, he bade adieu to the grateful people of Georgia, and set sail for England November 2, 1760, having served the Province a little less than four years.

He was afterwards appointed Governor of Nova Scotia, a position which he held for two and a half years, remaining in England, however, during this time.

To benefit his failing health he dismissed all public cares, and sought repose at Marseills in the south of France. He afterwards visited Italy, where on January 21, 1806, at a venerable age, he died, and was buried upon the shores of the beautiful bay of Naples.   OTIS ASHMORE.

David Emanuel.

I T is remarkable how soon Time's effacing fingers sweep into oblivion the unrecorded deeds of man. Only one hundred years ago David Emanuel was one of the most prominent and honored citizens of Georgia, and for a time Governor of the State, and to-day the records of this distinguished man may be expressed upon a single page. All men must die, but it is the duty of the living to posterity to see that the inspiring record of great men and noble deeds should live.

The memory of no prominent man of Georgia has suffered so much from neglect as that of David Emanuel. The writer has made extensive efforts to rescue from oblivion the records of this distinguished Georgian, but the ruthless tide of time has already overwhelmed all except a few fragments from which this sketch is prepared.

White, in his *Statistics of Georgia,* says: "David Emanuel came to Georgia about 1768 or 1770, and settled on Walnut Branch, near Waynesboro, from whence he moved to the head of Beaver Dam Creek."

The Rev. Adiel Sherwood, who lived in Burke County in 1818, in his *Gazetter of Georgia,* says: "Colonel David Emanual, of German extraction, was born in Pennsylvania in 1744. He came to Georgia before the war and married Miss Ann Lewis, by whom he had several children. He endured many hardships during the war, near the close of which his own and about thirty other families had built some cabins in a cluster below Augusta, and which the Tories denominated Rebel Town."

In *White's Historical Collections of Georgia,* page 39, we find among the signatures to the oath of Allegiance and Supremacy the names of "David Emanuel and David Lewis (Justices St. Geo. Paris, 17th December, 1766)."

In response to a letter of inquiry, the Rev. George G. Smith, of Macon, Ga., author of *The Story of Georgia and the Georgia People,* says: "David Emanuel, the *pro tem* Governor, was the son of John Emanuel, who was the son of David Emanuel, who came to Virginia probably from Pennsylvania, and who afterwards came to Georgia. John Emanuel had quite a family, among whom was David, who was a sturdy youth when the Revolution began."

In the list of Headrights granted by the Colonial and State governments from 1754 to 1800, we find the names of David and Asa Emanuel under the dates of 1760 to 1774, and again the name of David Emanuel under the dates of 1786 to 1789.

Whatever uncertainty may exist concerning the early life of David Emanuel it is clear that his family was prominent in Burke County before the Revolution, and that he himself took an active part in that great struggle. When Georgia was overrun by the British, Burke County was the scene of several sharp skirmishes between the American patriots on the one side and the British and Tories on the other. At that time David Emanuel was attached to the command of his brother-in-law, General John Twiggs, and many dangerous encounters took place. The following dramatic incident in the life of David Emanuel is related by Sherwood, and, with slight variations, by White:

"Near McBean's Creek he was taken prisoner while out on a scout, and condemned to be shot with two or three others. Divested of most of their clothing, and ready for execution, Mr. Davis, one of the unfortunate company, begged permission to go to prayer. This was granted, and as may be expected, he engaged most fervently at a throne of grace. He and the other prisoners were then shot down, and though a big mulatto man (who was to have his clothes as a remuneration for shooting him) stood ready to fire, Emanuel jumped among the horses, which were near, and made his escape. The night was dark, and jumping into the swamp, he sank up to his neck. His pursuers, muttering their curses, passed several times near him, but a kind Providence permitted him to escape their notice. When all was still he crept out, and in the morning made his way to Twiggs' army."

When the War of the Revolution closed, David Emanuel continued to reside in Burke County, and, by reason of his excellent judgment and sterling character, he became prominent in the political affairs of that county. He was a member of the two conventions which met in 1789 and 1795 to revise the Constitution of the State. He was elected several times as Burke County's Representative in the Legislature, and for several years he was a member of the Senate. He was a practical man of affairs, and possessed rare judgment and business ability. While a member of the Senate he was thrice elected President of that body, and when General James Jackson resigned the office of Governor, in 1801, to accept the position of United States Senator, David Emanuel, by virtue of his office as President of the Senate, discharged the duties of Chief Executive from March till the following November, when Josiah Tattnall was elected Governor.

When the notorious "Yazoo Fraud" threatened to debauch the morals of the State and rob it of a vast and valuable domain, the Legislature appointed a committee of its best and wisest men to investigate the infamous act and report the results to that body. Upon this committee David Emanuel was placed, and to his honesty and wisdom much of the credit is due for rescuing the fair name of the State in this memorable crisis.

Having for many years served his State in war and in peace, and having been honored by his fellow-citizens, he died at his home in Burke County in 1808, loved and respected by all who knew him. The name of one of the largest counties in the State perpetuates his memory.

David Emanuel is described as "a fine-looking man, amiable, of good judgment and inflexible integrity."

There is a tradition that he was of Jewish extraction, and while careful inquiry at this date fails to throw any direct light on the matter, his own name together with the names of other members of his family would seem to strengthen this tradition. David Emanuel had two sisters, Ruth and Rebecca. Ruth married General John Twiggs, of Revolutionary fame, and their children were named George L., David Emanuel, Levi, Abram C., Asa L. and Sarah L.

Sherwood, who was a Baptist preacher, says that David Emanuel was a Presbyterian in religion. One of the daughters of David Emanuel married Hon. Benjamin Whitaker, for a long time prominent in the political affairs of the State.

OTIS ASHMORE.

William Ewen.

WILLIAM EWEN was a native of England, and came to Georgia, probably, in 1734, as an apprentice to the Trustees. In a few years, by his correct behavior and business habits, he became very popular with his fellow-citizens. During the period in which the affairs of the colony were managed by William Stephens, Esq., much discontent existed among the people. Repeated complaints of grievances had been made, which were never effectually redressed; and a meeting of the disaffected citizens was called, at which Thomas Stephens, the son of William Stephens, was appointed to represent their interests in Great Brittain; and a committee was also appointed to correspond with Mr. Stephens, of which Mr. Ewen was an active member. In the discharge of his duty he was frequently brought into collision with the President of the colony, who, judging from several portions of his journal, did not award to him much credit for the course which he thought proper to adopt. When the struggle between Great Brittain and her colonies commenced, he was among the first of that "immortal band" who took up arms in defence of American liberty. On the 21st of June, 1775, he was appointed a member of the Council of Safety, and shortly afterwards President of the Council, the duties of which were very arduous. At this period Georgia occupied a very critical situation. Of all the colonies none were so illy prepared to dispute the claims of the mother country. On the South she was exposed to the attacks of the Spaniards of Florida; on the East her coast was at the mercy of the foe; on the North and West countless tribes of savages known to be in the pay of the British King were ready to make inroads upon the population. She was destitute of soldiers and all the means of war. A very large proportion of the people, although they felt that they had just grounds of complaint against the mother country, were disposed to postpone open resistance with a hope that their grievances would be redressed. The Sons of Liberty were, indeed, few. Says an actor in those days, "There are few righteous souls among them; a panic seems to have run among the people; assistance is wanted from Carolina to overawe such men as would sell their heritage for a mess of pottage." Happily for Georgia she had such men as William Ewen at the head of her government. The wisdom of the arrangements he proposed and his firmness in executing them baffled in many instances the designs of the foe. His letters, his proclamations and other official papers, breathe a spirit of determined opposition to tyranny. He lived to see the independence of his country established and to receive the plaudits of his grateful fellow-citizens for his devoted attachment to their cause. *—White's Historical Collections.*

Benjamin Few.

BENJAMIN FEW, Colonel of Richmond County militia during the Revolutionary War and one of the most active partizan officers of Georgia in that war, was born in 1744 at the "Three Sisters" plantation, near Hickory, Baltimore now Harford County, Maryland. He was the eldest son of William Few, Sr., and Mary Wheeler, deriving his given name from his maternal grandfather, Benjamin Wheeler.

In the fall of 1758 when Benjamin was fourteen years old, his father removed his family from the tobacco lands on Deer Creek in Northern Maryland to the frontier forests of North Carolina on the Eno River in Orange County, and here the boys of the family were inducted into the wielding of the axe to clear the wilderness, a new occupation, as the family chronicles record the blistered hands and strained muscles engendered by this unwonted task.

Here in North Carolina, outside of a short period at a country school, Benjamin assisted his father on the farm and at a saw and grist mill on the banks of the Eno, and here it was that he courted and won his wife, Rachel Wiley.

Ten years of peace the Fews spent in this frontier settlement, ten years of work and then the years of peaceful work were succeeded by the three years of the so-called War of the Regulators against the oppressive acts of the Colonial officers, who sought to enrich themselves at the expense of the people, and ending in the battle of Alamance, May 16, 1771, where the Regulators, poorly led and equipped, were defeated by the artillery and muskets of the British under General William Tryon, the royal governor, who bore the sobriquet of the Great Wolf of North Carolina.

The day after the battle James Few, Captain of the Regulators, the younger brother of Benjamin, refusing to take the oath of allegiance, was hanged at the head of the British camp, the first martyr in the cause of American independence. A few days after, the farm of the father, "a man dangerous to the State," according to the Governor's view-point, was overrun and the cattle and horses of the British driven in the fields to destroy the growing crops.

There is no positive evidence that Benjamin participated in the battle of Alamance, but it is believed that he was one of those who fought and escaped capture. His father was a sympathizer with the cause, and in 1768 was one of the bondsmen of Herman Husbands, the erstwhile leader of the Regulators, and Benjamin Few was not the kind of man to have remained peaceably at home when such an occasion offered. Certain it is that a few months after this battle, six more Regulators having been executed, the Few family, deeming North Carolina a dangerous place for longer residence, removed to the Quaker settlement in St. Paul's Parish, Georgia, near Wrightsboro, and the cruel execution of James Few was not calculated to make any of the family espouse the British cause in the sorrowful yet glorious years that followed.

The Revolution finds every male Few in arms: the aged father, William Few, Sr., according to the statement of his grandson, Rev. Ignatius A. Few, a Colonel in the Commissary Department; Benjamin, the subject of this sketch, Colonel of militia; his brother, William Few, Jr., Lieutenant-Colonel of militia, had a distinguished career elsewhere recorded in this work; and the youngest brother, Ignatius Few, Lieutenant, Captain and Brevet-Major of dragoons in the Continental Army.

The two brothers-in-law of Benjamin, Rhesa Howard, husband of Hannah Few, and Colonel Greenberry Lee, husband of Elizabeth Few, were also actively engaged.

The Revolutionary records of the State of Georgia having been nearly all destroyed, it is a somewhat difficult matter to follow the career of Benjamin Few through all the years of conflict. His earliest recorded action was not at the time deemed a creditable one. The patriots of Georgia had their hands full with the British and the Tories and did not want the horrors of an Indian warfare as well, so that it was but natural that the following, signed by Governor A. Bulloch, should appear under date of May 16, 1776, as part of orders to Captain Wm. McIntosh: "And as there has been information made of the murder of an Indian by one Few and a party of men under his command, you are therefore ordered to use your utmost efforts to apprehend the said Few and to bring him to Savannah, and at all times to do whatever may be in your power to prevent the murder of any Indian in the Back Country." But when Benjamin Few went to Savannah he went with the militia of Richmond County at his back.

Under the act of the Georgia Legislature of March 1, 1778, he was one of the Commissioners from the county of Richmond for the sale of the confiscated estates of Tories or those attainted of treason. The members of this committee were especially obnoxious to the British and those caught were hanged.

Colonel Few was with the troops that marched against but failed to meet the British General Prevost in his attempt to take Savannah from Florida, and was a member of the unfortunate St. Augustine expedition in the spring of 1778, planned in retaliation for Prevost's campaign. After the capture of Savannah by the British in December, 1778, the whole patriot force in the State of Georgia consisted of the militia of the upper three counties; the militia of Richmond being under the command of Benjamin Few. He successfully resisted the attack of the British under Brown and McGirth upon the patriot camp in Burke County, on their way to Augusta, this constituting the first successful engagement against the enemy on Georgia soil, and shortly afterward he defeated and dispersed a large body of the Creek Indians inspired by the British agent Tate upon the Ogeechee River. This last affair was after the Georgia militia had been driven into South Carolina, not having been strong enough to resist the capture of Augusta by Colonel Campbell, January 31, 1779, and the *Georgia Gazette* of February 15, 1779, a Tory paper, had gleefully announced the departure from Georgia of "a villainous tribe of plunderers under the celebrated horse thief, Captain Few."

It is not to be wondered at that the name of "Benjamin Few, Rebel Officer, Richmond," appeared in the historic black list promulgated by the British Governor, Wright, and that the *Georgia Gazette* of March 14, 1782, the Tory paper previously noted, printed within the British lines, further announced that "A Georgia Parole" [hanging] had been reserved for the "virtuous Few."

During the summer of 1779 Colonels Few, Twiggs and Jones were hanging around the outposts of the enemy, cutting off supplies and exerting themselves when opportunity offered. In December, 1779, Colonels Few and Twiggs commanded the Georgia militia at the unsuccessful siege of Savannah. Here Pulaski received his mortal wound and was carried from the field by some of Colonel Few's men, but otherwise the militia did not distinguish themselves in the battle.

June, 1780, finds Colonel Few in Hillsboro, North Carolina, his former home, on his way with the men of Richmond to join the Southern army. In December, 1780, he was at the battle of Long Cane Creek, South Carolina, and here was criticised for not properly bringing his men into action, more of a surprise as "he had previously given evidence of good conduct."

It would hardly be profitable to follow him and the varying fortunes of the Southern army, so long unfortunate, to the end of the war.

One anecdote of his Revolutionary life has come down hitherto unrecorded through the years. When the British had overrun the entire State of Georgia, and lukewarm patriots, unable to remove their families from the State, were hurrying homeward and taking the oath of allegiance to George III., Benjamin Few, unable to remove his family, said that "he would leave them with the God of battles." When he did return after the war was over, like the other Georgia patriots, he returned to a ruined estate.

Colonel Few represented the county of Richmond in the first Georgia Legislature after the treaty of peace, and was a Justice in this county in 1783. He acquired a headright in Wilkes County about 1784, but spent most of his time on his farm on Germany Creek, Columbia County. He removed from Columbia County, Georgia, to Alabama in 1803. The Land Records, American State Papers, note his transactions there in connection with some Spanish grants, and there he died in 1805. He and his wife are buried in the neighborhood of the Nanna Hubba Bluffs on the Tombigbee River.

He left two sons, William and Thomas. Dr. James E. Dickey, President of Emory College, Georgia, is a descendant of the latter.

In personal appearance Colonel Few was about five feet ten inches high, stout and powerfully muscled, bold, bluff, kind-hearted and magnanimous. He was a friend of the fatherless, as William and Sarah Few, the children of his murdered brother James, were reared in his family.

Feared and abused by his enemies, British and Tories, he was idolized by his soldiers; plain-spoken, brave and patriotic, a manly man, a soldier of many battles, he gave to Georgia, in times of peril, the years of his manhood.

L. D. Carman, M.D.

William Few, Jr.

THE great-grandfather of William Few was Richard, who, with his son Isaac, came to America with the Pennsylvania colonists in 1682, and settled in what is now Chester county, Pennsylvania, where he died in 1689. Isaac Few married Hannah Stanfield, whose father, Francis, was at one time a member of the Pennsylvania Provincial Assembly. Isaac Few died in 1734, leaving a large family, among whom was William Few, Sr., father of the subject of this sketch, who was born in 1714.

The colonist Fews—father, son, and a servant—had come from Lavington, Wiltshire, England, where the Quakers were and are still numerous. The family, presumably, continued in this faith until the elder William Few removed to Georgia, when he exchanged his faith for the fast growing and more virile Methodism.

The subject of this sketch was born in that part of Baltimore county which now forms Harford county, Maryland, on June 8, 1748. His mother, Mary Wheeler, was a devout Catholic, and had inherited a very nice property from her father, Benjamin Wheeler, who died in 1741. Her great-grandfather, Major John Wheeler, of Charles county, had been one of the early settlers in that section.

The foregoing authoritative account of Mr. Few's ancestry was gathered from old wills and court records; but his own autobiography is the best guide for the balance of this sketch. This document was prepared for family use shortly before Senator Few's death with no expectation that it would ever reach

6

the public. This work, from the pen of a conspicuous actor in the most fruitful period of the genesis of the American State, forms a very valuable contribution to the history of Georgia and the nation during and for many years after the Revolution. Mr. Few's extreme modesty is nowhere better shown than in this simple narrative of his life, dealing, as it does, more with events with which he was connected than with his own personal history. For the biographer's sake a more personal relation would have been far more useful.

The scope of this sketch will permit only a brief outline of William Few's career, as given in this autobiography. Its author states that his father, after two or three successive failures of the tobacco crop in Maryland, and for the additional reason that it was thought that his mother's health would be greatly improved by a southern climate, decided to move to North Carolina in 1758. The tide of immigration had already turned in this direction from the northern region, and it is not unlikely that its ebb had brought back many tales of the salubrious climate, the fertile soil, and the natural riches of field and forest to be found to the southward. So in the year 1758 the elder Few with his wife, six children, and several slaves journeyed to North Carolina, carrying with them their "household gods" and goods. A settlement was made on the River Eno, in what is now Orange county, not far from the town of Hillsboro. A sturdy and vigorous class of citizens had opened up this territory, which was included in the Granville grant, and this was in most respects a frontier settlement typical of the time and section. Virgin forests abounded everywhere, and the young sons as well as the servants were put to work making a clearing. William was ten years old at the time of the removal, and must have been a sturdy, well-grown lad, as he states that he, too, took part in the general activity necessary for forming a permanent settlement. We get from this narrative a little glimpse of pioneer life in respect to its isolation from all the real substance of civilization, from its conveniences, its associations, and its refining influences. It is stated, for example, that in this remote backwoods region two years passed without sight of an officer of the law, or of any other person in fact, save a very occasional itinerant preacher, who had strayed from the main highways into this almost uninhabited country in search of souls. However, a little later a straggling schoolmaster wafted into the settlement, and William was given his first opportunity for learning. This master, so-called, appears to have been a good representative of that forbidding class of pedagogues who outrage every kindly instinct of youth under the guise of their delegated authority and who by daily acts of incompetence and brutality make themselves the perpetual terrors of the youthful mind. Young Few, however willing, seems to have profited little from this schooling, but fortunately the following year a different type of schoolmaster appeared. William remained with the latter a year, and was indebted to him for almost the sole instruction he ever received in the rudiments of knowledge. Having learned to read he soon devoured the few books his father's library contained. We cannot but wonder at the statement when the author names among these such works as Tillotson's Sermons and Barclay's Apology. The Bible, of course, was a treasured possession of the family, and, between Catholic mother and Quaker father, doubtless its truths were not neglected.

The Fews later moved into the town of Hillsboro, which had then about forty families. This was the metropolis of the western frontier and was the headquarters of the court on the main thoroughfare. There young William gained access to several— for the time and place—good libraries, and he seems to have improved to the utmost the opportunities thus offered. He does not mention having gone to school any more, so we must conclude that the two years received back in the wilderness must have begun as well as completed all the formal education he ever received.

Soon after moving into Hillsboro he seems to have become filled with ambition to become a lawyer, and, although a good many years elapsed before his ambition was gratified, he must not have remained idle, as he states that he applied himself diligently to such law works as he could procure.

A most unhappy event terminated the Fews' residence in North Carolina. This was but one in a series of abuses of a kind and of a piece with those that finally drove the colonists into open rebellion against the mother country. Reference is made to what is known as the Regulator uprisings. James, the second of the Few children, just a little past maturity, seems to have been identified with the uprisings which contributed a most emphatic protest against governmental outrages. These troubles, which seem to have been led and taken part in by some of the most substantial citizens of that section, culminated in the battle of Alamance, which no less a historian than Bancroft names the first positive and overt act of rebellion against the mother country, and the first in the series that culminated in the achievement of separation.

James Few, following this battle, in which the Regulators were defeated, was taken and hanged without semblance of trial. Bancroft speaks of him as the first martyr of the Revolution. William Few omits all reference to this melancholy event in his autobiography, merely stating that his father removed to Georgia because of his having become involved financially. This embarrassment was due undoubtedly to his known connection with the Regulator affairs as bondsman for those outlawed. Young William was left to wind up the affairs in North Carolina.

Before the latter joined his family in Georgia, the Revolution had opened in earnest. Few had no moments of hesitation or doubt as to the side with which he should cast his lot. His narrative states that he was among the first who proposed to raise an independent company of infantry in Hillsboro. He was joined by twenty other young men, who chose officers, purchased uniforms and arms, and began systematic instruction in the manual of arms under an old British corporal. The North Carolina convention met at Hillsboro in 1776 and resolved to raise two regiments, in one of which young Few was offered a commission as captain, but this he was unable to accept.

In the autumn of this year the future senator joined his family in Georgia. He was just past twenty-eight at this time. He had hardly reached Georgia before he was induced to offer as a candidate for the constitutional convention, which was to organize a form of government to replace the colonial system just overthrown. He was elected to this body. The constitution provided for an assembly to be chosen by popular suffrage, and a governor and sixteen councillors to be chosen by the assembly. Few was unanimously elected a member of the popular body for Richmond county, and his election to this body was immediately followed by his selection as one of the sixteen councillors. The British soon after this outlawed all those prominent in the new government, and William Few was designated on this black-list "rebel councillor."

Georgia, up to the spring of 1778, had felt scarcely any evil effects from the Revolution, as the storm-center at this time lay far northward, and political liberty was more of an academic than a real question. At this date, however, General Prevost invaded the State from East Florida, and this invasion excited the indignation of the patriots to the highest pitch. As a result a retaliatory invasion was organized under General Howe, the invading party consisting of militia and six or eight hundred Continental troops.

Few was a member of the militia, but in what capacity he does not state. The invasion proved a complete fiasco; the time was ill-chosen, and the troops were forced to retreat without an engagement. Soon after the termination of this unfortunate expedition, Few was appointed Surveyor-General, and later one of the Commissioners of Confiscated Estates and Senior Justice for Richmond county.

Savannah fell in December, 1778, and following this the State got in a bad way indeed. The Governor fled to South Carolina, the Continental troops were withdrawn, and the country was entirely at the mercy of the British. The militia organization, confined at this time to the northern counties, did not number more than 500. Colonel Benjamin Few, the eldest brother of William, commanded the Richmond militia, and his troops, joined by a small body under Colonel Twiggs, successfully checked the advance of the enemy at Burke Court House. This engagement may be regarded as the opening of that fierce and relentless partisan warfare in this section, which continued until peace was declared. The limits of this sketch will permit only brief reference to this stirring period. William Few gained the rank of Lieutenant-Colonel of the Richmond county militia, and was an active participant in the almost daily skirmishes and forages in which this body of patriots engaged.

In 1779, the first panic having been overcome, the State government was partially reestablished, and William Few was again elected to the Legislature. In January, 1780, he was appointed a member of the Continental Congress. Henceforth he was identified continuously with that body and with its successor, provided for under the Constitution of 1787. He had hardly taken his seat before a matter of the deepest interest to his state arose. There were intimations of peace on the basis of the retention by the British of territory then in their possession. Georgia had by this time lost what little she had recently gained and had practically fallen under British control, and the state government had become badly disorganized. These rumors threw the Georgia delegates into a state of great alarm, and they deemed it of capital importance to take some immediate action looking to the rehabilitation of the Whig government. William Few was chosen for this work, and reached Georgia in September, 1781. As illustrative of the narrow resources of the government at the time, it may be noted that great difficulty was experienced by Congress in raising the $1,000 which it had voted for the expense of the trip.

Following Mr. Few's return, a legislature was soon assembled at Augusta, a full set of officers elected, and the militia reorganized. This important task completed, Few returned to Congress in May, 1782. Lord Cornwallis' surrender in the fall of 1781 put an end to the war. After the treaty of peace the following year Colonel Few returned to Georgia. General elections occurred about this time, and he was again sent to the Legislature from Richmond county. This was a most important session, as it was necessary to reorganize the government and provide in various ways for the future welfare of the State.

Colonel Few had consecrated the past eight years to the public service so disinterestedly that he had had little time to think of private affairs. Although he had received no formal instruction in law, he decided to devote himself to this profession. He was admitted to the bar in 1784, and, as he says in his autobiography, began the study and practice of law at the same time. In 1786 the Legislature again appointed him a member of Congress. The Congress now sat at New York instead of Philadelphia.

This session of Congress was a most important one, although in a negative way, exposing as it did the weakness and impotence of the then federal form of government. This inability to get results brought a realizing sense to Congress of the need of a stronger central power, and resulted in the call for a constitutional convention to convene May, 1787. William Few was named a member by his state, and was also at the same time reelected to Congress. He sat through the entire session of the memorable Constitutional Convention, and his conspicuous signature is one of the thirty-nine attached to the great instrument which it gave to the country. His connection with this monumental work will cause him to be remembered, even when his other many and honorable services in behalf of his state shall have been forgotten.

Congress adjourning, Few returned to Georgia, and was elected to the Legislature, which was among the first to adopt the new Constitution. This was done on January 2, 1788, three months after its transmittal by Congress to the different states (September 28, 1787). Under the terms of the new organic law of the nation, Few was appointed senator. The short term fell to his lot, and this expired March, 1793. He appears not to have offered for re-election, but returned to his plantation in Columbia county, having been for eight years a member of the Legislature, for four a member of the Continental Congress, and for an equal period a member of the Senate.

Mr. Few did not remain long in retirement before a public measure of immense import called him again to public life. This was the celebrated Yazoo Act, a measure growing out of the wild fever of the time for land speculation. Great indignation had been aroused by the sale on the part of a former legis-

lature of all the unlocated lands of the State to several companies of speculators, for sums which averaged about a cent and a
half per acre. Casual readers of the history of the celebrated
case might find cause to suspect Mr. Few of insincerity in throwing all the weight of his powerful influence in favor of the
annulment of the act granting these lands *pro bono publico,*
since it is a matter of record that his name appeared at one
time among a company of bidders whose offer had been rejected.

Few was one of the original opponents of the sale, and the
explanation of his appearance before the Legislature as a bidder
is that when he and some others who, like himself, were opposed
to the sale, had used all the power at their command to defeat
it, they hastily formed a company and made a bid greater by
$200,000 than the highest offer before the Legislature. This
bid, prepared as a *dernier resort,* was rejected on the ground
that its promoters were notoriously insincere in making the
same, and had no idea of carrying out its terms. The public
conscience finally became aroused, and annulment became the
paramount issue of the ensuing campaigns. Mr. Few was
elected a member of the Legislature from Columbia county,
and this Legislature promptly declared the Yazoo Act null and
void, and even went to the unusual extent of cutting from the
books, and burning every record and document relating to
the Act.

About this time Mr. Few again offered for the Senate, but
was defeated. He had been practically twenty years continuously in the service of his state, and this being the first defeat
he had known in his whole career, he takes no pains to conceal
his keen mortification. The Yazoo cabal, still strong in the
State, evidently concentrated all its fury against him, although
this does not account in full for his defeat.

Soon afer his defeat for the Senate, Colonel Few was appointed Judge of the Second Judicial District, and remained in this station three years. This was the last in the series of public services which he rendered for his adopted state, as he removed to New York City in May, 1799. He was called into public life there almost immediately, becoming a member of the Assembly for the years 1801, 1802, 1803, and 1804. From this time till his retirement from participation in active affairs in 1816, Mr. Few held several public offices, among which were Commissioner of Loans, Inspector of the State Prison, and Alderman of the city of New York. In addition to these public offices, Mr. Few was a director of the Manhattan Bank from 1804 to 1814, and President of the City Bank from 1814 to 1816.

His marriage presumably occurred in the year 1786. The lady of his choice was Catherine Nicholson, daughter of Commodore James Nicholson, known as the first commander of the American navy.

This useful and efficient life came to an end June 16, 1828, at Fishkill, on the Hudson River. His wife and three daughters survived him. The eldest of the daughters, Frances, married Major Albert Chrystie, and through this union the sole descendants of Senator Few now living are the members of the family of the late Wm. Few Chrystie, who reside on their estate, Postavern, Hastings-upon-Hudson, New York.

MARION LETCHER.

John Floyd.

THE father of this distinguished man was Mr. Charles
Floyd, a native of Virginia, who came to Beaufort
district in South Carolina. Here his son John was
born on the 3d of October, 1769. The devotion of Charles
Floyd to the cause of American liberty was remarkable. During the Revolution he was in the habit of wearing a silver
crescent about two inches long with the motto, "Liberty or
death," engraved on it. Few patriots of seventy-six were
doomed to greater suffering. Besides a long imprisonment,
his estate was ruined by the devastations and plunder of the
British soldiery and their infamous allies, the Tories. After
the close of the war the broken fortunes of the family demonstrated to the son the necessity of providing for his own
wants; and at the age of sixteen he, with the approbation of
his father, apprenticed himself to a house carpenter for the
term of five years. Having served four, his master, as a
compliment to his fidelity, offered to release the services of
the fifth year; but the apprentice gave proof of that conscientious estimate of moral obligation and high-toned self-
denial which shone so conspicuously through the subsequent
scenes of his life. When a boy he had promised the service
of five years, and nothing short of a plenary fulfillment could
satisfy the requirements of his own buoyant and honest
heart.

About the year 1791 or 1792 both father and son removed
to Georgia and established themselves near the mouth of
St. Illa River, in the county of Camden. The great demand

at that time for water craft adapted to the navigation of the numerous sounds, creeks, and rivers of the country, determined him to commence the business of a boatwright. Having procured at Charleston drawings and models of the most approved keels in that harbor, he hired the requisite number of timber cutters and without delay entered upon his new business. By nature he was endowed with great aptitude for mechanics, and by the habits of his life for great activity in business. With these qualifications he soon raised himself from a state of comparative poverty to one of opulence; and long after he had acquired an independent estate he still retained his chest of fine tools, and occasionally applied his own hands "to the labors of a boatwright as well as to housebuilding." He was frequently a Representative from the county of Camden in the General Assembly of the State; and in 1826 was elected one of the Representatives of Georgia in the Congress of the United States. Anterior, however, to his election to Congress, he received the commission of Brigadier-General in the militia service of Georgia, and on the occurrence of a vacancy he was advanced to the grade of Major-General of the first division.

Though not averse to politics, his predilections were decidedly military, and, considering the defects of his early education, his attainments in the history and art of war were quite remarkable.

The act of Congress, passed in June, 1812, declaring war between the United States and Great Britain, opened a theatre for the display of Floyd's military talents, although as the British did not attempt an invasion of the State, his action was confined to a limited sphere.

In September, 1813, the Federal government called for a levy of Georgia troops, and three thousand, six hundred men were ordered to rendezvous at Camp Hope, near Fort Hawkins on the Ocmulgee River. This force consisted of one company of artillery, one squadron of dragoons, one battalion of riflemen and two regiments of infantry, a majority of whom were volunteers, and considered at the time the flower of the State militia.

General Stewart, of Oglethorpe county, being the oldest brigadier, was ordered to the command of these troops; but, from age, infirmity or some other cause, he resigned his commission, leaving Floyd the senior officer of that grade in the State. Though unapprised of General Stewart's resignation, and, of course, unprepared for the executive order which conferred upon him the command, he accepted it and promptly repaired to the place of encampment of the army, and without subsistence or means of transporting military stores.

Energy and dispatch in all things were characteristic of General Floyd, and, on assuming the command, he proceeded to make immediate arrangements for taking the field. Unfortunately it was not in his power to control the commissariat of the army—it could not march. Either the perfidy of the contractors, or, what they alleged in case of themselves, the default of the Federal government in supplying promised funds, prevented the army from moving into the country of the Creek Indians, then the allies of England, before the middle or latter part of November. Even then the march of the army would have been impracticable had not the General succeeded in an application to the Legislature then in session for a loan out of the State Treasury. This loan was placed in the hands of Captain Samuel Butts, a special commissioner, who, under the orders of the General, procured a temporary supply of provisions and transportation.

Though the troops could anticipate but little glory in contending with an undisciplined army, they marched with alacrity, and bore with patience the heavy labor of constructing a line of forts and block-houses, extending from the Ocmulgee to the waters of the Alabama river.

They missed no opportunity of encountering the enemy, but by reason of the great distances which were to be traversed before the hostile towns could be reached, and the unfortunate, if not culpable, delinquency of the Federal government in failing to supply provisions and transportation, it was not in the power of General Floyd to meet the Indians in any considerable force at but two places. Having completed a work on the right bank of the Chattahoochee, called Fort Mitchell, he put himself at the head of a detachment of nine hundred troops and hastened to the attack of Autossee, one of the most populous towns of the Creek nation.

It was situated on the left bank of the Tallapoosa river and in the immediate vicinity of a considerable town called Tallassee. On the expedition every man, for the want of other conveyance, carried his rations in his own knapsack; and after a rapid march over a distance of sixty miles a successful and simultaneous attack was made on both towns. The action lasted more than an hour, when the Indians fled from the field and the towns were burnt to ashes. This victory over a superior force, however, was not achieved without serious loss to the detachment as well as to the enemy. The General received a dangerous wound from the effects of which it is believed he never entirely recovered.

Soon after the battle of Autossee, as General Floyd found himself able to ride on horseback, he determined to make another inroad; and having received information that certain bands of savages, known as the Upper Creeks, had collected in great force and fortified Hatlewaulee, a town on the same river, he determined to attack it, and for that purpose detached from the army fifteen hundred rank and file. The march of these troops was badly obstructed by continued falls of rain and the want of bridges and roads. When the detachment had advanced to a point within fifteen or twenty miles of the town it was attacked about an hour and a half before daybreak, and by such a superiority of numbers as to render the issue at first doubtful.

Everything except the firmness and discipline of the detachment was in favor of the enemy. The darkness of the hour, the covert afforded the Indians by a thick forest of pines with which the camp was surrounded, the total want of breastworks or other defenses, the surprise which the first yell of the savages occasioned, and the estimated numerical superiority of the enemy's force were well calculated to put the courage of the militia to a severe test; but they had been in service six months, had become hardened to the privations and hardships of camp life, had met the enemy before, and now they encountered him with the coolest intrepidity.

Not a platoon faltered, but every one brought into action kept up a brisk fire until the dawn of day enabled General Floyd to order a charge. In less than fifteen minutes every hostile Indian but the dead and dying had fled from the battlefield.

In this action, known in the official report as the battle of Chalibbee, the detachment sustained severe losses in both killed and wounded. Among the former was that gallant soldier and true patriot, Captain Samuel Butts. The loss of the enemy was doubtless greater; but, as it is the known custom of Indians to carry off their wounded in time of battle and as many of the killed as practicable, their actual loss was never ascertained.

Within a few days after the battle of Chalibbee, the term for which this army had been called into service expired, and the several corps, after due inspection, received an honorable discharge. But the war continuing, new levies were made, and another brigade was placed under command of General Floyd for the purpose of repelling an apprehended assault on Savannah. This, however, turned out to be a bloodless campaign. The British troops never appeared in that vicinity until the President's proclamation announced the treaty of peace.

After the close of the war in the spring of 1815 General Floyd served several sessions as a member of either the State Legislature or of Congress—everywhere and at all times esteemed and honored as one of the most meritorious citizens of Georgia. Though his public and private life exemplified to a great extent the circle of social and moral virtues, it has been said by those who knew him best that the sturdiest and most effective element of his character was patriotism. With him it was a deeply seated passion, a fixed sentiment that seemed to modify all his estimate of human merit. He died on the 24th of June, 1824.

Joel Crawford, *in White's Collections.*

Robert Forsyth.

THE subject of this sketch was born in England and was a descendant of the Scotch family of the name, whose history is identified with that of Scotland for centuries. Coming to Virginia early in life, he joined his fortunes to those of the new republic, served in the Continental army, and left it with the rank of major. His home, until about 1784, was in Frederick county, whence he removed with his family, first to Charleston, South Carolina, where he remained but a short time, and thence to Richmond county, Georgia, where he made his home for the remainder of his life. He was the first United States Marshal for the State of Georgia, and lost his life in the performance of his official duty, having been assassinated by one Beverly Allen, whom he had arrested and allowed too much of privilege. His slayer fled to Texas, the then Mecca of law-breakers, and was never apprehended by the law.

An old but well preserved tombstone in the Augusta cemetery marks Major Forsyth's grave. His only son, John Forsyth, lived to honor his name, being Governor of the State, United States Senator, Secretary of State for the United State, and Minister to Spain, during a life of only sixty years.

GEORGE H. AUBREY.

7

George Galphin.

WE are indebted to White's Historical Collections for
the following:

Prior to the year 1773 George Galphin was a licensed
trader to the Creek and Cherokee tribes of Indians, then
within the limits of the colony of Georgia, and to whom these
tribes were largely indebted, in his own right or by the assignment of the claims of other traders. In the same year
Sir James Wright, Governor of Georgia, pursuing the instructions of the parent government, concluded at Augusta
a treaty of cession of land for the sole purpose of discharging the indebtedness of the Indian traders, and by which
was annexed to the British crown a large extent of territory,
embracing the present counties of Wilkes, Lincoln, Elbert
and parts of Greene, Oglethorpe and Franklin.

In 1775 the treaty was ratified by the British crown, and
commissioners were appointed to ascertain and liquidate the
claims under it. Accordingly, on the 6th of June the claim
of George Galphin was proved for 9,791 pounds, 15 shillings
and 5 pence, and duly certified by the "Governor in Council"
and payable out of such moneys as shall or may arise by
the sale of lands lately ceded to his Majesty by the Creek
and Cherokee Indians.

The menace of hostilities and open war in the succeeding
year arrested, and, by its result, entirely destroyed the pros-
pect of payment from this source.

In January, 1780, the Legislature of Georgia, under the
exigencies and pressure of the war, appropriated these ceded

lands and applied them to the uses of the war. An important reservation was, however, made in behalf of such Indian traders as were "friends to America." They were requested to lay their claims before "the then or some future House of Assembly" to be examined, and whatever claims should be allowed as just and proper were to be paid by Treasury Certificates, payable within two, three and four years, and bearing 6 per cent interest.

This act of Georgia brought into view the inquiry, What was the relation of George Galphin to the Revolution? As preliminary to the answer, it is proper to state that George Galphin was a native of Ireland, emigrated soon after manhood to America, and died at Silver Bluff, his residence, on Savannah river in South Carolina, on 2d of December, 1780, in the seventy-first year of his age.

By his enterprise he extended his mercantile transactions with several Indian tribes far into their country, and, by fair dealing and uniform kindness, acquired a controlling influence over their temper and conduct, which were always predisposed to resentment and war.

His position commended him to the notice and employment of the colonial government, and, as a commissioner of Indian Affairs, his official duties were discharged with promptitude and fidelity. To the period of his death, his conduct during the war of the Revolution was consistent, uniform and patriotic.

In 1777 General Howe wrote General Washington from Charleston, "The temper of the Creek nation, by the unwearied exertions of Mr. Galphin and by the liberality of this State in supplying them, upon generous terms, with those goods they wanted, seems at present to promise peace, which I consider a very happy event for this State and that of

Georgia." The Honorable George Walton, a signer of the Declaration of Independence and chairman of the committee which reported the act of Georgia in 1780, and knew its motives, its sincerity and intention of justice, was called upon in the year 1800, by the representatives of George Galphin, for his knowledge and recollection of and concerning the objects, terms and conditions of a treaty made at Augusta in the year 1773. To that call he responded and spoke highly of Mr. Galphin. He said, "Having enjoyed his friendship in his lifetime, having fully known his sentiments as to the Revolution, and been a frequent witness of his exertions in favor of it, I cannot resist the occasion of paying my own individual tribute of gratitude to his memory and services. Who is there that has forgotten the exercise and right of his influence in restraining the inroads and consequent murders and ravages of the savages, especially the Creeks? None. The undersigned is of the opinion, therefore, that to dispense with the claim of this venerable man, founded as it is, is to dispense with the justice and laws of the land."

By the side of this full statement of Mr. Walton may fitly be placed that of his compatriots, Major Joseph Habersham, Honorable William Stephens and Major Peter Deveaux, who unite in testifying that Mr. Galphin was a decided friend of the American Revolution from its early origin to his death; that he, with others, suffered very considerably, indeed largely, in property during the war.

The act of Georgia was an open invitation to all claimants, friends of America, on the ceded lands, to apply to her Legislature for payment. The heirs of Galphin have been the only applicants.

Their first petition was in 1793, when the United States

Senate passed a bill by eight to three to carry into execution the promise of the State, made in 1780, to the whole amount of Galphin's claim.

The Royal Assembly, which met in Savannah in 1780, attainted George Galphin of high treason only four months before he was carried to his grave. In 1790 the British Parliament appropriated two hundred and fifty thousand dollars for the payment of the claims of the sufferers by the cession of Georgia to the Americans. The heirs of George Galphin were not allowed to participate in this because they were informed that it was intended only for British loyalists. His estate was sold to satisfy ·debts incurred in his trade with the Indians, for the payment of which he relied upon the proceeds of these ceded lands.

The matter was referred to the Judiciary Committee which reported the claim a just one, which should be assumed by the general government. Accordingly, the Secretary of the Treasury was directed to pay the claim, amounting to $234,871. Mr. Crawford's connection with the claim will be told in his sketch.

Compiled from *White's Collections.*

William Gibbons.

THE Honorable Thomas Spalding, then far advanced in years, in 1850 thus narrates his recollections of the subject of this sketch: "Mr. Gibbons was my law instructor. After my own father he was the best friend I ever knew. He was a great lawyer, well read in his profession, which he acquired in Charleston under the direction of a Mr. Parsons—an Irish gentleman of high grade in the law. The result from his professional labors while I lived with him was three thousand pounds sterling a year. This I knew, as I was his collector and Mrs. Gibbons his treasurer. There was then no bank paper. His note-book was to him of great value, for he had distinctly noted every important case that had occurred during his whole practice, giving the points on which it turned and the opinion of the judge; and as these judges in those times were Judge Walton, of Augusta, and Judge Houstoun, of Savannah, these decisions carried more weight with the jury than the decisions of the King's Bench.

"Mr. Gibbons was not a very fluent speaker. He was very quick in discovering the weak point of his opponent, and his memory was always ready to give the law that bore upon it. His commentary upon the law was in short, clear, distinct terms, very pointed; and sometimes he indulged in witticisms, which increased as he grew older from his intimate association with Peter Carnes the elder—the wittiest lawyer I ever have known, and whose wit obscured his profound law knowledge in the eyes of the many. Mr. Gibbons in his nature was very open, frank, and manly, and very determined. This gave him a few warm friends and many bitter enemies.

"It gives me pleasure to state that General James Jackson, the noblest man with whom it has been my lot to be acquainted, when I called upon him as Governor to give me a letter to Mr. King, our then minister in London, kept me to dine with him; and he asked me what were Mr. Gibbons' receipts from his profession? I replied: 'Three thousand pounds per annum.' His response was: 'My own were about that amount when I unwisely left my profession for politics. Mr. Gibbons, *as a whole*, was the greatest lawyer in Georgia.' Let me say to you that General Jackson and Mr. Gibbons had exchanged three shots at each other; they were considered the bitterest enemies by the public. A high-minded man feels no enmity."

Mr. Gibbons was a gentleman of large wealth, accumulated, it is believed, by judicious investment of his professional income. It was upon one of his rice plantations, situated not far from "Mulberry Grove" on the Savannah River, and while as the guest of Mr. Gibbons inspecting his growing crop, that General Nathanael Greene, on the 13th of June, 1786, contracted the illness which so speedily terminated his valuable life. His residence in Savannah was noted for its comfort and bountiful hospitality. It was the day of rich brown sherry, Madeira wine and good brandy.

Upon another of Mr. Gibbons' plantations General Wayne, in June, 1782, met and overcome the famous Indian Chief Guristersigo.

While intent upon the practice of his profession and busied with his private affairs, he was not indifferent to the claims of country or an idle spectator of passing events. His sympathies at the outset were cordially enlisted on the side of the "Sons of Liberty," and his time and services were cheerfully given to furthering the aims of the rebels.

He was one of the party which, during the night of the
11th of May, 1775, broke open the magazine in Savannah
and removed therefrom some six hundred pounds of the
King's powder, to be exploded not in the honor, but in defiance of his Majesty.

In the Provincial Congress of July, 1775, he appeared
as a delegate from the district of Acton, and was a member
of the committee raised to acquaint the president of the
Continental Congress with the proceedings of the Georgia
Congress.

Of the Council of Safety selected on the 11th of the following December he was chosen a member. It was by direction of this council that Governor Wright was arrested and
confined. So far as we can learn, Mr. Gibbons never bore
arms during the struggle, but he was almost continuously
in the civil service of the commonwealth. Of that Executive or Supreme Council which, in July, 1779, was invested
with extraordinary powers, he was an active member.

Aside from the distinction of representing Georgia in the
Continental Congress he was complimented in 1786 with the
position of Associate Justice of the county of Chatham; in
the following year with the speakership of the House of
Representatives; and in 1789 with the presidency of the
constitutional convention. The act of a formal acceptance,
by Governor Walton, from Mr. Gibbons of the new Constitution concluded upon by that convention in Augusta on the
6th of May, was announced to the town by a salute of eleven
guns.

Mr. Gibbons died in Savannah in 1800. His will bears
date the 14th of June, 1799, and was admitted to probate
on the 26th of November in the following year. It is now
of record in the office of the ordinary of Chatham county,
Georgia.   C. C. Jones, Jr.

Tho: Glascock

2:nd Jany. 1785.

Thomas Glascock.

THE Revolutionary annals of Georgia may well be proud of the noble and patriotic career of Brigadier-General Thomas Glascock. In the year 1779, before and after the Continental troops attacked Savannah, then in the hands of the British, we find two Glascocks, father and son, high in the civil and military service of Georgia. The father, William Glascock, an eminent lawyer and politician, was Speaker of the House of Assembly; and the son, Thomas Glascock, was a young captain of cavalry in the Legion of Count Pulaski, the immortal Polish refugee, who, fleeing from political proscription at home, came to America and, at Savannah, fought, bled and died for American liberty.

Thomas Glascock was born in Virginia in 1749 or 1750, and preceded the rest of his father's family to Georgia some years before the Revolution. He was educated at the best institutions of both the South and the North, and the eventful days of 1776 found him in the full vigor and enthusiasm of young manhood. He entered heart and hand and soul into the great struggle for American independence, and for a year or more before the battle of Savannah, had been in command of a company of cavalry, doing bold and signal service in the lower part of the state. He exhibited great bravery and military genius by attacking and defeating, with a small force, a large body of the enemy.

Young Glascock conceived a romantic and devoted attachment to Count Pulaski; and the attachment seems to have been appreciated by the noble Pole, and to such an extent, indeed, that the older man treated the younger as if he had been a son or a much younger brother. Early in the battle of Savannah Count Pulaski, attempting to lead his men past an abatis of the enemy's works into the town, received a cannon shot in the groin from which he fell and in three days after died. On the retreat of the Continental troops it was recalled, and with bitter mourning by his legion, that the Count had been left dangerously wounded near the abatis. And now was shown the high courage and noble personal devotion of Captain Glascock, who, having chosen a few of his men, ready and willing, boldly volunteered to return and rescue the dying soldier. And this he did through fire and smoke and shot and shell; and, three days after, when the illustrious Polish patriot breathed his last, the young captain of cavalry was by his side, a place he had not vacated from the hour of the rescue.

During an expedition against the Indians, who had become troublesome on the western frontier of the young and struggling commonwealth, he was appointed colonel. A year after, in the fall of 1780, Captain Glascock, having risen through all the intermediate grades, was appointed and commissioned Brigadier-General in the Continental army. At this time he was in his thirtieth or thirty-first year, and soon after married Miss Mary Bacon, a sister of Edmund Bacon, Esq., of South Carolina, the eminent lawyer and wit, whom Judge Longstreet has handed down to us as Ned Brace in *Georgia Scenes*.

In 1785 he served on an Indian commission, and on the 18th of November of that year was present at a meeting with the Cherokees at "Hopewell on Kiowee." On the 28th of the same month, he, with his colleague and the North Carolina delegation, issued a protest against the treaties as signed.

In 1793, General Glascock, at the call of Governor Telfair, met in Augusta with Major-Generals Twiggs, Jackson and Clarke, and Brigadier-Generals Morrison, Irwin, Gunn and

John Clarke to consider the condition of affairs as it related to the Indians. Having applied in vain to the Federal government for protection, it was decided to make an expedition against the Creeks the following October. The expedition was abandoned on the disapproval of President Washington.

On June 5, 1794, President Washington commissioned him Marshal of Georgia. Descendants of General Glascock in Augusta still have the original commission.

During Governor Irwin's administration he was appointed to the command of that quota of the militia which was designated by the general government to be furnished by Georgia. He was a member of the Georgia Mississippi Company.

He was a member of the Constitutional Convention in 1798, but with General Gunn, of Camden, "asked and received leave to decline to sign the constitution because, by section 23, article 1, the state claimed and re-asserted its right of possession and jurisdiction over territory which they claimed as grantees under the usurped act of 1795."

General Glascock was a bold financier and left large estates. He died in Richmond county about the age of 54, and was buried at his country place, "The Mills," some miles to the northwest of Augusta. White says of him: "In every situation to which he was elevated he never exhibited one mark of presumption, one mark of assumed authority over those with whom he was associated, but always exhibited that character with which we are mostly pleased—the friend of mankind."

HARRIET GLASCOCK GOULD JEFFERIES.

William Glascock.

WILLIAM GLASCOCK was descended from one of two brothers who immigrated to this country from England in the year 1630. He was born in Virginia and followed his son Thomas to Georgia before the war of the Revolution. In *White's Historical Collections,* page 58, will be found the resolution of a Provincial Congress convened at Savannah January 18, 1775. This Congress met to devise means to redress American grievances, and resolved that non-importation, non-consumption, and non-exportation the best methods to be pursued with the mother country to obtain a proper recognition of the rights of the Province of Georgia. On page 61 of the same work the name of William Glascock is enrolled as a delegate to this Congress. This Provincial Congress chose delegates to the Continental Congress. These delegates were Noble Wimberly Jones, Archibald Bulloch, and John Houstoun. When Savannah was overrun the seat of government was moved to Augusta. The election of delegates was directed to take place on the first Tuesday in 1779, and the Legislature was to meet in Augusta thereafter. William Glascock was elected a delegate and was chosen Speaker of the House of Assembly of the State of Georgia January the 4th, 1780.

In *White's Historical Collections,* page 98, appears a Disqualifying Act, passed July 6, 1780, directing Sir James Wright, Baronet, Captain-General, Governor and Commander-in-chief of his Majesty's Province of Georgia, to disqualify certain persons who had taken up arms against his

Majesty from ever thereafter holding any position under the Crown. William Glascock, "Rebel Counsellor," appears on the roll of the disqualified, and was attainted of high treason by the British in 1780. In January, 1780, by an act of the Legislature, William Glascock was appointed, in conjunction with George Walton, one of the signers of the Declaration of Independence, Daniel MacMurphy, John Twiggs, and George Wells, Esquires, a board of commissioners for granting lands to such citizens as might be induced to come into the State, also for the improvement and enlargement of Augusta, laying out streets, straightening roads, building a court-house and "gaol," reserving desirable lots for church and school. This act is signed William Glascock, Speaker, and will be found in *Watkins' Digest of the Laws of Georgia.* William Glascock acted as Governor of Georgia at one time during the Revolution. He was appointed by an act of the General Assembly which met at Savannah July 31, 1783, William Gibbons, Speaker, as trustee to establish the Richmond County Academy, Augusta. The same body also made him one of the trustees to found Franklin College, now the University of Georgia, signed Joseph Habersham, Speaker, Savannah, January 27, 1788. The minutes of the said university show that Hon. William Glascock died in 1793. He was buried on his plantation below Augusta, called "Glascock's Wash." There is no picture of him extant.

HARRIET GLASCOCK GOULD JEFFERIES.

John Glen.

JOHN GLEN, the first Chief Justice of Georgia, was the son of James Glen, one of the royal governors of South Carolina. His standing as a lawyer and as a patriot is clearly indicated by the positions which he held. The *Georgia Gazette* of July 20, 1774, published a call signed by Noble W. Jones, Archibald Bulloch, John Houstoun, and George Walton requesting "that all persons within the limits of this province do attend at the Liberty Pole at Tondee's Tavern in Savannah, on Wednesday, the 27th instant, in order that the said matter [Boston Port Bill] may be taken under consideration, and such other constitutional measures pursued as may then appear most eligible."

John Glen was chosen chairman of the Savannah committee and as such sent notices to the different parishes, requesting that they would send to the meeting of August 10th, which was an adjourned meeting of the one called in July, delegates "to join the committee agreeable to the number of representatives each parish sends to the General Assembly."

On the 18th of January, 1775, a Provincial Congress met in Savannah upon invitation of a committee of the citizens of Christ Church parish and elected John Glen chairman.

On June 22, 1775, he was made a member of the first Council of Safety, along with a number of other leading patriots of his day. He was also a member of the Provincial Congress which met July 4, 1775. In fact there was scarcely a patriotic movement during those stirring times which marked the beginning of the Revolution with which he was not in some way connected.

The Council of Safety, as originally created, had almost arbitrary powers. The Provincial Congress, feeling the need of a broader basis of action, on April 15, 1776, adopted a set of resolutions amounting to a constitution. Among other things this constitution provided for a Chief-Justice and two assistant judges, etc. They were to be "appointed by ballot and to serve during the pleasure of the Congress." Mr. Glen was chosen as the first Chief-Justice of Georgia, and his salary fixed by the statute at one hundred pounds per annum. Judge Glen was mayor of Savannah in 1797, and on January 26th of the following year was appointed judge of the Superior Court.

He married Sarah Jones, a daughter of Noble W. Jones, about 1755. He died May 13, 1799.

A. B. CALDWELL.

Nathanael Greene.

MAJOR-GENERAL NATHANAEL GREENE was the second son of a Quaker preacher and was born at Warwick, Rhode Island, August 7, 1742. He was of English extraction and his ancestors came to this country during the reign of Charles the Second, among the first settlers of the little colony. Like most men of his calling, the good divine was not rich in this world's goods, and Nathanael was given far more training at the plow and in his father's blacksmith shop than in the school-room. The boy's mind was naturally keen, however, and he had the good fortune to meet with two men whose influence affected his whole career. One of these was a youth named Giles who had been to college and who filled his companion with a desire for the companionship of books. The other was the noted Lindley Murray, and the impetus thus received from association with them carried young Greene forward until he was the possessor of a very fair education. Over his forge he pursued his studies as far as Latin, higher mathematics and metaphysics, until at the beginning of the fierce discussions which arose with the mother country at the outbreak of the Revolution he was well prepared to take an active part as a leader.

In 1770 he was elected to the General Assembly of the colony and aided in the discussions, but as the Stamp Act and other aggressive measures on the part of England gave evidence of the approaching conflict, he turned his attention to military studies. Cæsar's Commentaries and Turenne's

Nath Greene

Engd by H.B. Hall & Sons, New York.

Memoirs were his constant companions until Cupid superceded Mars one evening when he looked into the eyes of a damsel by the name of Catherine Littlefield. He married this lady in July, 1774.

A year later the battle of Lexington was fought and the colonies called the patriots of America to arms. Rhode Island responded with a force of sixteen hundred men and Greene was made the leader with the rank of Major-General. His military bent of mind had already attracted the censure of his Quaker friends, and finding him bidding defiance to the principles of non-resistance he was formally expelled from the society. The young officer took command of the troops in May, 1775. He was thirty-three years of age, and well fitted by nature for the duties of his difficult position. At Cambridge, where he went with his command to join the regular army, he met with Washington, and the great Virginian early perceived his ability and formed with him a friendship that endured throughout life.

After the evacuation of Boston, Greene was placed in command on Long Island. To his great mortification he was sick with bilious fever while his forces were engaged with the enemy. He soon recovered, however, and had the experience of his first battle at Harlem. Other engagements followed in which he had a prominent part. In December, 1776, Greene crossed the Delaware, and was in command of the left wing of the army in the brilliant movements that resulted in the victories of Trenton and Princeton.

In the disastrous battle of Brandywine, Greene covered the retreat of the Continental forces and stopped the advance of the exulting enemy. Shortly afterward at Germantown it was the skillful leadership of the same general that brought off the American army in safety and disappointed the fresh

8

troops of Cornwallis, confident of success. Greene thwarted the designs of the same officer when he advanced against Fort Mercer a few days later.

During the winter which followed, the terrible Valley Forge experience occurred. The American army was destitute of food and clothing and suffered terribly. Washington was helpless, but this did not prevent a movement on the part of several unscrupulous and ambitious officers for his overthrow. This plot was called the Conway cabal, and its prime movers were Generals Conway, Gates and Mifflin.

It failed completely, but General Greene, who remained faithful to his Commander-in-chief, long felt the hostility engendered by the wretched conspiracy. The situation of the army was improved, when, at the request of Washington and Congress, he undertook temporarily the duties of the Quartermaster and by energetic effort gave some relief to the suffering soldiers.

At the battle of Monmouth, Greene bore himself with coolness and intrepidity and played no small part in turning retreat into victory. In the unsuccessful attack upon Newport—a failure because the French commander, Count D' Estaing, thought it best to abandon the enterprise, to the great disgust of his American allies—he was a prominent figure and protected the rearguard of the army as it was drawn off.

He had now been Quartermaster for two years, in addition to his other military duties, but criticism of his thankless task on the part of some members in Congress furnished him the welcome opportunity of resigning it, and of devoting himself exclusively to the more agreeable work of fighting the enemies of his country. At Elizabethtown, Greene repelled the advance of Clinton, and fought successfully in the face of an army three times as large as his own.

His next service to his country was in connection with the treason of Benedict Arnold and the capture of the ill-starred Major Andre. Greene was called to preside over the court-martial which convicted the young British officer, and the safety of the nation demanded that this unfortunate spy should be sacrificed. In spite of his sympathies, Greene showed himself possessed of the true warrior spirit, and was alike unmoved by the tears of the sentimentalists or the threats of the English general.

The defeat of General Gates at Camden rendered it necessary to send Greene to the South. The conqueror of Burgoyne at Saratoga was too rash and it was necessary to supersede him with a man who was more endowed with the Fabian quality of prudence. The new commander found the Southern forces at Charlotte, but they were small in number and utterly dispirited. He had splendid assistance, however, in the partisan leaders, Marion, Sumter, Pickens and others. These brilliant soldiers lay hidden in the swamps of the Carolinas with small bands of ragged but devoted followers, and at unexpected times would sally forth to harass the armies of their foes. With their assistance Greene soon put new life into his troops and found himself in condition to meet the enemy. Lord Cornwallis was in command of the British, and the two armies met on the banks of the Catawba river. The Americans were defeated and retreated to Salisbury. An incident occurring at this place well illustrates the spirit of the Southern women. Greene had stopped at an inn for refreshment. He had ridden all day through the rain and storm, his clothes were wet and covered with mud, he looked depressed, and in response to inquiry he said that he was "tired, hungry, and penniless." As soon as he had dined the good landlady took him aside and placed in his hands two bags of money—the savings of a lifetime—and said: "Take these; I can do without them and they are necessary to you."

The British army followed the retreating Americans, and so determined was Cornwallis to crush his foe that he destroyed all his baggage in order that his advance might not be impeded. The eyes of the whole country were upon the two leaders, and Greene proved himself equal to the emergency. Reaching the Yadkin he barely had time to throw his forces across the river and destroy the boats when the pursuers appeared. The enraged British opened fire with their cannon upon the Americans, but were impotent, especially as severe rains had swollen the stream. Their shot tore the shingles from the roof of the cabin where Greene was writing dispatches, but they did not disturb his composure nor cause him to stop until he had finished his labors.

His movements were so skilfully managed as to win praise from all. Washington wrote, "Your retreat is highly applauded by everybody." Even the enemy praised him. Tarleton, their famous cavalry leader, said, "Every measure of the Americans during their march from Catawba to Virginia was judiciously designed and vigorously executed." And this movement was made by raw militia without sufficient clothing or food in the face of a foe that far outnumbered them.

Greene soon received supplies and reenforcements. After getting his army in shape he turned southward to again meet his foe. At Guilford Court-House, North Carolina, they joined in battle with no decided success for either commander. Cornwallis claimed the victory, but a British speaker in the House of Commons declared they were undone if they suffered another such "victory."

At Hobkirk's Hill and at Ninety-Six Greene again met the enemy in doubtful contest. Later he turned still further southward and attacked the British General Stewart at Eutaw. The first onset was successful, but unfortunately the half-starved Americans succumbed to temptation as they found in their possession the tents filled with all the comforts to which they had so long been strangers. They broke ranks and ate and drank to their hearts content as they gave themselves up to the gratification of their appetites. While they were thus occupied the British returned and scattered the disorganized forces. The Americans rallied and the British soon retreated to Charleston. It was a victory for the Continental troops but a most disappointing one.

By a series of skilfull maneuvers the American commander, aided as he was by the brilliant exploits of Marion and Sumter, the "Swamp Fox" and "Game-cock" of the Revolution, soon recaptured from the British the whole of the Carolinas with the exception of Charleston. Into this city General Leslie had led the army under his command, and Greene threw a strong cordon of troops about the place to begin a siege. Desperate, the British leader endeavored to accomplish by bribery what he feared to attempt in the open field. There were several mutinous spirits in the American army and the plot was formed with them to capture Greene and carry him into the city. The treacherous scheme was laid bare through the courage and fidelity of a woman. The leader of the movement, Sergeant Gornell, was hanged, and four others were put in chains.

The failure of this plot discouraged the British General, and the capture of Cornwallis at Yorktown made it certain that further continuance of the war was useless. As the Americans drew closer to the city the garrison soon felt the need of provisions, and finally on the 14th of December evacuated the city. Greene entered with the Governor by his side, and the long siege was at last over.

Greene was everywhere congratulated for the splendid part he had taken in the struggle. Congress, on his arrival at Princeton, voted him two pieces of ordnance taken from the enemy and a medal. South Carolina and Georgia, more practical in their patriotism, presented him with two plantations. The Carolina land he had to give up on account of the pressing debts he had incurred during the war.

In 1785 he removed with his family to the Georgia farm, which was at Mulberry Grove, twelve miles above Savannah. Here he spent the last days of his career, enjoying his domestic happiness in the midst of the pleasures of plantation life. One unpleasant incident marred this period. Captain Gunn, who had been associated with him in the army, deeming himself wronged about some military decision with reference to the capture of a horse, challenged the General. Greene refused to meet him in the duel, after consulting Washington, and thus helped in the formation of a better public opinion with regard to the foolish code of honor.

But he did not long enjoy the comforts of private life. On the 19th of June, 1786, he died from brain fever at the age of 44. The whole country was in sorrow at the untimely taking away of this great man. Especially was he mourned by the people of Georgia, among whom he had cast his lot and by whom he was sincerely loved. He was buried in the old Colonial Cemetery at Savannah, and, not being marked, the identity of his burial place soon became lost. In 1819 the City Council of Savannah appointed a committee to locate the grave, but the investigation was unsuccessful.

In March, 1901, the Rhode Island State Society of the Cincinnati took up the matter, and, together with several gentlemen of Savannah, prominent among whom was Superintendent Otis Ashmore, undertook a systematic search for the grave. On the 4th of that month their efforts were successful, and they fully identified the remains by means of the coffin plate, military buttons, etc. The bones of General Greene and his son, George Washington Greene, were enclosed in a zinc-lined box and placed in the vaults of the Southern Bank until their ultimate disposition should be definitely determined. It was finally decided to re-inter them at the base of the Greene monument in Savannah where they now remain. The occasion was made a solemn public ceremony on November 14, 1902, and an address was delivered by the president of the Rhode Island Society of the Cincinnati, Hon. Asa Bird Gardiner. Thus fittingly was honored the memory of this great patriot by the people of his native and adopted States. M. L. BRITTAIN.

James Gunn.

BORN of humble parentage and in straitened circumstances in Virginia, in 1739, and having acquired such education as was offered by the common schools in the neighborhood, Mr. Gunn applied himself to the study of the law, and was in due course called to the Bar.

When the united colonies took up arms against the mother country he espoused the cause of the Revolutionists, and in his native State joined the rebel army.

As a captain of dragoons he participated, under General Wayne, in the movement for the relief of Savannah in 1782; and upon the termination of the war selected that town as his home, and there resumed the practice of his profession.

He was fond of military affairs, and, as Colonel of the First Regiment of Chatham County Militia, led a detachment of State troops which succeeded in dispersing a formidable body of runaway slaves, who, having been trained to arms by the British during their occupation of Savannah, upon the cessation of hostilities styling themselves the "King of England's soldiers," and refusing to return to the abodes of their respective owners, formed a fortified encampment on Bear Creek, and from this place of conjectured security sallied forth by night, plundering and burning adjacent plantations on both sides of the Savannah River.

Subsequently he rose to the grade of Brigadier-General of Georgia militia, and was, by Governor Telfair, summoned to a council of war to devise measures for the protection of the State against the incursions of the Creek Indians.

Of violent temper and inclined to quarrel, shortly after General Greene became a resident of Georgia, General Gunn challenged him for an alleged wrong which he conceived the General had inflictd upon him during the war of the Revolution. At the time of the conjectured injury General Greene had been Gunn's commanding officer. Declining the meeting, and disavowing all responsibility in the premises, General Greene planted his refusal upon the broad ground that any admission of accountability under the circumstances would prove totally subversive of all military discipline. The whole matter was referred to General Washington, who unhesitatingly justified the course pursued by his favorite Lieutenant.

The Georgia Legislature, then in session at Augusta, on the 10th of February, 1787, elected General Gunn as a delegate to the Continental Congress; but it is believed he never took his seat as a member of that body.

Of the first Congress which convened under the Constitution framed by the Convention of 1787, General Gunn was a member. He was also a United States Senator from Georgia in 1795 and 1796. While holding this high office he became implicated in the Yazoo speculations, involving personal disgrace and impairing the fair fame of the commonwealth which he represented in the Upper House of the national Congress. He was one of the three grantees of *The Georgia Company,* and exerted his influence to compass a cession of public lands in direct violation of established principles of justice and equity.

Alluding to this scheme to rob the State of Georgia of its western territory, Doctor Stevens observes:

"The whole State was heaving with excitement. The bribery which had been so openly used by men high in office,

on the Bench, at the Bar, and in the Senate, and the corruption, intrigue, intimidation, and violence which had been
employed to gain over the Legislature to the plans of the
speculators constitute a dark page in the political history of
Georgia. One of the most zealous advocates of this scheme
was James Gunn. This man, who had risen from almost
obscurity to power by truckling to the vulgar tastes of the
populace, and by some show of military genius, was, at the
period of which we write, a Senator of Georgia in Congress,
and his presence there was needed to guard the interests of
the State. Yet, sacrificing all public considerations to private advantage, he remained in Georgia, repaired to Augusta,
and by his influence and efforts, at once overbearing and unscrupulous, became the main manager of this nefarious
business. Having secured the passage of the bill he then
repaired to Congress, which he reached only the last day of
February—four days before the constitutional close of the
session—and there sought to carry out his Georgia schemes
by involving the general government also in these questionable
transactions."

In these efforts he was thwarted by his co-Senator from
Georgia—a gentleman of the sternest probity, jealous of
personal and national honor, and of conspicuous courage—
the honorable James Jackson. It was chiefly through his
potent intervention that the *rescinding act* was passed, that
the scheme to rob the commonwealth of its valuable western
territory was exposed to public apprehension and reproba-
tion, and that the legislative proceedings of Georgia were
purged of this flagrant iniquity. Disgrace and disappointment followed hard upon exposure. Senator Gunn died suddenly at Louisville, Jefferson County, Georgia (then the
capital of the State), on the 30th of July, 1801. In the

Georgia Gazette of August 6, 1801, appears the following notice of his death: "Extract of a letter from Louisville, dated July 31. General Gunn arrived here last Sunday, and died last night at eleven or twelve o'clock; a very short illness indeed. It is said that his death was greatly owing to a draught of cold water after the taking of medicine; and, what is strange, the doctor and several gentlemen were in the room, and not one observed his death till some time after he expired. He is to be buried this afternoon with the honors of war."

His will was probated in Chatham county, Georgia, on the 10th of May, 1808, and letters testamentary were granted to Sarah Gunn, executrix. He was one of those who voted for locating the seat of government on the Potomac.

While an active and brave subaltern in the Continental army, and a man of determination and of considerable force of character, General Gunn was violent, aggressive, addicted to extravagant statement and profane swearing, overbearing, disposed to pander to the lowest prejudices of the populace, unscrupulous in the means employed for the accomplishment of his ambition, vain, boastful, negligent of public duty when intent upon schemes of personal advantage, and intolerant of opposition. The architect of his own fortunes, he builded a reputation quite marked, but in some respects unenviable.

C. C. JONES, JR.

Button Gwinnett.

THE public career of Button Gwinnett furnishes a notable example of the power one man can exert over the life and destiny of another.

Dr. Lyman Hall, who was Gwinnett's closest friend, was largely, if not entirely, responsible for the attitude taken by Gwinnett towards the colonies in the struggle for independence. Whilst Gwinnett was a man of convictions and moved at times by strong prejudices, he had great respect for the opinions and character of Dr. Hall. Some time after the beginning of the Revolution, Gwinnett was in doubt as to the course he would take, whether to ally himself with the colonies or take position against them.

Dr. Hall convinced him of the justice of the American cause, and, in 1775, he began taking an active part in public affairs, and from that time forward became prominent, pronounced, and aggressive in his defence of the political fortunes of the Province then on the eve of a mighty struggle.

Button Gwinnett was born in England in 1732, about the time Oglethorpe was settling the colony in Georgia. He had splendid physique and handsome face. He was quite well educated and a gentleman of polite address.

He began life as a merchant in Bristol, England. He left England and came to America in 1772, settling at Charleston, S. C. Here he resumed his business as a merchant; but being attracted by the steadily growing Province of Georgia, he moved his property and his business to Savannah. In 1768 he converted his property into money and bought a large part of St. Catharine's Island. He at once established a plantation and gave his attention to agriculture.

This purchase put him in easy access to the home of Dr. Lyman Hall, in the Midway District. Dr. Hall was the leading physician of the community. There sprang up between the two a strong personal and political friendship that resulted, as stated, in changing Gwinnett's views on public questions, making him a strong and helpful adherent to the cause of the colonies.

Gwinnett's first public service was rendered as a delegate from the parish of St. John to the Provincial Congress, which convened in Savannah January 20, 1776. By this Congress he was selected a delegate to the Continental Congress, his associate delegates being Archibald Bulloch, John Houstoun, Lyman Hall, and George Walton. He attended the session of that national assembly on the 20th of the following May. It was at that session, as one of the members, together with Lyman Hall, and George Walton, he affixed his signature to the Declaration, proclaiming the independence of the United Colonies, July 4, 1776. About two months later, August 30, 1776, he presented to the Council of Safety certified resolutions by the Continental Congress, authorizing the enlistment of a regiment of rangers, horse, and foot—two battalions, two companies of artillery to garrison the forts at Savannah and Sunbury, to be erected at the expense of Georgia, and the construction of four galleys, to be built at the charge of the general government and under the supervision of the Governor of Georgia,—all intended for the defence of the State. Gwinnett was largely instrumental in securing the passage of these resolutions.

Still retaining his position as a delegate to the Continental Congress, on October 7, of the same year, he became a member of the Council of Safety.

He had much to do with the framing and the enactment

of the Constitution of 1777, which for twelve years defined and supported Georgia as an independent State. Many of the provisions of that constitution withstood the changes of more than a century, and their beneficial influences are felt to this day.

In February, 1777, Archibald Bulloch, the first President and Commander-in-Chief of Georgia, suddenly died.

On the 4th of March following Button Gwinnett was elected to succeed him. He was to serve until such time as a Governor could be duly elected under existing constitutional provisions.

Gwinnett was unduly ambitious for preferment, and upon the day of his election as President, at his urgent solicitation, the Council of Safety passed an order, "requesting President Gwinnett to march into Florida with a competent force of militia and volunteers, erecting the American standard as he went, and proclaiming protection and security of person and property to all who would take the oath of allegiance to the United States."

The troops had been increased to a brigade. Colonel Lachlan McIntosh had been promoted to the rank of Brigadier-General and assigned to the command of these forces. Gwinnett had been a candidate for this position and he became intensely embittered by McIntosh's success. Because of a spirit of revenge, Gwinnett intervened in military matters to such an extent as seriously to impair the discipline of the troops and create insubordination toward the commanding general. All this was humiliating and mortifying to General McIntosh and caused great demoralization in the army.

Ambitious to signalize his administration by a feat at arms, Gwinnett planned the expedition against Florida. Instead of entrusting its command to General McIntosh, who was the ranking military officer of the State, Gwinnett, heaping affront upon affront, set him aside and took command in person. The expedition failed most signally.

At the session of the Legislature in 1777, John Adam Treutlen was a candidate for the office of Governor against Gwinnett, and he was elected. McIntosh became a warm partisan of Treutlen against Gwinnett and had much to do with Treutlen's election. McIntosh was open and violent in his abuse of Gwinnett, having publicly pronounced him a scoundrel. This was more than Gwinnett could endure, and the quarrel resulted in a challenge from Gwinnett, which McIntosh promptly accepted. The two met and a duel was fought on the morning of the 16th of May within the present limits of the city of Savannah.

At the first shot both were struck, Gwinnett's thigh was broken and he fell to the ground. He was asked if he cared to exchange another shot. He replied, "Yes, if I should be helped up." To this the seconds would not consent, and Gwinnett was taken from the field.

The weather was very warm for the season and the wound proved fatal a few days later. McIntosh was confined to his bed for some time, but finally recovered. Gwinnett's death created great excitement and the threats of his friends foreboded trouble.

Dr. Lyman Hall brought the matter to the attention of the Legislature and charged the officers with great remissness in not arresting McIntosh and bringing him to trial for murder. As soon as his condition would permit, McIntosh surrendered to the officer of the law and gave bond for his appearance. He was tried and acquitted. This settlement did not satisfy the people nor allay the animosity of the friends of Gwinnett. McIntosh finally surrendered his military command in Georgia and, securing an order from the Continental Congress, he took with him his deputy adjutant-general, his son, Captain Lachlan McIntosh, and his brigade major, Captain John Berrien, and reported at Washington's headquarters for assignment to another field for service.

Gwinnett was an able, patriotic citizen, devoted to American institutions, but he was over-ambitious and intense in his prejudices. An implacable enemy and intolerant of opposition, his career was brief but brilliant. He died May 27, 1777. In front of the City Hall in Augusta a monument has been erected 150 feet high in honor of Gwinnett and the two other signers of the Declaration of Independence. No one knows where his remains were deposited.

W. J. Northen.

James Habersham.

ONE of the most prominent of Georgia's early settlers was James Habersham, the ancestor of a long line of descendants, many of whom have been distinguished in the history of the State.

He was born at Beverly, Yorkshire, England, in January, 1812. In company with his friend, the Rev. George Whitefield, he left England for Georgia in December, 1737, and according to his letter dated May 15, 1771, he arrived in Georgia on May 8, 1738. Soon after his arrival he opened a school for orphans and destitute children, and co-operated with Whitefield in establishing and maintaining the Orphan House of Bethesda, an institution dear to the hearts of both throughout their lives.

When Whitefield returned to England in 1741 he left Habersham in charge of the Orphan House, and under his wise management it flourished greatly. He selected the site for the new Orphan House at Bethesda, and on November 3, 1741, he moved his orphans to their new home.

In 1744 he resigned his position at Bethesda, and entered into a copartnership with Colonel Francis Harris to carry on a general mercantile business in Savannah. The house of Harris and Habersham was the first commercial enterprise established in Georgia, and to it much of Savannah's prosperity and importance was due. Extensive trade relations were established with the principal cities of the North, with the West Indies, and with London, and through it was transacted a large import and export business. James Habersham raised and exported the first cotton ever shipped from America.

In 1750 James Habersham was appointed, in conjunction with Mr. Pickering Robinson, Commissioner to advance the culture of silk in the Colony, and his letters upon this subject show how deeply interested he was in this new industry.

In 1754 he was appointed, by the King, Secretary of the Province and one of the Councillors, and in 1767 he was made President of the Upper House of the General Assembly.

When Governor Wright left Georgia, July 10, 1771, on a leave of absence to England, James Habersham, by virtue of his position as President of the King's Council, assumed the duties of Governor, and for nineteen months he discharged these duties with dignity, ability and fidelity. The cares and responsibilities of the office, however, during these stormy times were not congenial to his calm and peaceful nature. The rising tide of the Revolution filled his heart with sadness and apprehension. In common with many of the older men of the time he remained loyal to his King, but at the same time he sympathized deeply with the Patriots in many of their grievances.

To the cares of his office were added those of his own private affairs, as well as those of Governor Wright and Mr. Knox, the Provincial Agent living in London. James Habersham was a successful man of affairs, and of considerable fortune. He owned several farms; among them was Beverly, his country seat, about nine miles southwest of Savannah, and Silk Hope, on the Little Ogeechee, about seven miles from the city. At one time he owned 198 slaves. Governor Wright had eleven plantations in Georgia, and at one time he owned 523 slaves. William Knox, the Provincial Agent in London, and a warm personal friend of Habersham, was a large rice planter also. The supervisory care of all this vast interest for his friends added no little to the weight of his responsibilities. When, therefore, Governor Wright returned to Georgia, in February,

1773, Habersham gladly turned over to him again the reins of government.

By this time his health was much impaired by frequent attacks of gout, from which, at times, he suffered greatly. He planned to visit England for the benefit of his health, and to renew his old acquaintances. These plans, however, were frustrated by a threatened Indian uprising in Georgia, and he was destined never again to see his native land.

In the summer of 1775 he visited New Brunswick, New Jersey, with a hope that the change of climate would benefit him; but he soon grew worse, and at that place he peacefully passed away on the 28th day of August, 1775. Two of his sons were with him at the time of death, his wife having died several years before. His body was taken to New York and interred in a vault of Trinity church, preparatory to its removal to Georgia. On November 14th his body was landed in Savannah and deposited in the family vault in the old Colonial Cemetery, where it now remains.

James Habersham was married on December 26, 1740, to Mary Bolton, at Bethesda, his friend, Whitefield, performing the ceremony. Mary Bolton, the daughter of ...... Bolton, of Philadelphia, was born April 5, 1724, and died January 4, 1763. Ten children were born of this marriage, three of whom, James, Joseph and John, survived their father. James Habersham, Jr., was a prominent merchant of Savannah. He had poor health, and from his quiet and polite manner he was called "the gentleman of the family." All three of the sons were educated in part at Princeton, and all of them warmly espoused the patriot cause. Joseph and John became prominent in the Revolution, and distinguished in State and National affairs afterwards.

Of the character of James Habersham, Col. C. C. Jones truly says, he was "one of the sweetest, purest, most useful, and noblest characters of the long line of Colonial worthies." He was deeply religious, and profoundly interested in the spiritual welfare of his fellowman. In all of his correspondence there is not an unworthy line. His letters breathe a spirit of Christian faith and feeling that permeated his whole life.

He was in no sense a politician. Though loyal to his King, he did not approve the unjust acts of England against America, and he deeply deplored those conditions which finally broke into revolution.

When we consider the loyalty of James Habersham to the mother country and his affection for Georgia as well, in connection with those dramatic events which swept nearly all the people of the Province, among them his own sons, into the whirlpool of the Revolution, we cannot but feel that his death was fortunate for him. In his letter of April 7, 1775, he says: "I would not chuse to live here longer than we are in a state of proper subordination to, and under the protection of Great Britain, altho' I cannot altogether approve of the steps she has lately taken." He saw with prophetic vision the coming storm, but death kindly drew the curtain and closed his eyes forever to the bloody fulfillment of his prophecy.

OTIS ASHMORE.

Painted by John Sartain Philaᵈᵃ

MAJOR JOHN HABERSHAM.

CONTINENTAL ARMY

John Habersham.

THIS distinguished Georgian was the third and youngest son of the Hon. James Habersham and Mary Bolton. He was born December 23, 1754, at Beverly, one of the country residences of his father, nine miles southwest of Savannah, Georgia. When quite young his mother died, and ever afterwards his kind hearted father was tenderly devoted to him.

He was baptized by the Rev. Bartholomew Zouberbuhler, the rector of Christ Church, of which his father was a leading member. His early education was obtained in Savannah, and serving from a mere youth as the secretary of his father, he became practically acquainted with his extensive public and private business. When only thirteen years old his father regarded him as "one of the best clerks in the Province." For some time he was with the commercial house of Mr. Clay, and here he acquired those habits of industry and close attention to business which later contributed so much to his success. He afterwards went to Princeton College, from which he was graduated with distinction.

When the issues of the Revolution were forced upon the Colonies, John Habersham, who had scarcely attained to manhood, together with his two brothers, promptly took sides with the patriots, though his aged father, who was the President of the Royal Council, and for a time Acting Governor of the Province, remained loyal to the last to the Crown of England.

On January 7, 1776, he joined the Continental service as First Lieutenant of the first company of the battalion raised for the defense of Georgia. With three hundred of this battalion, of which his brother, Joseph Habersham, was Major, he assisted Col. Lachlan McIntosh, from hastily constructed works on Yamacraw Bluff, in repelling the British troops led by Maitland and Grant in their attempt to take to sea the vessels in the harbor laden with rice. He soon afterwards was made Brigade Major of the Georgia troops under General Lachlan McIntosh, ranking officer, and Colonel Samuel Elbert, second in command.

He accompanied the unsuccessful expedition planned for the subjugation of Florida, and when dissensions arose in the American camp concerning the conduct of the campaign, Major Habersham was appointed upon a council of war, which reported against the further prosecution of this ill-advised and badly-managed expedition.

The British in Florida planned, in turn, an attack upon the settlements in Georgia, having for their special object the capture of the town of Sunbury, and the investment of Savannah.

Led by Colonels Fuser and Prevost, the British troops advanced to St. John's Parish, burned the Midway Meeting House, and laid waste the county with fire and sword. At this juncture Colonel Elbert commissioned Major Habersham to hold an interview with Colonel Prevost for the purpose of protecting the invaded territory from needless pillage and conflagration. The English commander, however, declined to grant the request, insisting that, inasmuch as the people were in rebellion to the authority of the Crown, they would have to suffer the consequences, however disastrous they might be.

In one of the skirmishes near Midway Meeting House the brave General Screven was severely wounded, and captured by the enemy. Desiring to render medical aid to his fallen companion in arms, Colonel Elbert sent Major Habersham, under a flag, to Colonel Prevost, and in response Dr. Braidie and Dr. Alexander were permitted to attend him, but their examination showed the wound to be mortal, and the gallant Screven died upon the field.

At the capture of Savannah by the British under Colonel Campbell, on December 29, 1778, Major Habersham was entrusted with a part of the artillery on the American left, just east of the city. Finding it impossible to withstand the deadly assault of the enemy and threatened by a flank movement on the right, he directed his cannoneers to save themselves, but himself refused to quit his guns till completely overwhelmed by the foe. At this critical moment, it is said, Major Habersham, perceiving personal capture inevitable, broke his seal upon one of the cannon to prevent it from falling into the hands of his captors. In the unfortunate rout which ensued many of the Americans were killed or captured. Among those taken prisoners was Major Habersham.

His imprisonment, however, does not seem to have been of long duration, for at the unfortunate battle of Brier Creek Major Habersham again appears with McIntosh and Elbert, stubbornly holding the left of the line of battle after the right and centre had broken and fled, till nearly every soldier in their command was either killed or wounded. Here it appears he was exchanged in time to take part in the memorable siege of Savannah, in October, 1779.

In January, 1782, General Greene, who then had command of the Southern Department, detached General Anthony Wayne, the hero of Stony Point, "to reinstate, as far as might be possible, the authority of the Union within the limits of Georgia."

This officer, desiring to win over to the American cause the parties of Creek and Cherokee Indians who frequently visited Savannah since its capture by the British, and who by presents were inspired to annoy the outlying settlements, appointed Major Habersham to intercept and conciliate them. In this he was partly successful, but through the imprudence of some of his associates the mission was, in a large measure, defeated.

When Savannah was evacuated by the British, in 1782, the civilians who had remained loyal to the Crown and who could not readily depart with the military and officials, were anxious to ascertain what their status would be under the American occupation, and to secure pledges of immunity from molestation either in person or property. To Major John Habersham, on the part of the patriots, these negotiations were entrusted, and by him they were conducted with wisdom and fairness.

Lieutenant-Colonel James Jackson with his legion, and Major Habersham with his recruits, were detailed by General Greene to take charge of the town till the Civil Government could be restored. So far as Georgia was concerned, the Revolution was now at an end.

In 1784 Major Habersham was elected President of the Executive Council, and in that capacity he opened the Land Court in Augusta.

In 1785-'86 he was a member of the Continental Congress, and in October, 1786, he was the chairman of a commission appointed by the State of Georgia to make a treaty with the Indians at Shoulder-Bone Creek, in Hancock County. At this meeting fifty-nine chiefs and warriors of the Creek nation were present, and on November 3, a treaty was signed providing for the peaceful conduct of the Indians, and agreeing upon the boundary lines, about which there had been some dispute.

In 1787, he was appointed as one of the commissioners from Georgia to settle a dispute between this State and South Carolina concerning the boundaries between them. The commission met at Beaufort in April, and adjusted in an amicable manner the pending differences between the two states, and the agreement was ratified by Congress and by the General Assembly of Georgia.

After the Revolution, Major Habersham resided in Savannah, much respected for his patriotic services and his business ability. On January 27, 1785, he was appointed a member of the first Board of Trustees to establish a State University,— a compliment to his intelligence and wisdom.

In 1789, he was appointed Collector of the port of Savannah, an office which he continued to hold till his death, which occurred November 19, 1799, at the early age of forty-five years.

On March 27, 1786, he married Ann Sarah Camber, and seven children were born to them.

In all the public and private relations of life Major Habersham exhibited a most commendable character. He was honest, public-spirited, and a true friend to those in distress. He forms one of a noble group of patriots in the early history of Georgia whose memories will live so long as heroism and high purpose find a lodgment in the human heart.

OTIS ASHMORE.

Joseph Habersham.

JOSEPH HABERSHAM, the second son of James Habersham and Mary Bolton, was born in Savannah, Ga., July 28, 1751. His mother having died when he was quite young, he was sent, at the early age of eight-and-a-half years to Princeton, N. J., to be educated, where he remained six and a half years. About the age of fifteen he returned to Savannah, a disappointment to his practical old father so far as his education was concerned, for in a letter to William Knox, Esq., dated May 7, 1768, the father says, in referring to John, his younger son, "I truly lament that I ever sent my other two sons to the northward. Joe went there at eight-and-a-half years of age, and under the idea of stuffing his head with useless criticisms of phrases and words in Latin and Greek, he was neither taught to write legibly nor with propriety in the Language."

Not being very strong physically, his father determined to send him to England for the benefit of his health, as well as of his education. Accordingly, in May, 1768, his father placed him aboard ship, tenderly consigning him to William Knox, Georgia's Provincial Agent in England, and placing in his hands an advisory letter of deep paternal solicitude, which the son was to read on the first day of every month for one year after his arrival in London.

He remained in England three years engaged in the mercantile business, and returned to Savannah November 17, 1771, much improved in health and in his practical knowledge of business affairs. By the aid of his father, he entered into a commercial business, first with his brother James, and afterward, on January 1, 1773, with Mr. Clay.

In the dramatic events that formed the political prelude to

Engraved by J Gross from a Painting by W. G. Comaron after Douglass.

JOSEPH HABERSHAM.

Jos. Habersham

the Revolution, Joseph Habersham aligned himself with the patriot cause, and throughout that eventful struggle for liberty, he bore a conspicuous and honorable part. When the tidings of the battle of Lexington reached Savannah, Joseph Habersham, in company with Dr. Noble W. Jones, Edward Telfair, William Gibbons, Joseph Clay, John Milledge, and a few others,—most of them members of the Council of Safety—broke open the powder magazine in Savannah on the night of May 11th, and took therefrom about six hundred pounds of powder, which was afterwards used with good effect in the American cause.

There is a well approved tradition that a part of this powder was sent to Cambridge and used in the battle of Bunker Hill.

In July, 1775, Captain Maitland's ship direct from London, and loaded with gunpowder and military supplies, appeared at the mouth of the Savannah River. This ship, Joseph Habersham and Captain Bowen, with a picked body of men, determined to capture. Conveyed in a Georgia armed schooner, the first commissioned for naval warfare in the Revolution, these daring men succeeded in their hazardous undertaking, and at the earnest solicitation of Congress, five thousand pounds of the captured powder was sent to Philadelphia to be distributed to the Continental armies.

Mr. Habersham was a leading member of the Provincial Congress, which assembled in Savannah July 4, 1775, and on January 7, 1776, he was appointed Major of a battalion raised for the protection of Georgia under the command of Colonel Lachlan McIntosh and Lieutenant-Colonel Samuel Elbert.

At a special meeting of the Council of Safety, on January 18, 1776, it was decided to place under arrest the Governor, Sir James Wright, and his Council, and Major Joseph Habersham, then a member of the Council of Safety, volunteered to accomplish this bold plan. With a party selected by himself, he proceeded to the residence of the chief executive, the site on which now stands the Telfair Academy of Arts and Sciences, and passing the sentinel at the door, he boldly laid his hand upon the shoulder of the Governor, and said, "Sir James, you are my prisoner." The members of the Council who were in consultation with the Governor at the time, fled precipitately from the building. The Governor was confined to his house for some time, cut off from communication with his officials, but wearied and mortified at his harassing situation, he effected his escape on February 11th, through the rear of the house, and made his way to a warship at the mouth of the Savannah River.

The physical and moral courage required to perform this daring act indicates the heroic quality of Joseph Habersham's character, and in those eventful times, its accomplishment was as important as it was startling and dramatic.

Throughout the Revolution, Colonel Habersham bore a conspicuous part, and he was always ready to respond to the calls of duty when courage and patriotism were demanded. He was present at the memorable siege of Savannah, and aided in directing the military operations upon this eventful occasion.

After the close of the war he was elected a member of the General Assembly of the State of Georgia, and was twice honored by that body as Speaker of the House.

He was a delegate to the Continental Congress from 1785 to 1786, and in 1788 he was a member of the Convention which ratified the Federal Constitution.

In 1790-'91 he was a member of the city council of Savannah, and in 1792-'93 he served as its Mayor. When President Washington visited Savannah in 1791, Joseph Habersham delivered an address of welcome to that distinguished guest.

In 1795 he was appointed by Washington as Postmaster-General of the United States, a position which he filled with credit till Mr. Jefferson was elected President. By Mr. Jefferson he was tendered the office of Treasurer of the United States while yet Postmaster-General. Regarding this as a delicate hint from the President that his resignation would be acceptable, he promptly surrendered his portfolio and returned to his home in Savannah. This incident is one of the earliest illustrations of the application of the doctrine, "To the victor belong the spoils." Colonel Habersham had accepted the position tendered him by Washington from the highest motives of patriotic duty, and he filled the office without cringing or political favoritism. He finally refused to remove, from the subordinate position in his department, postmasters who were of opposite political views to those of the administration, but regarded only efficiency and good behavior as factors for continuance in office.

Having retired to private life, Colonel Habersham entered upon a commercial business in his native city, and in 1802 he became President of the Branch Bank of the United States in Savannah. This position he held till his death, which occurred November 17, 1815.

In May, 1776, he married Miss Isabella Rae, daughter of John Rae, who was living at Brampton plantation, near Savannah. Of this union ten children were born.

Colonel Habersham was a man of strong and positive character, with the most exalted conceptions of honor and patriotism. Though of a quick and ardent temper, he was ever ready to make amends for any wrong, and to the needs of the poor and unfortunate his heart and his purse were always open. Tolerant of the views of others, he expressed his own with freedom, and guided by the great principal of right, he was ever found loyal to the best interests of his people. His services to his state and to his country, and the inspiration of his exalted life, will place him for all time among the foremost of Georgia's early patriots. OTIS ASHMORE.

Lyman Hall.

LYMAN HALL, one of the signers of the Declaration of Independence, was born at Wallingford, Conn., April 12, 1724. He was the son of the Hon. John Hall and Mary Street. Four generations before his birth his paternal ancestor, John Hall, came from England in the ship *Griffin*, and, after residing for a time in Boston and New Haven, he established his home at Wallingford, Conn.

In 1747, Lyman Hall was graduated from Yale College in a class of twenty-eight members, and under the direction of his uncle, Rev. Samuel Hall, he entered upon the study of theology. He soon abandoned this course, however, and adopted medicine as his profession, in which he became very proficient. About this time he married Mary Osborne.

In the twenty-eighth year of his age he removed from Wallingford to Dorchester, South Carolina, and cast his lot among the Puritan colonists, who had moved from Massachusetts to that place a few years before, and who were prospering greatly in their new home. Here he was warmly welcomed, and for many years he ministered to the needs of these sturdy people.

Owing to the unhealthfulness of this situation, and the impoverished condition of the lands, many of these settlers removed to the Midway district of what is now Liberty County, Georgia. Along with this secondary stream of immigration came Dr. Hall, who purchased a small plantation a few miles north of Midway Meeting House. Owing to the swampy conditions of the adjacent country, much sickness prevailed in the new settlement, and Dr. Hall found ample opportunity for the exercise of his professional skill. After some time Dr. Hall removed to Sunbury, where many of the settlers had summer homes, and he soon became the leading physician of the town and country around. His sympathetic nature, his politeness, and his learning, endeared him to the people, and they trusted his honest judgment, not only in matters pertaining to his profession, but in public affairs as well.

When the storm of the Revolution began to lower, Dr. Hall promptly took sides with the patriots, and to the infant cause of liberty he was a tower of strength. Of him Col. C. C. Jones aptly says: "On the revolutionary altars erected within the Midway District were the fires of resistance to the dominion of England earliest kindled; and of all the patriots of that uncompromising community, Lyman Hall, by his counsel, exhortations, and determined spirit, added stoutest fuel to the flames."

Dr. Hall was chairman of the meeting, assembled at Midway on February 9, 1775, which sent delegates to the meeting at Charlestown, when the other districts of Georgia declined as yet to break loose from the mother country.

On March 21, 1775, Dr. Lyman Hall was elected by the people of St. John's Parish to represent them in the Continental Congress. The other districts of Georgia had not yet acted, and after some discussion of his eligibility to membership to that body it was unanimously agreed by Congress that he be "admitted as a delegate from the Parish of St. John in the Colony of Georgia, subject to such regulations as Congress should determine relative to his voting."

In the deliberations of this body, he declined to vote upon questions which were to be determined by the colonies, but took part in the discussions, and in every way in his power he aided the Congress in its work. In a few months, however, Georgia took decisive action in the election of delegates, and Dr. Hall was among the representatives with full power to vote and to speak. In this capacity he continued to serve Georgia till the close of the Revolution.

When the Declaration of Independence was signed, Lyman Hall, Button Gwinnett and George Walton, in behalf of the inhabitants of Georgia, affixed their names to the famous document.

When the British troops overran Georgia, the property of those who had espoused the patriot cause was confiscated and destroyed, and Dr. Hall's residence at Sunbury and his plantation near Midway were despoiled.

With his family he removed to the north, where he resided till 1782, when he returned to Georgia, and settled in Savannah. Here he resumed the practice of his profession and endeavored to repair his shattered fortunes.

In January, 1783, Dr. Hall was elected Governor of Georgia. During his administration an act of the Legislature was passed confiscating the property of those who sided with England in the Revolutionary struggle, and an important treaty was made with the Indians by which large tracts of land were ceded to the State. Of the many important acts of his administration was that portion of his message to the Legislature which assembled at Augusta on July 8, 1783, commending the establishment and maintenance of "seminaries of learning," as follows:

"In addition, therefore, to wholesome laws restraining vice, every encouragement ought to be given to introduce religion, and learned clergy to perform divine worship in honor of God, and to cultivate principles of religion and virtue among our citizens. For this purpose it will be your wisdom to lay an early foundation for endowing seminaries of learning; nor can you, I conceive, lay a better than by a grant of a sufficient tract of land, that may, as in other governments, hereafter, by lease or otherwise, raise a revenue sufficient to support such valuable institutions."

This wise suggestion from Governor Hall undoubtedly paved the way to the establishment of the University of Georgia.

After the expiration of his term of office as Governor he returned to Savannah, where he again took up the practice of medicine. Having resigned the position of Judge of the Inferior Court of Chatham County, to which he had been chosen, he removed to Burke County in 1790, and settled upon a fine plantation near Shell Bluff on the Savannah River, and engaged in large farming operations.

Here on October 19, 1790, he died at the age of sixty-seven years, and was buried in a brick vault upon a bold bluff overlooking the river. In 1848 his remains were removed to Augusta and placed with those of George Walton beneath the monument erected by patriotic citizens in front of the court-house in honor of the Georgia signers of the Declaration of Independence. The remains of Button Gwinnett could not be found, but they are believed to rest in the old Colonial Cemetery at Savannah in an unmarked grave.

Gwinnett and Hall were close friends and when Gwinnett was killed by Gen. Lachlan McIntosh in a duel, Dr. Hall, one of Gwinnett's executors, and some other citizens of influence, brought the matter to the attention of the Legislature, and charged the judicial officers with neglect of duty in failing to arrest McIntosh. Whereupon, McIntosh surrendered himself to Judge Glen and demanded a trial. Although acquitted by the Court, McIntosh never recovered from this unfortunate incident, and at the suggestion of friends he applied to General Washington for duty outside of his State, where he remained for nearly two years.

10

The marble slab inserted in the brick vault in which the remains of Dr. Hall were first interred was, after the removal of the remains to Augusta, sent to the corporate authorities of the town of Wallingford, Conn., where it is carefully preserved.

Dr. Hall left a widow and a son, John, both of whom died soon after the death of the husband and father.

In person Dr. Lyman Hall was six feet tall and finely proportioned. Though not brilliant, he was dignified in manner and of great force of character. He was a man of great courage and discretion, and withal gentle and easy in manner.

He was eminently fitted to guide the ship of state in the storm of the Revolution, and though he never bore arms, or won distinction as an orator, the people felt safe with his hand at the helm.

The State of Georgia has fitly perpetuated his memory in naming one of its counties for him, and so long as liberty and patriotism shall live so long shall the name of Lyman Hall be remembered. Otis Ashmore.

Engraved by J. J. Barber

HON. SAMUEL HAMMOND.

OF GEORGIA.
A.D. 1787.

Samuel Hammond.

SAMUEL HAMMOND was the son of Charles Hammond, and was born in Farnham's Parish, Richmond county, Virginia, September 21, 1757. His ancestors were among the early settlers of the eastern shores of Virginia and Mary-land and were a sturdy stock of patriots. Young Hammond was not lacking in the family traits, nor in the training which makes for patriotism, as his subsequent career shows. He entered the public service in 1774, when but seventeen years of age. He then volunteered in an expedition, ordered out by Governor Dunmore, against the Indians of the frontier. On this expedition he was engaged in the decisive battle of Point Pleasant under General Andrew Lewis, October 10, 1774.

On the breaking out of hostilities with the mother country, Mr. Hammond at once aligned himself with the American patriots and was commissioned captain of a company at the head of which he fought at the battle of Great Bridge, near Norfolk, in December, 1775. From 1775 to 1777, he served under General Maxwell, and, in 1778, was a volunteer aide to General Hand in the expedition against Pittsburg. In 1779, he joined the army under General Lincoln and went South.

During Prevost's invasion, Captain Hammond was attached to the commands of Colonels Henderson and Malmudy. It always seemed his fortune to be in the thick of the fight. At the siege of Savannah, his command was united with that of General Huger in the gallant charge on the left of the British lines. He was near the brave Pulaski when he fell.

He participated in most of the important engagements of the

South—Augusta, Stono Ferry, Blackstocks and Ninety-Six. At the battle of Eutaw Springs, he was promoted major for distinguished gallantry. Of his further services, White, in his *"Historical Collections,"* says: "He continued with General Williamson's command until the fall of Charleston, when Williamson took protection, with a considerable number of his followers.

"Young Hammond, however, who was courteously permitted to take part in the council which was called to decide upon the terms of capitulation at Charleston (his rank and age not justifying such participation), protested against the decision of the majority, and refused to take the British protection.

"He withdrew from his former associates, raised a few choice spirits (seventy-six in number), and with them proceeded toward the North, determined to find assistance or die with arms in their hands. But more than half of this number, in consequence of the discouragements of the times, subsequently left Hammond's party, and in hiding about fell into the hands of the Tories, who now overran the country and from whose cruelties they suffered vastly more than if they had continued with their companions in arms. Hammond's little band, consisting now of only thirty-three persons, proceeded as they best could to make their way towards North Carolina. They were, however, compelled to conceal themselves during the day in swamps and canebrakes and push on with all possible speed at night, depending entirely on chance for subsistence. One night while passing along the foot of the mountains, they came to the house of a good Whig, who was then absent from home, and learned from his wife (Mrs. Jones) that she had been ill-treated and plundered by a party of Tories, seventy or eighty in number, who had the day before passed her house on their way to join the British army. Hammond and his associates determined to pursue and chastise them if possible. Guided by a lad along the trail they had taken they succeeded in surprising them the next morning at breakfast, and, in a spirited charge, routed them completely.

"On their arrival in North Carolina, they were joined by Captains McCall and Liddle, of Pickens' regiment, and a small detachment of men. Here in July, 1780, they fought the battle of Cedar Springs under command of Colonel Clarke, of Georgia, against a party of dragoons under Dunlap, of Ferguson's regiment, who attempted to surprise them about half an hour before day; but owing to timely notice, which was brought into the camp by two noble Whig ladies, the dragoons were repulsed and defeated.

"In the following month, August 19, 1780, Captain Hammond was engaged with Colonels Williams, Clarke, and Shelby in the battle of Musgrove's Mills on the Enoree River. Here the British were defeated, their commanding officer, Colonel Innis, wounded, Major Fraser killed, and a number of prisoners taken.

"At Hillsborough, he received from Governor Rutledge the brevet commission of major, with orders to take charge of all the refugees, as they were called, belonging to Colonel Leroy Hammond's regiment of militia and others who might come into service. In the ever memorable battle of King's Mountain, which occurred on the 7th of October, 1780, Major Hammond bore himself gallantly and lost many of his men. After this battle, he was attached for a short time to the command of General Davidson, and acted under Colonel Davy on the retreat of Lord Cornwallis from Charlotte toward the Catawba, but was soon transferred to the command of General Sumter and with him took part in the battle of Blackstocks.

"Previous to the battle of Cowpens, he joined General Morgan. In this celebrated action, he commanded on the left of the front line and rendered the most important service throughout the engagement. After the battle he was detached by General Morgan with a small portion of his command to reconnoitre the British army, which, after its defeat, had taken position on the north side of Broad River, some distance below Cowpens. This service he performed efficiently.

"On the arrival of Cornwallis at Ramsour's Mill, Major Hammond passed over to the north side of the river and joined General Greene. He continued with him, however, only a few days when he was again attached to General Pickens' command, with whom he passed to the rear of the British army.

"He was joined by Major James Jackson, of Georgia (afterwards Governor Jackson), who was charged to pass into Georgia to harass the enemy. They proceeded together through the district of Ninety-Six, enlisting numbers of people in their enterprise. Hammond rejoined General Pickens, and the Georgia and Carolina forces, acting in concert, advanced upon Augusta, drove in the outposts and commenced the siege of that place. Hammond, having now been promoted to the rank of lieutenant-colonel, was ordered with two companies of State troops to storm Fort Grierson. On the capitulation of the enemy at Augusta, Colonel Hammond, with the other troops under Pickens, marched and joined General Greene at the siege of Ninety-Six; but on the advance of Lord Rawdon the siege was raised and Pickens' command retreated westward, and thence turning northeastwardly rejoined Greene on the Congaree, below Broad River. Through the summer of 1781, Colonel Hammond continued actively employed as a partisan and gave hot pursuit to the Tories in every direction. He, however, rejoined General Greene in the fall of the year and was with him at the glorious battle of Eutaw Springs on the 8th of September, 1781.

"On the 17th of the same month, he was appointed to the command of a regiment of cavalry by Governor Rutledge and instructed to raise and equip it like that of Mayham's for three years, or the war. A number of his State troops who had long served under him as volunteers now enrolled themselves in his regiment. He was also joined by a portion of Colonel Leroy Hammond's militia, and, with these, he remained in service under General Greene until the preliminaries of peace were signed and announced. Being then encamped with General Greene at Bacon's Bridge, near Charleston, he received orders to discontinue recruiting for his new regiment, and in a short time afterwards the greater part of his men were discharged."

Soon after the Revolution, Colonel Hammond settled in Savannah. In 1783 he married Mrs. Rebecca Rae, of Augusta, widow of Colonel John Rae. Mrs. Hammond died at Savannah in the spring of 1798.

He was elected to the State Legislature several terms from Chatham county. He also held the office of Surveyor-General and was one of a commission to arrange treaties with the Indians. In 1793 Governor Telfair appointed him to the command of the first battalion of the Chatham county militia and sent him on an expedition against the Creek Indians, in which capacity he rendered efficient service in checking their depredations.

Prior to this time, Colonel Hammond had engaged in mercantile pursuits in Savannah, and this had taken him to France and to South America, where he gained a knowledge of both French and Spanish which he was able to use later.

On the 25th of May, 1802, he was again married, uniting himself to Miss Amelia O'Keefe, a young and beautiful lady. The same year he was elected to represent the State of Georgia in Congress, defeating Joseph Bryan, Esq., and William Harris

Crawford who was just entering public life. In Congress, he renewed his acquaintance with Thomas Jefferson, then President, whom he had known before the Revolution. The new Territory of Louisiana had been divided into the Territory of Orleans and the District of Louisiana. This last comprised the whole region west of the Mississippi and north of the thirty-third degree of latitude.

President Jefferson appointed him Military and Civil Commander of the District of St. Louis, and, in the spring of 1804, accompanied by his wife and about two hundred family servants, he set out on his journey overland to St. Louis, which was then only a little French village on the extreme western border of civilization.

His house soon became headquarters, as it were, for army officers and their families. He kept open house and dispensed old-time Virginia hospitality. Polished in manners, brilliant in conversation and of attractive personality, he was an ideal host. Add to this the presence of his charming and accomplished wife and it will be understood why "Governor Hammond's Mansion" became noted in government circles. In 1816, he organized and was first president of the first bank in St. Louis. He was also president of the first Territorial Council. White says he bought a large amount of valuable property which his public duties and advancing age prevented him from managing properly. Some of this property has been recovered by his family in recent years. On account of the failure of local banks he became involved in a large debt to the United States, but the historian records to his credit that by the sale of other property he discharged the last farthing of this indebtedness.

In 1824, to gratify his wife, he returned South with a large number of slaves, the trip requiring three months. Returning to South Carolina he was honored with the office of Surveyor-General and elected to the Legislature. The last office he held was Secretary of State of South Carolina. After adjusting his affairs he settled on Varello Farm on Horse Creek, three miles below Augusta on the South Carolina side. Here he died the 11th of September, 1842, in the eighty-fifth year of his age. His body lay in state in Augusta, and was interred in the family cemetery known as Mt. Airy. The military of Augusta and Hamburg, the Masonic fraternity and a large number of citizens attended to the grave. As the procession passed Schultz Hill, the site of his old fort, the artillery fired a last salute in honor of the veteran of 1776.

The late Mrs. James H. R. Washington, of Macon, was his daughter. Colonel Hugh V. Washington, of that city, is his grandson. A. B. CALDWELL.

George Handley.

GEORGE HANDLEY was a native of England, having been born near Sheffield, England, February 9, 1752. We know but little of his boyhood and education. At the age of twenty-three he came to America, arriving in Savannah May, 1775.

These were stirring times—times when the lines were clearly drawn, and men were forced to take sides. Georgia patriots were busy concerting measures of resistance to British encroachments. If Mr. Handley had not decided on his course before reaching America, he seems not to have hesitated for a moment in identifying himself with the principles so zealously advocated by such radical organizations as the "Liberty Boys."

When, in January, 1776, by direction of the Legislature, a battalion of Continental troops was organized, Mr. Handley was made first lieutenant of the second company of the battalion. In October, of the same year, he was promoted to the captaincy. He bore himself bravely in numerous engagements in South Carolina and Georgia, sharing the fortunes, good and ill, of his command, till July, 1780, when he had reached the rank of major. Then it was that he fell into the hands of the enemy, on account of the treachery of Brigadier-General Andrew Williamson, who abandoned his command and the town of Augusta to the British. Major Handley was sent a prisoner of war to Charleston, South Carolina. There is no record of the time or manner of his exchange, but it is known that when he retired from the service in July, 1782, it was with the rank of lieutenant-colonel.

After the close of the Revolution Colonel Handley removed from Savannah to Augusta. Young, active, and popular, it was but natural that he should become prominent in local political circles. He was made Sheriff of Richmond county and several times represented the same county in the Legislature. In 1785, Colonel Handley was one of the Georgia commissioners to the State of Franklin, which it was proposed should be carved out of the territory of western North Carolina. Two years later he was made Inspector-General of his adopted State.

In January, 1788, only a little more than a dozen years after landing in Savannah, he was chosen Governor of Georgia. At this period the governor was elected by the Legislature and the term was only one year.

Retiring from the chief magistracy in 1789 Governor Handley was, in August of that year, appointed by President Washington Collector of the Port of Brunswick, Georgia. He continued to hold this position till the time of his death. He died at Rae's Hall, Georgia, September 17, 1793.

Compiled by the Publisher.

Stephen Heard.

STEPHEN HEARD; planter, patriot, soldier, and Governor was among the most active officers of the war of the Revolution. He was born in Hanover county, Virginia, in 1740. It is claimed that he was of an English family to whom large estates were granted in Ireland. The family spent a part of the time in England and a part in Ireland, and so some members of the family were born in England and some in Ireland, just as they happened to be spending their time in one country or the other.

Earlier writers have asserted that Stephen Heard was born in Ireland, and when a boy came with his father to America. Close investigation, however, shows this to be an error. He was born in America in 1740, at least twenty years after his father's family had left Ireland for America.

A story is told of how, in 1719, Stephen's grandfather used a pitchfork upon a minister of the Established Church of Ireland, about "tithes," and fearing the consequences left the country for America. He settled in Hanover county, Virginia, in 1720. The next year thereafter, all his family followed him except one son, who remained in Ireland to settle up his father's business and come out the next year. When the old gentleman had his trouble with the minister he lived in county Tyrone, Ireland. His son John was the father of Stephen, the subject of our sketch.

Stephen was the recipient of a good elementary education, but as the French and Indian War came on while he was quite a boy, and as he, together with several of his brothers, joined

General Washington's regiment, he never had the advantage of classical training. For gallantry displayed whilst in this regiment he was soon promoted by General Washington to the captaincy of a company. From this time as long as he and Washington lived there continued between these two great men a feeling of mutual love and esteem.

In 1769, in his old age, John Heard, together with his sons, removed to Georgia, settling in the upper part of the State, in what was then known as St. Paul's Parish, the upper part of which was organized into Wilkes county in 1777, parts of which have since been added to five other counties.

Here Stephen Heard married Miss Germany (commonly pronounced Garmany). After Lord Cornwallis had overrun North Carolina, South Carolina, and Georgia, the Tories made living in upper Georgia almost insupportable. All good men were forced to flee the country in self-protection. Among other wanton acts the Tories forced Stephen Heard's young wife with her tender babe out into a snow storm. They both died from the exposure.

About this time Colonel Boyd, of the British army, was ordered from New York to notify the disaffected and excite the Tories in this part of North Carolina, South Carolina, and Georgia to immediate action. Soon after Boyd commenced operations, Lieutenant-Colonel Pickens, with a few Americans hastily gotten together, began at once to pursue them, forcing them to cross the river into Georgia. Here Stephen Heard, who was in charge of civil affairs, joined General Elijah Clarke in exciting all the Whigs in the country to meet the Tories at once. The Americans felt once more prepared to contest for the supremacy of Georgia, although at a great disadvantage as to numbers. Much depended upon this battle. If Boyd should succeed in driving back the Americans this part of the country,

Georgia and South Carolina, would yield to the British power. While on the other hand, if Pickens and his men should succeed, it would not only arrest the Tory power, so galling to the people, but protect them from other insult and give a stimulus to American courage, which a long series of disasters had made especially necessary. Truly it was a moment big with fate for Georgia.

Here General Clarke, nobly seconded in all his efforts by General Heard, formed a junction with Pickens. At the same time they mustered all the brave Whigs in their reach and rapidly pursued Boyd, who had taken a circuitous route through the Cherokee nation, until they overtook him on Kettle Creek in Wilkes county.

With a carelessness evincing great want of military skill and prudence, amounting almost to criminality, the Britisher halted his men for the night at a farm and allowed them to scatter, catching, killing, and cooking beeves, when the Americans surprised him.

Pickens divided his men, attacking Boyd on both right and left, at the same time giving orders not to fire till within thirty-five paces of the foe. Boyd was a brave man, but early in the engagement was shot down, and after close fighting for at least an hour or more, the Tories were utterly routed. Col. Heard here greatly distinguished himself, "encouraging his men and leading them to points of danger and vantage." The result was a complete victory for the Whigs, who had only four hundred men actively engaged against Boyd's eight hundred Tories. So complete was the victory that not more than three hundred Tories escaped.

This success was of far greater importance than the numbers engaged would indicate. It broke up the Tories throughout that section, who never afterwards assembled except in small numbers. They still plundered and murdered individuals and were sorely dreaded for their desperate outrages, but this battle of Kettle Creek so affected their fate that they never afterward went into permanent organization. Georgia became free once again from the galling yoke of the Briton.

At one time, when this part of the country was so terrorized by the British, Stephen Heard, with most of the good men, was taken prisoner. But a faithful old negro woman, Mammy Kate, was allowed to visit him twice a week to get and return his clothes for washing. She never failed to bring food—usually the "Georgia ash-cake." Of course she had to conceal it. "Lord a massey, honey," she would say, "I hid dat bred in my busson to git to ole Master," nodding with a shake of her head, "but I allus took it out 'fore I got dar, 'cause he was mighty particular." After remaining in prison a few weeks he effected his escape. All chronicles have failed to give the details of the manner of his escape. There is a tradition, however, fondly treasured till to-day in the memory of his descendants, that Mammy Kate, being a stout, strong negress, smuggled him through the lines safely concealed in a large basket on one of the occasions of her coming for "ole Master's clo'es." Col. Heard continued to discharge the important duties of Chairman of the Executive Council of the State till the suspension of hostilities.

The brother of Stephen Heard, Major Barnard Heard, was taken prisoner by the Tories in Wilkes and carried to Augusta in irons, where he was sentenced by a court-martial to be hanged. On the day before the siege of the town commenced, however, he made his escape and fought on that occasion under Clarke and Jackson. After the battle, he went to the British garrison where he found his father, John Heard, a prisoner, quite advanced in years and almost exhausted by hunger, and another old man, both of whom he took by the hand and brought to the American post.

Soon after their arrival in Georgia, the Heard brothers built a fort for the protection of themselves and their father's family. This was at such a prominent place that it became known all over the country as Heard's Fort. In 1777, when the eleven parishes of Georgia were organized into eight counties, St. Paul's Parish was changed into Wilkes county. On account of its prominence Heard's Fort was chosen as the county site, and the name changed to Washington, being the first place in the whole country which was given a local name in honor of George Washington the Father of his Country.

During a portion of the time in which Georgia was overrun by the British, Col. Heard did all in his power to inspire the desponding people with hope. When about the middle of February, 1780, the capitol at Augusta was abandoned and Governor Howley had gone to Philadelphia to take his seat in the Continental Congress, George Wells, by virtue of his position as president of the council, became *de facto* Governor and Stephen Heard president of the council. Two or three days later Wells was killed in a duel with General James Jackson, and Stephen Heard succeeded to the chief magistracy of the embattled commonwealth. He continued to discharge all the duties of this office till late in 1780, when he retreated into North Carolina and Myrick Davies succeeded to the presidency of the Executive Council.

At this time affairs in Georgia were gloomy indeed. Devastation and ruin stared the people in the face from every quarter. When the British took possession of Augusta only Richmond and Wilkes counties of the whole State remained loyal to the American cause.

The pay for a Captain for a month was not enough to buy

a pair of shoes. McCall says, "The value of paper money was at that time so much reduced that the Governor dealt it out by the quire for a night's lodging for himself and party; and if the fare was anything extraordinary the landlord was complimented by two quires."

Whilst Heard was Governor of the State, being aware of its defenceless condition, he moved the capital from Augusta to Heard's Fort.

Most difficult was it to maintain even a show of civil authority. Many good men leaving the State went into voluntary exile. Thus were the affairs administered by Governor Heard to the very verge of political death. Dissensions occurred among good men and the land was a prey alike to internal as well as external foes.

Immediately after the close of the Revolutionary War Mr. Heard settled down to quiet life on his farm known as "Heardmont," eight miles north of Washington. Here located in a primeval forest of oaks, hickory, walnut and pine, presenting a most commanding appearance, his house was a model of beauty and comfort. For at least ten years it was the only plastered and lathed house north of Augusta, a distance of about sixty miles. The mechanics were about three years in collecting the material and building it. Many country people for miles around visited it as an object of curiosity. He imported solid mahogany furniture from London. It took this three months to reach him after the order was placed in London.

But his talents and integrity, together with the reputation he bore for much service which he rendered his people during the war in many capacities, gave him such leading influence in society that his services were often called for in behalf of his people. In 1790, when that portion of Wilkes County was organized into Elbert County, he was the foreman of its first grand jury. He was also a leading Justice of the County Court for several terms and one of the delegates representing Elbert in the Convention of 1795.

He married the second time Miss Elizabeth Darden, of Virginia, who bore him five sons and four daughters, all of whom he was careful to have well educated. From these have sprung many noble men and women, who are to-day found in all our Southern States. In educating his daughters he was one of the first and leading patrons of the Moravian School established at Salem, North Carolina, which was a prominent place for at least a hundred years as an educational center for girls. Delighting in books and a lover of learning, he filled the shelves of his library with the best of books, carefully selected for the benefit of his children.

In the seventy-fifth year of his age, highly esteemed all over the nation, he died, very much regretted.

In the family graveyard at Heardmont there is a plain monument over his grave bearing the following inscription:

SACRED TO THE MEMORY OF
COL. STEPHEN HEARD.

He was a soldier of the American Revolution, and fought with the Great Washington for the liberties of his country. He died on the 15th of November, 1815, in the 75th year of his age, beloved by all who knew him.

"An honest man is the noblest work of God."

There is no portrait of Governor Heard extant.

R. J. MASSEY.

Reb. Henry Holcombe.

HENRY HOLCOMBE was born in Prince Edward County, Virginia, September 22, 1762. His mother's name was Elizabeth Buzbee. His father, Grimes Holcombe, and his grandfather, John Holcombe, both born in Virginia, were descended from an old English family, the earliest ancestor of which, Walter de Holcombe, came from Normandy and settled in Devonshire, England, shortly after the Conquest, nearly 800 years ago.

Grimes Holcombe moved from Virginia to South Carolina when his son Henry, the subject of this sketch, was but a boy, and, where before attaining his majority, he entered the Revolutionary army and rose to the rank of Captain. He was hopefully converted when in command of his company, at the age of twenty-two. He began at once to proclaim the unsearchable riches of Christ, making his first religious address on horseback at the head of his command. On the 11th of September, 1785, he was ordained to the ministry and soon became a distinguished preacher and met with extraordinary success in his work. Among his converts were his wife and an only brother of hers and their mother; and by him his own father, Grimes Holcombe, was converted from Pedo-Baptist views. All these he had the pleasure of baptizing.

He was a member of the South Carolina State Convention which met at Charleston in 1788 and approved the Constitution of the United States, and afterwards was pastor of the Eutaw church, though residing at Beaufort until 1799. About that time he was invited to Savannah, Georgia, as a supply to the Baptist church, which occupied the house now known as the Independent Presbyterian church of that city. The few Baptists in Savannah had erected a house of worship which was rented then by the Presbyterians, whose church edifice had been destroyed by fire; and for two years Dr. Holcombe preached to the pew-holders of the building at a salary of $2,000, which was then considered enormous.

He was practically the father of the Georgia penitentiary system. Shocked by the execution of a man named Rice for the comparatively small crime of stealing a gun, he was the first to urge in the State a milder system of punishment. This he did in a memorial to the Legislature in September, 1802; following up this effort with great zeal and pertinacity. The result was that the penitentiary system was adopted instead of the bloody code of earlier days.

He was the founder of the Savannah Female Asylum. Touched by the forlorn condition of some wretched little orphan girls whom he discovered in the city of Savannah, he founded the Savannah Female Orphan Asylum in November, 1801, an institution which still exists, and which has been the means of incalculable benefit to poor and destitute female orphans. The first meeting of those who took part in its organization was held at his suggestion and convened in his parlor. The constitution, drafted by him, was adopted. Under this the first Board of Directors was elected on the 17th of the following December at a meeting in the Presbyterian church of which he was pastor. It was composed of fourteen ladies, among whom was Mrs. Frances Holcombe, the doctor's wife.

He was the founder of Mount Enon Academy, and was the first to urge the establishment of an institution of learning by the Baptist denomination. The idea was his own; he had but little sympathy and met with poor encouragement, nevertheless he pressed the matter with immense power, and finally succeeded in establishing an academy at a place in Richmond County which he called Mount Enon. In 1805 application was made to the Legislature for a charter for the institution, but for some reason the charter was not granted. The intention of the founder was to establish an institution of high grade for literary and theological education, of which the academy was to be merely the beginning. The academy flourished under his fostering care until he left the State in 1811, when it immediately began to decline, and soon came to an end. Even after it was established and on a good foundation the Baptists of the State were too lacking in public spirit and too regardless of the value of education to keep it up. Indeed, in those early days a very large proportion of the Baptists of Georgia entertained a prejudice against education and took no interest in institutions of learning, except to oppose them. So long as Dr. Holcombe remained, his great personal influence with all classes, from the highest to the lowest, overcame, to some extent, this prejudice, but as soon as he left the cause failed. However, there were some who caught from him the spirit of progress and improvement, and this continued to diffuse itself until desire began to be publicly expressed for the establishment of another institution as the successor of Mount Enon Academy. Josiah Penfield, of Savannah, one of Dr. Holcombe's former deacons in the church at that place, and who had been baptized by him, proposed to give $2,500 towards the founding of such an institution, provided the rest of the denomination would raise an equal amount. His condition was promptly met and Mercer University, in a place called Penfield, in honor of the good deacon, was the result. Mount Enon Academy was the first institution of learning established by Baptists in the Southern States, and one of the first in the United States. So Mercer, to-day one of the noblest institutions of the land, may safely attribute its origin to the brain of this great and good man.

The first Baptist periodical, and certainly one of the first, if not the very first, religious periodical ever published in the United States, was published by Dr. Holcombe in Savannah in 1802. There was not enough literary spirit in the people to sustain it, and its career was closed in two years. It was called *"The Analytical Repository."*

Although, to use his own words, "At eleven years he had completed all the education he had ever received from a living preceptor," before he was fifty he had not only received a degree of A.M., at that time quite a distinction, but the degree of Doctor of Divinity, which meant much more then than it does now, was conferred on him by Brown University, Rhode Island, in 1810.

Of the many illustrious descendants of Dr. Holcombe we mention Hon. A. O. Bacon, who has in the United States Senate so nobly illustrated Georgia for the last fifteen years. Also another grandson, the late Rev. H. H. Tucker, A.M., D.D., who for many years was president of Mercer University and afterward Chancellor of the State University, and a leading Baptist divine for over a quarter of a century.

R. J. Massey.

John Houstoun.

JOHN HOUSTOUN, Governor, member of Congress, Chief Justice, etc., was a son of Sir Patrick Houstoun, Baronet, Registrar of Grants and Receiver of Quit Rents, and Priscilla (Dunbar) Houstoun. He was born in the Parish of St. George, near what is now Waynesboro, August 31, 1744, and attended school in Savannah, where he received a good education. He was by profession a lawyer. Allied with the younger men of the colony, he early took the side of the people against the aggressive acts of the English Parliament.

Accordingly on the 20th of July, 1774, he, with Archibald Bulloch, John Walton and Noble W. Jones, issued a call to the people of Georgia to meet at the Watch House in Savannah to consider their rights and liberties as American subjects. A number of citizens responded to the call and a committee, of which Mr. Houstoun was a member, was appointed to prepare and report to a later meeting resolutions setting forth their attitude toward the recent unjust and oppressive acts of Parliament and their determination to use every lawful means to assert their constitutional rights.

Governor Wright proclaimed the meeting illegal and revolutionary, but it was held at Tondee's Tavern, in Savannah, on the 10th of August, 1774, regardless of his wishes. The resolutions adopted at this meeting were the groundwork for dissolving the ties which bound the colony of Georgia to the mother country. At this meeting Mr. Houstoun was made a member of a committee to secure and forward supplies to Boston, whose port had arbitrarily been closed. The second Convention met at Savannah on the 8th of December, 1774. Mr. Houstoun, Archibald Bulloch and Noble W. Jones were named as delegates to the Continental Congress.. These and other young men of the colony—"Sons of Liberty"—now, thoroughly aroused and intent upon moulding public sentiment and controlling the political destinies of the struggling colony, called a Provincial Congress to meet on the 18th of January, 1775. Owing to the power of the royal Governor, Wright, and the loyalty of many of the older men of the colony a general response to the patriotic invitation was prevented, so that only five of the twelve parishes of which Georgia was then composed were represented, and the delegates from some of these were seriously hampered by restrictions imposed upon them by the more conservative. Though, thus crippled and thwarted in their efforts to capture the House of Assembly by Governor Wright who prorogued the session, the Provincial Congress, nevertheless, chose Mr. Houstoun, Archibald Bulloch and Noble W. Jones to represent Georgia in the Continental Congress. These advocates of popular government, feeling that they would be inconsistent should they undertake to represent the entire colony in the Continental Congress when elected by a minority of the parishes, accordingly on the 6th of April carefully prepared an address to the president of that august body, setting forth the reasons why they could not serve as members of the Congress, but significantly adding that when the proper time arrived they would be found ready.

It might be said that John Houstoun was a leader of the revolutionary spirit in Georgia. He was one of the four original organizers of the "Sons of Liberty."

They had paved the way for a bloody war, and when tidings of the battle of Lexington reached Georgia her citizens were filled with a determination to cast in their lot with the other colonies in an effort to throw off the galling yoke of bondage by which they were so unjustly held.

Events now crowded upon each other. On June 5th the Liberty Pole was erected at Tondee's Tavern, in Savannah, at the corer of Whitaker and Barnard streets, since appropriately marked by the Daughters of the American Revolution.

On June 21st John Houstoun, Noble W. Jones, Archibald Bulloch and George Walton requested the inhabitants of the town and district of Savannah to meet at the Liberty Pole at ten o'clock in the forenoon of the following day, to select a committee to bring about a union of Georgia with the other American colonies. The response was generous. A Council of Safety was chosen, with instructions. to maintain a correspondence with the Continental Congress, with Councils of Safety in other provinces and with committees in other Georgia parishes, with a view to the consummation of the proposed union. The correspondence began, similar meetings were held in the other Georgia parishes, and as a result of these combined efforts on the part of the patriots there assembled in Savannah on the 4th of July, 1775, a Provincial Congress at which every parish in the colony was represented. Mr. Houstoun was present as a delegate from the town and district of Savannah. He was the first delegate chosen to represent the Province in the Continental Congress. Archibald Bulloch and J. J. Zubly were also chosen, and together they journeyed to Philadelphia and participated in the session of September, 1775.

Mr. Houstoun was returned to the Continental Congress by the Provincial Congress which met in Savannah in January, 1776. In that year he was called home to neutralize the influence of Dr. Zubly. But for this unfortunate situation, which required his presence in Georgia at that perilous time, Mr. Houstoun's name would have appeared on the Declaration of Independence with those of Hall, Gwinnett, and Walton.

On the 8th of May, 1777, he was made a member of the Executive Council of which Benjamin Andrew was president. On January 18th of the following year, 1778, he was chosen Governor.

At this time the entire commonwealth, and especially South Georgia, was threatened by the Indians, British and Tories. It was a difficult matter to get the Executive Council together on short notice, so the Governor was given, by that body, almost absolute power in all matters pertaining to the State affairs. This remarkable exhibition of personal confidence he highly appreciated and discharged his duties without fear or favor. As Commander-in-Chief of the Georgia militia he lead the troops, about 350, for the invasion of Florida. On the St. Mary's River a disagreement arose between Gen. Robert Howe, in command of the southern department, and Governor Houstoun as to who should command the Georgia militia. This caused Howe to withdraw his Continental troops and return. Gov. Houstoun, finding himself with insufficient troops to make an attack, led his command back to Savannah and discharged them. As a result of this most unfortunate occurrence South Georgia was overrun by the enemy and Savannah fell into his hands.

John Houstoun was again elected Governor in 1784, and it was during this administration that the Legislature at Savannah passed the act appropriating forty thousand acres of land for the foundation and support of a State college. Governor Houstoun was first named in the list of trustees, who were empowered the next year to put this education act in operation.

A great portion of his time this year was given to the administration of the land courts and the granting of lands to the Georgia soldiers who had fought in the war against Great Britain.

The next year, 1786, Mr. Houstoun was made Chief Justice of the commonwealth, and the year following, with Major John Habersham and Gen. Lachlan McIntosh, was elected by the Legislature to settle the boundary line between Georgia and South Carolina. Carolina was represented by Gen. C. C. Pinkney, Gen. Andrew Pickens and Hon. Pierce Butler. From the conclusions arrived at Gov. Houstoun dissented and his reasons are found in Marbury and Crawford's Digest, pp. 666 and 677. His arguments are strong and forceful. The next year he was defeated for Governor but served his people as a Justice for Chatham County. This year, 1789, the act was passed incorporating the city of Savannah, and Mr. Houstoun was elected Mayor. So he had the unusual distinction of having been twice Governor and a Chief Justice of Georgia before he was elected the Mayor of "Oglethorpe City" in 1790.

In 1791 Gen. Washington visited Savannah and Mr. Houstoun was a member of the committee who welcomed and entertained this distinguished man. In 1792 he was commissioned Judge of the Superior Court of the Eastern Circuit of the State.

Gov. Houstoun married Miss Bryan, a daughter of Jonathan Bryan. They had no children.

This incident has come down in the family. "While the seat of government was at Savannah Gov. Houstoun's elder brother, Sir George Houstoun, had a country seat nine miles from the city on the Vernon River, called White Bluff. The Governor was accustomed to spend much of his time at this country place. The British got wind of this, and on one occasion sent a boat and crew up the river to capture the Governor. He heard of this raid in time and ran through the garden into the woods behind the house, climbed a tree and remained hid until the raiding party left."

No son of Georgia was ever more faithful to the trusts committed to his care, none left a more stainless record. On the 20th of July, 1796, he departed this life at White Bluff, the old family home, nine miles from Savannah. Georgia perpetuates the name and the memory of this distinguished son of hers in Houstoun County in the central part of the State.

A. B. CALDWELL.

William Houstoun.

LAWYER, commissioner, member of the Continental Congress, William Houstoun was a native of Savannah, Georgia, where he was born about 1755. He was a son of Sir Patrick Houstoun, Baronet, and a brother of Governor John Houstoun. He was educated for the law in Great Britain and was admitted in 1776 to the Inner Temple, London. At the commencement of the Revolution he returned home and took an active part in the cause of liberty. He was twice elected to the Continental Congress and served in that body from 1784-'87. In 1785 he served as a commissioner in the dispute between South Carolina and Georgia over their boundary line. In 1787 he was deputized by Georgia to attend the Convention to revise the Federal Constitution, and, although he attended and participated in the deliberations of that august body, he declined to sign the Constitution. With his brother John he was one of the original trustees for the establishment of a college to which the State granted forty thousand acres of land in 1784, chartered in 1785 as Franklin College, now the University of Georgia. He resigned this position in 1787.

Mr. Houstoun was a lawyer of note in his day. Loyal to his native State and section, he was quick to avenge any insinuation that reflected against either. On one occasion the Rev. James Manning, delegate from Rhode Island, made some remarks which he construed as reflecting on the people of the South, and the next morning he appeared in Congress armed with a sword. His friends intervened and the fiery young Georgian was persuaded to send his sword back to his room by his servant, thus closing the incident.

The portrait of Wm. Houstoun as well as that of Governor John Houstoun, together with the family plate and his historic papers of great value, were destroyed by fire in southwestern Georgia, where the family had sent them during the war between the States, for protection and safe-keeping. There is no record of the date and place of his death.

W. Berrien Burroughs, M.D.

Richard Howley.

RICHARD HOWLEY, farmer, lawyer, member of the Continental Congress and Governor was born in Liberty County or as it was then called, St. John's Parish, about 1740. During the Revolution this county was completely overrun by the British and Indians, and after the fall of Fort Morris, the strongest fort in Georgia, Mr. Howley, with other soldiers and civilians, made his way to Augusta, Savannah, having been previously taken by General Prevost, commanding the forces of Great Britain.

Mr. Howley took an active part in the affairs of the State. These were times that tried the souls of men. The refugees of the southern counties, who had been members of the previous Legislature, elected George Walton Governor, but this was unconstitutional. The General Assembly met in December, 1779, and on the 4th of January, 1780, elected Richard Howley Governor. On account of the defenceless condition of Augusta the assembly passed the following law: "That his Honor, the Governor, or in his absence the President and Executive Council might do and transact all and every business of government in full, ample authoritative manner, in any other State within the confederation, touching and respecting of this State, as though it had been done and transacted within the limits of this State."

Governor Howley issued a strong proclamation, "commanding and requiring the people to stand firm to their duty, and exert themselves in support and event of the great and glorious independency of the United States; and also to remember with gratitude to heaven that the Almighty Ruler of human affairs hath been pleased to raise up the spirit and might of the two greatest powers in the world (France and Spain) to join with them and oppose and destroy the persecutors of their liberties and immunities.

At Savannah a terrible defeat had followed the unsuccessful attempt of the Americans, under General Lincoln, and the French, under Count D'Estaing, to raise the siege.

Governor Wright, the Royal Governor, was again in his seat and those loyal to the Crown had assembled, and the House of Commons passed the Confiscation Act at Savannah, by which more than one hundred and fifty Georgia citizens, that were attainted of high treason, lost their property. Their names with their occupations have been preserved.

Governor Howley, knowing the defenceless condition of Augusta, "which might be surprised and captured by twenty men," decided it unwise to remain there, and the assembly designated Heard's Fort (where Washington, Ga., now stands) as a proper place of meeting to transact government business. Governor Howley had been elected to the old congress, so he held the dual offices of governor and congressman, a compliment never before or since paid any Georgian. The British occupied every county in the state except Wilkes. Leaving Honorable George Wells, the president of the council, with three members of the board to transact business, Governor Howley took several members of his cabinet with the archives of the state and a large quantity of paper money and fled to New Bern, North Carolina. From New Bern John Milton, a member of his cabinet, carried the archives to Baltimore, where they remained until several years after the war. Governor Howley went to Philadelphia and took his seat as a member of Congress. Our currency had so depreciated in value that his expenses to Philadelphia cost the state half a million dollars.

Colonel Brown had occupied Augusta and issued his edict confiscating all the property of the patriots, and banishing from the colony all who remained unless they took the oath of allegiance to the King.

Governor Howley was always active in the interest of his state and section, and fearing that Congress would make a treaty with Great Britain by which South Carolina and Georgia would remain British possessions, he prepared and published an able remonstrance which was signed by William Few and George Walton, our other members of Congress. It will be remembered that the British army held both sides of the Savannah River as well as the principal towns of South Carolina and Georgia. It was boldly hinted that in the negotiations England's claim to these colonies would be pressed on the ground that they "had been again colonized to England by new conquest." Mr. Howley's original letter to Henry Laurens on this subject is in the possession of the writer of this sketch and reads as follows:

"PHILADELPHIA, January 2, 1781.

SIR:—I cannot but consider it an indispensable duty, as Governor of the state of Georgia, to communicate to you the situation of the unfortunate country previous to your departure to France. Long distinguished for its exertions and opposition to the measures of the British tyrant, and exposed to the weight of his forces in proportion to the display of its firmness, its condition, I am persuaded, will be considered not unworthy the attention of the ministers of that great monarch to whom you will soon have the honor of being introduced.

When the illustrious and puissant ally, who generously yielded himself to support the independency of Georgia in common with the other states in the union, is informed that the glory of his reign and the prosperity of his people continue ob-

12

jects as ardently desired by the citizens of that state, as their own freedom it will be an act of justice which the uniform tenor of their conduct is entitled to, and which they are solicitous to have represented in the most perfect manner.

Overrun at different times by numerous bodies of the British troops, their virtue and heroism have stood an ordeal test, nor can the savage cruelties of their enemies depress the generous ardor prevailing among them which will always display itself in maintaining their independence and the alliance between France and the United States—an alliance which the Georgians cherish with enthusiasm.

As the Southern states are now become the theatre of the war, and the greatest part of the British force is embarked for that quarter, the declarations which are contained in the New York and Charleston *Gazettes* grow more serious, should the court of London indeed offer independence to eleven of the states on condition of having Georgia and South Carolina ceded to them. Such allurements thrown out to a people harassed by a long and bloody war might possibly give birth to discussions of a most interesting nature, and which may ultimately promote the views of that perfidious court.

Should these extensive and fertile countries be sacrified to Britain in addition to the Floridas, her northern and southern possessions in North America would contain the greatest part of the wealth and commerce in that continent from whence wisdom and policy direct should be entirely expelled. Our enemies would in such a situation acquire means of again blazing in their former insolence and perhaps of carrying into effect designs dictated by a turbulence and ambition unacquainted with restraint. A paper respecting the State of Georgia, which will be put into your hands by the delegates now representing Georgia in Congress, will demonstrate what numerous resources Britain would derive from an establishment of this point. The enlightened mind of the Count DeVergennes and the other wise ministers who conduct the affairs of our august friend and ally, will, I am persuaded, see this important matter in a proper and timely form, and take measures for disconcerting the insidious plans of a perfidious and active enemy. The full information which you have of our affairs generally renders it unnecessary for me to say any more on this matter; and the opinion I entertain of your abilities and honor possess me with assurance of having true and forcible observations suggested to Count DeVergennes. I have the honor to be, sir, your most humble and obedient servant, RICHARD HOWLEY.

His Excellency, HENRY LAURENS, ESQR.,
Minister of the United States to Versailles.''

Henry Laurens was our minister plenipotentiary to negotiate a treaty with that country; was captured on the high seas on the Mercury by the British frigate Vestal, and for fifteen months was incarcerated in the Capital Tower of London. He was exchanged for Lord Cornwallis after the surrender of the latter.

After the war Governor Howley returned to his native county, Liberty, in 1783. He died in Savannah in December, 1784.

WM. BERRIEN BURROUGHS, M.D.

Jared Irwin.

AUTHENTIC information about the boyhood and early manhood of Jared Irwin is meagre. His father, Thos. Irwin, came from Ireland about the middle of the eighteenth century and settled in Lunenburg county, Virginia; later the family removed to Rowan, now Mecklenburg county, North Carolina. It was here, in 1751, that the subject of this sketch was born. When he was seven years of age his parents moved to Georgia and settled in the parish of St. George, or what is now Burke county. His subsequent career would indicate that he was a man of education, but it is not known where he attended school. In fact, we hear nothing at all of him till the outbreak of hostilities with the mother country, when he looms up as an ardent patriot and, for nearly half a century, serves his adopted State with satisfaction to his constituents and with honor to himself. He entered the Revolution as captain and rose to the rank of colonel. He was active in the Georgia and Carolina campaigns.

At the close of the war, he began in the state legislature a long and honorable career in the public service which was not interrupted by his removal, about 1787, to Washington county, then a vast wilderness. His services included membership in all the state's leading conventions, the presidency of the senate, and two terms as governor of the commonwealth. It was during his first term that he performed the act which, had he done nothing more, would have given him a permanent place in Georgia history. He signed the famous Rescinding Act by which the Yazoo Fraud was wiped from the statute books.

There is no record as to whom he married; but he had four

children, Jared, Jr., John, Isabel and Jane. The boys were in the first class graduated from the University of Georgia.

Although descended from Presbyterian ancestry, Governor Irwin was a Congregationalist. He donated a church and several acres of land near his place, Union Hill, for the use of all denominations. It was named Union Church in honor of his place. This church has more recently passed into the possession of a Baptist congregation and is now called Ohoopee. It is near Sandersville. Governor Irwin lies buried in this churchyard.

He has been accorded the distinction of being the only individual, up to this time, to whom the State of Georgia has erected a monument. A shaft to his memory was placed in the street in front of the court house in Sandersville. When Sherman entered the little town on his march through Georgia, one of Wheeler's men fired a shot, which left its mark on the marble, where it can still be seen. Later, in removing the monument to the Court Square, the shaft was broken, but has been cleverly mended. It bears the following inscription:

"Erected by the State of Georgia to the memory of Governor Jared Irwin; he died at his residence, Union Hill, Washington county, on the first day of March, 1818, in the 68th year of his age.

General Irwin was one of the convention which met at Augusta in 1788 and ratified the Constitution of the United States. He was a member of the convention in 1789, which formed the Constitution of the State of Georgia; in 1798, he was president of the convention which revised the Constitution of the State of Georgia. He rendered distinguished services to his country as commissioner in concluding several treaties with the Indians.

At the close of the war of independence he was a member of the first legislature under our present form of government; which he occupied for several years. He was elected president of the senate frequently, at various periods from 1790 to the time of his death.

He was governor of Georgia from January 17, 1796, to the 11th of January, 1798, and again from the 23d of September, 1806, to the 7th of November, 1809. His administration was distinguished for his justice and impartiality; and his was the honor, after several years' labor in that behalf, of signing the act rescinding the Yazoo Law.

A true patriot, he entered the service of his country as captain and soon rose to the rank of colonel during the Revolutionary War. As a soldier he was brave and gallant. He distinguished himself at the siege of Savannah and Augusta; and in the battle of Camden, Briar-Creek, Black-Swamp, and several other engagements, he was at all times foremost leading his gallant band to victory. And not with his sword and in his person only did he do service for his country. From his private means he erected a fortress in Burke County for the protection of the people of the surrounding district.

His pure devotion to the cause of liberty marked him in the eyes of the enemy, and, on more than one occasion, was he plundered of his property and his premises reduced to ashes.

At the close of the war of the Revolution, with the rank of general, he was actively engaged in the service of the state, in repelling the attacks of their merciless foes.

In his private relations, Gov. Irwin was beloved by all who knew him; the spotless purity of his character, his benign and affable disposition, his widespread benevolence and hospitality, made him the object of general affection. To the poor and distressed he was a benefactor and a friend.

In every position of public life, as a soldier and statesman, as a patriot, the public good was the object and end of his ambition. And his death was lamented as a national calamity.

But his memory will ever be embalmed in the hearts of his countrymen; and the historians award him a brilliant page in the record of his country.

Peace to his ashes. Honor to his name!"

A. B. CALDWELL.

James Jackson.

O F the many heroic men cast from the crucible of the Revolution, none deserves a more grateful remembrance by the people of Georgia than James Jackson.

He was born at Moreton-Hampstead, in the county of Devon, in England, September 21, 1757. He was the son of James Jackson and Mary Webber, whose sympathies for the patriotic cause of America early aroused in the heart of their son a burning desire to alleviate the oppressions of England upon the colonies.

At the early age of fifteen, he left his ancestral home and cast the fortunes of his life among those daring spirits who were then peopling the new world.

In 1772 he landed in Savannah, and placed himself under the protection of John Wereat, Esq., an old and intimate friend of his father.

Samuel Farley, Esq., a prominent and successful lawyer of that city, recognizing the fine quality of young Jackson's mind and character, received him into his office and directed his studies. When Archibald Bulloch was chosen president on January 20, 1776, Jackson was elected clerk of the court.

But these were times of great political unrest. Patriotic feeling was at a high tension, and the gathering storm of the Revolution demanded action. With Jackson's strong inherent conceptions of human liberty we find him actively associated with those stirring events which form the dramatic prelude to the great struggle soon to follow. With such daring spirits as Bulloch, Habersham, Houstoun, Jones and Hall, his ardent nature found congenial company.

Jas Jackson.

He first distinguished himself in 1776, when an attack was made against Savannah by Commodore Barclay and Majors Maitland and Grant, for the purpose of capturing the rice-laden ships in the harbor. To dislodge the enemy who had already captured some of the vessels, the Council of Safety resolved to set fire to the shipping. Among the volunteers to accomplish this perilous act was James Jackson, then only nineteen years old.

His gallantry at the attack upon Tybee merited the thanks and approbation of President Bulloch, who led the expedition, and who witnessed his exhibitions of bravery.

Shortly afterwards, he was made lieutenant, and then captain, of a volunteer company of light infantry, but, owing to some trouble between himself and his men, in which he believed he was not properly supported by his colonel, he resigned his position about the time that General Howe resumed the invasion of East Florida.

In the latter part of the year 1778, he was appointed brigade-major of the Georgia militia, and with his command he bravely resisted the invasion of the British under Colonel Prevost in many skirmishes southwest of Savannah. He took an active part in the battle near Midway Meeting-House, in which the gallant General Screven lost his life, and in which he himself received a wound in the ankle.

On that ill-fated day in December, 1778, when the British under Colonel Campbell captured Savannah, and the hopes of the patriots went down in defeat, Major Jackson was among those who escaped in the general rout of the American forces under the short-sighted leadership of General Robert Howe. The greater number of the Georgia troops having been killed or taken prisoners in this assault, and there being no longer a field for his services in his own state, General Jackson, accompanied by Mr. Milledge, barefoot and penniless, friendless and unknown, crossed the Savannah river and joined the command of General Moultrie as a common soldier.

Upon this "barefoot expedition," as he calls it, they were arrested as spies by some American soldiers, and, but for the timely arrival of Major Peter Deveaux, both would have been hanged.

He returned to Georgia in time to take part in the unsuccessful siege of Savannah in October, 1779. Upon this memorable occasion the name and services of James Jackson will ever be associated with those of Pulaski, Jasper, Lincoln, Habersham, McIntosh and Estaing.

Georgia, now being almost in entire possession of the British, Major Jackson once more crossed to Carolina and joined Colonel Clarke in August, 1780. On the 20th of the same month, General Sumter was attacked at Blackstocks, near Tyger river, by Lieutenant-Colonel Tarleton. In this obstinate battle, General Sumter was dangerously wounded, and Major Jackson was ordered to pursue Tarleton, who had fled from the field. Owing to the fleetness of Tarleton's steed, he made his escape, but Jackson captured thirty or forty horses in the chase. His action upon this occasion gained for him a high and well-earned reputation among the militia of Georgia and South Carolina.

At the battle of the Cowpens, Major Jackson again distinguished himself for bravery and military skill. General Andrew Pickens, who commanded the Georgia and Carolina troops upon this occasion, bears the following testimony to his gallant services:

"Major Jackson, by his example and firm, active conduct, did much to animate the soldiers and insure the success of the day. He ran the utmost risk of his life in seizing the colors of the 71st British regiment, and afterwards introducing Major

McArthur, commanding officer of the British infantry, as a prisoner of war, to Gen. Morgan."

After this battle, he performed conspicuous service in the Carolinas in checking the advance of Cornwallis, and at one time narrowly escaped death at the hands of Tarleton's troops at Tennant's Tavern. General Greene, now in charge of the Department of the South, was so well pleased with Major Jackson's record that he was authorized to raise a partisan legion of infantry and cavalry for service in Georgia. This Major Jackson soon accomplished, and with his eloquence and enthusiasm he fired his legion to the highest pitch of patriotic duty. "Liberty and Jackson forever" was the battle cry of this determined band of men, thus described by Jackson himself: "My dragoons were clothed and armed by themselves, except pistols; even their caps, boots and spurs. Their coats were made of deer-skins, dressed, and turned up with the little blue cloth I could procure. My whole corps for months were without anything to quench their thirst but the common swamp water near Savannah, and for forty-eight hours together without bread, rice, or anything like it."

Colonel Baker, having undertaken an expedition against Augusta, Major Jackson felt it his duty to return to Georgia. In the memorable attack upon Augusta, his services were of vital importance. Here his eloquence and military ardor aroused the drooping spirits of the American troops, and, under great difficulties, the British were dislodged from this important stronghold. After the surrender, Major Jackson was ordered to level the fortifications, to collect as many men as possible, and to join the army of General Greene. Having marched about thirty miles, he found it impossible to reach the main army and he returned to Augusta and took charge of the city.

In July, he received orders to take position with his troops midway between Augusta and Savannah, and here was discovered a conspiracy to kill Colonel Jackson in his bed. The plot was found out by a soldier named Davis, who acted as a waiter to Colonel Jackson, and the ringleaders were promptly arrested and executed. Davis was afterwards rewarded by the state with a gift of five hundred acres of land, a horse, saddle and bridle.

From this time to the close of the Revolution, Colonel Jackson served with General Wayne in the military operations before Savannah, and when that post was evacuated by the British, he was designated to receive the keys of the city in consideration of his conspicuous services in the campaign. He was the first American soldier to enter the city since its capture in 1778.

On July 30, 1782, the Legislature of Georgia adopted the following resolution:

"*Whereas,* Lieutenant-Colonel Jackson has rendered many great and useful services to his country, for which he is entitled to the notice of the legislature: Be it, therefore, resolved, that the house which heretofore belonged to Mr. Tattnall, in Savannah, be granted to Colonel Jackson as a mark of the sense entertained by the legislature of his merits."

When the cause of liberty had been won, Colonel Jackson sheathed his sword and engaged in the practice of law to which he had been educated. Aided by the instructions of George Walton, and by his own genius for forensic achievement, he soon rose to distinction in his profession.

On January 30, 1785, he was married to Mary Charlotte Young, daughter of William Young, a gallant patriot of the Revolution. She died July 5, 1795. Their children were William Henry Jackson, State Senator and first alumnus and a trustee of the University of Georgia; James Jackson, professor in the University of Georgia, Jabez Young Jackson and Joseph

Webber Jackson, member of Congress. Chief Justice James Jackson, of the Supreme Court of Georgia, was the son of William Henry Jackson, noted above.

Though eminently successful at the bar, Colonel Jackson's ardent nature soon led him into public life. For several years in succession, the people of Chatham county elected him their representative in the Legislature, where he performed conspicuous service.

In 1786, he was made Brigadier-General, Grand Master of the Grand Lodge of Masons in Georgia, and an honorary member of the Society of the Cincinnati. In January, 1788, when only thirty years of age, he was elected Governor of Georgia, an office which he modestly declined, saying that his age and experience would not justify his acceptance.

He was engaged for some time in directing the military operations against the Creek Indians, who were harassing the lower counties by their depredations.

In 1789, he was elected to the first Congress of the United States held under the new constitution, and in the debates of that body he took a prominent part. In 1792 he won a notable contest for his seat in that body against General Anthony Wayne, who had opposed him in the election. He held almost every important office in his State. He was made Major-General, and he was a member of the Constitutional Convention of 1798. He himself wrote a great part of that important fundamental law.

In 1796, he resigned his seat in the United States Senate at the request of his constituents to oppose in the Legislature of his state the infamous Yazoo Fraud. There cannot be found in all history a nobler, and a more patriotic self-sacrificing spirit than that which moved General James Jackson in exposing and crushing this gigantic scheme of villainy. This dark chapter in the history of Georgia is too long to be related here, but throughout this great struggle with the powers of bribery and corruption in high places, the strong, honest, and determined character of James Jackson will forever stand as a model of integrity and as an inspiration to generations to come. This bold scheme for defrauding the state of millions of acres of her territory was completely crushed, chiefly through the efforts of General Jackson, and upon the dramatic occasion of purging with fire drawn from the sun, the records of the corrupt act, he as the central figure kindled the flames with a burning glass, as he denounced as villains the men who had voted for the law.

In 1798, he was again elected Governor of Georgia, and he served in this office till March, 1801, when he was sent back to the United States Senate. In this capacity, he served his state till his death, which occurred in Washington on March 19, 1806. His remains rest in the Congressional Burying Grounds of that city.

Some years before his death, he prepared a manuscript volume of notes on "Ramsay's History of the Revolution in South Carolina," and also a full biographical sketch of himself. Both of these valuable documents are still preserved in the archives of the Georgia Historical Society at Savannah.

In estimating the character of General James Jackson, we are at once impressed that he was a man of heroic mould. If true greatness is the ability to meet a crisis, then James Jackson was truly great, for he lived in critical times. He was by nature a soldier, and an orator of high order. His mind was alert, and his intuitions were almost unerring. Quick in thought and action, he sometimes became involved in personal encounters, and on several occasions he engaged in duels, so common in his day. In one of these he was severely wounded.

Though relentless towards his enemies, he was generous in their defeat. If at times he appears to us with too much self esteem, we should remember that he was also brave, patriotic, and self-sacrificing to an extraordinary degree. In person he was about five feet and seven inches tall, slender, very erect in his carriage, with light hair and intensely blue eyes. His manners were dignified and affable, and his whole bearing was such as to impress those who knew him with absolute confidence in his integrity and the loftiness of his purpose.

The name of one of Georgia's most prosperous counties perpetuates his memory, and the record of his noble life will for all time remain a rich and inspiring heritage to the people of his beloved state. OTIS ASHMORE.

William Jasper.

WILLIAM JASPER was born in South Carolina about the year 1750. Very little, indeed, is known about his early history. One thing is certain, however, and that is his school facilities were limited to such an extent that in after life he was so illiterate that he could scarcely read or write.

Dr. W. B. Burroughs says, "We are entitled to claim Sergeant Jasper as a Georgian; for while he was born in South Carolina, he spent his early days on a farm in Georgia. Captain Barnard Elliott, who, under Colonel William Moultrie, commanded the first company of the second South Carolina regiment, known as the 'Grenadier Company' states in his diary, pages 221 and 222, that he enlisted Sergeant Jasper in Halifax county, Georgia. The settlement referred to as Halifax county included parts of Screven and Burke counties."

He distinguished himself in the attack on Fort Moultrie, June 28, 1760. In the midst of the engagement the flag-staff was shot down, and the flag fell to the bottom of the trench on the outside of the breastworks. Fearlessly, at once, Jasper leaped from the embrasure and caught the colors which he tied to a sponge staff, the only available staff in reach, and replaced it on the parapet where he supported it until another flag-staff could be procured. In recognition of this brave and heroic deed, Governor Rutledge, presented him with his own sword, accompanying it with a commission for the lieutenancy. Jasper was a modest man, and, knowing that he could neither read nor write, he most respectfully declined the commission. He, however, accepted a roving commission, which authorized him to come and go at will. In these forays he was in the habit of selecting five or six men of like daring and enterprise with himself. Often they would go out and gather as many prisoners as he and his men could guard and bring them into camp before General Moultrie knew of his absence. On one occasion he entered the British lines in disguise, and, ascertaining their strength, returned to the American camp and communicated it to the commander.

The recapture of certain prisoners by Jasper, with the aid of his friend Newton, near Savannah, is peculiarly interesting. Learning that a number of American prisoners were to be brought from Ebenezer to Savannah for trial he determined to release them at all hazards. With Newton as his companion, at a spring two miles from Savannah and about thirty yards from the main road, he awaited the arrival of the prisoners. When the escort, consisting of a sergeant, corporal, and eight men, and the prisoners in irons, stopped to refresh themselves at this spring; only two of the guards remained with the captives. The others leaned their guns against the trees, when Jasper and Newton sprang from their hiding place, seized the guns, and shot down the two sentinels. The remaining six soldiers were deterred from making any effort to recover their arms by threats of immediate death and were forced to surrender. The prisoners were immediatly released and Jasper and Newton with their redeemed friends and captive foes crossed the Savannah river and joined the army at Purysburg.

In the disastrous siege of Savannah, the gallant Jasper lost his life. Shortly after the battle of Fort Moultrie, the wife of Colonel Barnard Elliott presented an elegant pair of colors to the second regiment, to which Jasper was attached. Her address on this occasion concluded thus: "I make not the least doubt, under heaven's protection, you will stand by these colors so long as they wave in the air of liberty." In reply, a response was made that they should be honorably supported and never should be tarnished by the second regiment. This engagement was literally fulfilled three years afterwards. The colors had been planted on the British line at Savannah by Lieutenant Bush, who was immediately shot down and Lieutenant Hume who was also killed. Lieutenant Gray, while supporting them, received a mortal wound. A storm of shot drove back the patriots, and cut down the staff of the flag. Sergeant Jasper, seeing that it would fall into the hands of the enemy, leaped on the wall, seized the fallen flag, and carried it back to his regiment. At that moment he received a death shot and was borne bleeding from the field. When an officer called to see him he said, "I have got my furlough. That sword was presented to me by Governor Rutledge for my service in defense of Fort Moultrie. Give it to my father and tell him that I have worn it with honor. If he should weep, tell him his son died in the hope of a better life. Tell Mrs. Elliott that I lost my life in supporting the colors which she presented to our regiment. If you should ever see Jones, his wife, and son, tell them that Jasper has gone, but that the remembrance of the battle which he fought for them brought a secret joy to his heart when it was about to stop its motion forever."

In 1812, the legislature honored Georgia and the memory of this hero who died for her freedom by giving his name to one of her most prosperous counties. The patriotic citizens of Savannah have also nobly done their part by erecting to his honor, in one of their beautiful squares, a monument surmounted by a heroic figure of Jasper. One of the city wards also bears his name.

Sergeant Jasper married Miss Elizabeth Marlow while he was stationed at Fort Moultrie. They had two children, William and Elizabeth, both of whom were educated in Charleston.

R. J. MASSEY.

Noble Jones.

D R. NOBLE JONES was bred to the profession of physic, and lived at Lambeth, a village in the county of Surrey, seated on the south side of the river Thames, opposite Westminster, in which county his ancestors were born and resided. Being intimately acquainted with General Oglethorpe, he was induced by the general to accompany him to America on his first voyage in 1732. This friendship lasted all their lives. After General Oglethorpe's return to England to live, he sent Colonel Jones his portrait, with his Indian pupil standing by his side reading. It was lost when Savannah was captured by the English.

Dr. Noble Jones' family then consisted only of his wife and two children, a daughter and a son, Noble Wymberley. It was his first intention to accompany the General without his family, but his wife objected to being left. Having promised the General to accompany him, he concluded to bring his family, not, however, with an intention of residing permanently, but after his arrival he was pleased with the country and decided to remain. Before leaving England, Dr. Jones, by Deeds, to which the Seal of the Corporation of the Trustees of the Colony of Georgia was affixed, was appointed November 7, 1732, Conservator of the Peace, and the next day, November the 8th, 1732, Recorder in the place of Thomas Christie. How long he remained Recorder is not certain, but he still held that office in 1735, and was succeeded by Thomas Christie. He was appointed Surveyor by General Oglethorpe February 1, 1734-5, but did not give satisfaction and was discharged by the Trustees, and also suspended from the office of constable which he had held for some time. To the last office he was soon reappointed. That he was a good surveyor is testified to by Mr. Stephens in a letter to the Trustees 31st December, 1740. Other letters endorse Mr. Stephens' opinion.

He was also appointed by General Oglethorpe "Agent for the Indians," and for Tomo-chi-chi, in particular.

During this time he was very active protecting the southern frontier. He writes to General Oglethorpe July 6, 1735, "I have been twice to the most southern parts of the Province, the first time upon an alarm with about fifty men (all volunteers except ye scout-boat) the particulars of which voyage (for fear a false account should come to your hands) I will send by next. The second time was with Captain Dunbar, who I do not doubt has informed you thereof before now."

The constables were responsible for the colonists attending to their military duties, and Jones and Fallowfield are mentioned as the two constables, "in whom the civil and military power was lodged." Each of these two controlled three wards.

On the 10th of April, 1738, Mr. Stephens writes: "The two constables Jones and Fallowfield (which was all we had) came early to town on the present occasion, from their distant Plantations and took breakfast with me, conferring on the affair they came about, which was more immediately to look into the condition of the arms. It was resolved (for experiment sake) to order the drum to beat immediately to arms, that thereby we may see how alert the people were and what number would get together on a sudden, without previous notice; it was so done and in less than an hour's time we saw eighty-odd men in the center of the town, with their proper arms well appointed, and all able men, freeholders; such as were absent, were almost every man abroad busy in planting."

When General Oglethorpe invaded Florida and laid siege

to St. Augustine, some forty volunteers under Noble Jones joined the South Carolina regiment, in which he held a lieutenant's commission. On their return, the company was disbanded in Savannah, according to the General's orders, and Noble Jones was sent by him to Charlestown to collect the pay due them. Soon after Noble Jones' arrival in the Colony, he leased from the Trustees the southern end of the Isle of Hope; later he received a grant from the Trustees, which in turn was exchanged for a royal grant, when the Crown took charge of the colony. He named his place Wormsloe and built on it a watch-house, to protect Jones' Narrows, and later he built a large tappy fort, the ruins of which are still well defined. This fort was successfully defended by his daughter Mary against a party of Indians, during her father's absence. The other two-thirds of the Isle of Hope were owned by Messrs. Fallowfield and Parker. All three acted as Magistrates at the same time "by Colonel Oglethorpe's order till the Trustees' further pleasure be known." Wormsloe is mentioned in the London Magazine of August, 1745:

"We arrived in somewhat more than two days at the *Narrows*, where there is a kind of *Manchecolas* Fort, for their defence, garrison'd from *Wormsloe*, where we soon arrived. It is the settlement of Mr. *Jones*, 10 miles S. E. of Savannah, and we could not help observing, as we passed, several very pretty plantations. *Wormsloe*, is one of the most agreeable spots I ever saw, and the improvements of that ingenious man are very extraordinary; he commands a company of Marines, who are quartered in huts near his house, which is a tolerable defensible place with small arms. From this house there is a vista of near three miles cut thro' the woods to Mr. *Whitefield's* orphan house, which has a very fine effect on the sight."

When the Spaniards invaded Georgia in 1742, Noble Jones

was in command of a company of scouts, with General Oglethorpe's regiment on St. Simons, prepared to resist the Spanish
army which had landed there. It was through his vigilance that
General Oglethorpe was able to surprise and thoroughly defeat
them at Bloody Marsh. Captain McCall gives the following
account of this affair: "Capt. Noble Jones, with a detachment
of regulars and Indians, being out on a scouting party, fell in
with a small detachment of the enemies' advance, who were surprised and made prisoners, not deeming themselves so far in
front of the main army. From these prisoners information was
received that the whole Spanish army was advancing: this was
immediately communicated by an Indian runner to the General,
who detached Capt. Dunbar, with a company of grenadiers, to
join the Regulars and Indians, with orders to harass the enemy
on their advance. These detachments having formed a junction, observed at a distance the Spanish army on the march;
and taking a favorable position near a marsh formed an ambuscade. The enemy fortunately halted within a hundred paces
of this position, stacked their arms and made fires, and were
preparing their kettles for cooking, when a horse observed some
of the party in ambuscade and, frightened at the uniform of
Regulars, began to snort and gave the alarm. The Spaniards
ran to their arms but were shot down in great numbers by Oglethorpe's detachment, who continued invisible to the enemy, and
after repeated attempts to form, in which some of their principal
officers fell, they fled with the utmost precipitation, leaving their
camp equippage on the field, and never halted until they got
under cover of the guns of their battery and ships."

The first official notice of the appointment of Noble Jones as
a captain is on the 26th of March, 1742-3. *Egmont's Journal*
has this reference: "Noble Jones made a Captain by General
Oglethorpe," but he fulfilled the duties of a captain and was

called so before that date. After his return from the Spanish campaign, he seems to have devoted himself to his scout-boat duties (Captain of which he had been named by General Oglethorpe), and to the improvement of Wormsloe. He raised mulberry trees and silk-worms and the colony in a measure depended upon him for worm-seed.

He and Capt. Demetree cruised together with their scout-boats to intercept unlawful trading at Tybee.

On December 22, 1739, "with boat well armed he captured a schooner in *Ossybaw Sound,* and carried her around to Tybee."

Meanwhile he did not neglect his military duties in Savannah, and when, in 1749, Mary Musgrave, now Mary Bosomworth, assumed the title of Independent Empress, and putting herself at the head of a large body of warriors, set out for Savannah to demand from the President and Council a formal acknowledgment of her assumed rights, the militia was ready to receive her. President Stephens put the town in the best state of defense possible, and received the Indians boldly. Jones' History of Georgia says, "The Militia was ordered under arms, and as the Indians entered the town Capt. Noble Jones, at the head of a troop of horse, stopped them and demanded whether their visit was of a friendly or of a hostile character. Receiving no reply, he commanded them to ground their arms, declaring that his instructions were not to suffer an armed Indian to set foot in the town, and that he was determined to enforce these orders at every hazard. The Indians reluctantly submitted. Later, at their solicitation, their arms were returned to them, but strict orders were issued not to allow them any ammunition.

When at last an amicable adjustment of existing difficulties had been effected, Mary, drunk with liquor, rushed into the Assembly, and told the President that the Indians were her people, and that he had no business with them. Mary had been arrested and locked up and had just been released. The President calmly threatened to confine her again. Turning to Malatche in a great rage she repeated to him with some ill-natured comments what the President had said. Malatche thereupon sprang from his seat, laid hold of his arms, and called upon the rest to follow his example, and dared any man to touch his Queen. In a moment the whole house was filled with tumult and uproar. Every Indian having a tomahawk in his hand, the President expected nothing but instant death. During this confusion Captain Noble Jones, who commanded the guard, with wonderful courage, interposed and ordered the Indians immediately to surrender their arms. This they reluctantly did. Mary was conveyed to a private room, where a guard was placed over her, and all further communications with the Indians was denied her during her stay in Savannah."

About this time the expediency of subordinating Georgia to South Carolina was in certain high quarters seriously discussed, and gave the Trustees much concern. Before they could communicate with President Stephens, Captain Demetree landed at Causton's Bluff with boats, which having brought the last of Oglethorpe's disbanded regiment to Charlestown, on their way to England, were returning to Frederica in his charge. He had a small detachment of ten or twelve men, and said that he was on his way to Frederica to assume command at that point, that he took orders only from the Governor of South Carolina, and that the Trustees were cognizant of the fact. "As he failed to report to the President and his assistants, and disclose to them either his orders or intentions, they were at a loss to understand his extraordinary conduct, and ordered Capt. Noble Jones to wait upon him and demand an explanation of and an apology for his discourtesy. Capt. Demetree's reply to Capt. Noble Jones was that he was acting under instructions from his Grace, the Duke of Bedford, communicated with the consent of the Trustees, and that he was to receive his orders from, and report only to the Governor of South Carolina. He reluctantly appeared before the Council in answer to their summons." "After Capt. Demetree had made ample apology to Council he was permitted to assume command of the military force stationed at Frederica. The annexation of Georgia to South Carolina was to be accomplished at this time by stationing soldiers from three independent South Carolina Companies, in proper places in Georgia, 'to preserve the possession of the Province.' "

On July 13, 1750, the Trustees recommended to Common Council that Noble Jones be appointed an Assistant in and for the Province of Georgia and the appointment under seal was sent to him July 16, 1750.

On April the 8th, 1751, the Trustees recommended to the Common Council, his appointment as Register of the Province, and his appointment followed on May 24, 1751.

About the middle of May of this year, news came from Augusta that there was fear of an Indian invasion. "Accordingly the Magazine was examined, officers were appointed, and ordered to muster and discipline the militia, a troop of horse was ordered to be raised, composed of such inhabitants as were possessed of three hundred acres of land. Noble Jones was appointed Colonel, and his son, Noble Wymberly Jones, who had been a cadet in Oglethorpe's regiment was appointed to command the dragoons."

The alarm was exaggerated but it served to bring out the militia, which consisted of 220 men, infantry and cavalry, and when they paraded (on the 16th of April, 1751, under the then Captain Noble Jones) "behaved well, and made a pretty appearance." He was appointed "to accompany Mr. Robinson in his inquiry into the state of the Colony." According to Mr. Habersham he was a stiff churchman and took a great deal of voluntary trouble, in building the church, and in all church matters, aiding greatly his friend Rev. Mr. Zouberbuhler.

In the last year of the Trustee's government of the Colony, he was Captain of the Marines and Scout-boat at Wormsloe, Assistant to the President, Register of the Province, Commissioner to treat with the Indians, Member of the Council to report on the state of the Colony, and Colonel of the regiment.

The Trustees surrendered the Colony to the British Government the 23d of June, 1752, and Benjamin Martyn was appointed agent of the Colony in England. Upon the death of President Parker, who had succeeded President Stephens (the first President of the Colony appointed in April, 1741), Patrick Graham became President. His assistants were James Habersham, Noble Jones, Pickering Robinson, and Francis Harris, they reported to the Lords Commissioners for trade and plantations, who on the 6th of August, 1754, appointed Captain John Reynolds Governor of the Province, and Noble Jones was confirmed as Member of Councils. On the 27th of November, 1754, Gov. Reynolds, with the advice of the board, appointed Noble Jones and Wm. Spencer, Esqrs., Judges to hold the approaching court of oyer and terminer, and on December 12, 1754, Noble Jones and Jonathan Byran were appointed as Judges to hold the first general court in the Province.

On March 29, 1757, "Noble Jones, of His Majesty's Council, was appointed one of the New Commission of Peace." This appointment was made before the Lords of Trade had heard from Gov. Reynolds, who on Wednesday, 15th of December, 1756, "acquainted the Board that he had thought proper to suspend Noble Jones, Esq., from all his offices, for reasons which he would lay before the King." Gov. Reynolds "removed Mr. Noble Jones from the Board and Bench to gratify Mr. Little, and it is positively affirmed to promote the establishment of Bosomworth's titles to the Indian lands with a view to share the spoils." Gov. Reynolds was summoned to England to answer for his conduct in Georgia. He embarked in a merchant vessel in February, 1757, resigning the government into the hands of Lieutenant-Governor Henry Ellis, who became Governor-in-Chief on the 17th of May, 1758. Noble Jones was reinstated, by an order of the English Council to Governor Ellis, May 31, 1759, with his former precedence as Councillor, and also as Senior Justice of the General Court.

Under Gov. Ellis, he was one of His Majesty's Council, Senior Justice of the General Court, Colonel of the Regiment and Treasurer of the Province, having been appointed to this last office by Gov. Ellis on the 16th day of February, 1760. . . . "He has no salary but commission of five per cent, which on the last year's tax amounted to about sixty-five pounds, and may this year amount to eighty pounds." Gov. Ellis resigned his office on account of ill health, and handed over the government to Lieutenant-Governor James Wright, who was appointed Governor-in-Chief on the 20th of March, 1761. In the following letter to the Lords of the Board of Trade, Governor Wright commends Noble Jones' services as Chief Justice of the Colony, after Mr. Simpson's death and before Mr. Anthony Stokes' arrival.

Sav., Ga., 28 Sept., 1769.

"My Lords:—I take the liberty to acquaint your Lordships "that Noble Jones, Esq., Senior Judge of the Courts here, has "in every respect done and performed the office and duty of "Chief Justice from 20th of October, 1768, when Mr. Simpson "died, to the arrival of Mr. Stokes on the first of this instant, "Sept.: and altho' Mr. Jones was not bred to the law, yet I "believe that Justice was only administered during that time and

"with integrity, and I have not heard any complaint or fault
"found with his conduct. I therefore submit to your Lordships
"whether it may not be reasonable that Mr. Jones shall receive
"the salary from the death of Mr. Simpson to the appointment
"of Mr. Stokes, and half of it from the appointment of Mr.
"Stokes until his arrival here. I have given Mr. Jones two
"certificates of his having done his duty and have the honor to
"be My Lords, Your Lordships most obliged and obedient servant.　　　　　　　　　　　　　　　　JAMES WRIGHT."

"The Right Hon. Lords of Trade."

On the 10th of July, 1771, Governor Wright availed himself
of a leave of absence, and three days afterwards Mr. James
Habersham took the usual oaths of office, and entered upon the
discharge of the gubernatorial duties.

In a long letter to the Earl of Hillsborough Governor Habersham relates that the Assembly had, against royal orders, elected
Noble Wymberley Jones three times Speaker in succession, and
that they refused to leave this fact out of their minutes, on the
subsequent election of Archibald Bulloch, and that he had dissolved the Assembly. Noble Wymberley Jones was the son of
Noble Jones, and as ardent a patriot as Noble Jones was a
thorough royalist. His opposition to the Crown and his uphold-
ing of the cause of liberty seems to have embittered Mr. Habersham, who, not able to punish the son, brought his spleen to bear
upon the father. He writes to the Earl of Hillsborough April
30, 1772:

"My Lord, it is very painful to me to say or even insinuate
a disrespectful word of anyone, and every person who knows
me will acknowledge that it is contrary to my disposition to dip
my pen in gall, but I cannot help considering Mr. Jones' conduct
for some time past in opposing public business as very ungrateful and unworthy of a good man, as his family have reaped

more advantages from government that any I know in this Province. He was several years First Lieutenant and Surgeon in a company of Rangers paid by the Crown, and in these capacities met with great indulgence. His father is the King's Treasurer, and if I am not mistaken reaps very considerable emoluments from it by his accounts having never been clearly stated and examined by any Assembly that I know of: and such an inquiry may not be agreeable. Gov. Wright, in his speech to the Assembly in October, 1770, recommended our Finances and Publick Accounts be examined into; but that Assembly was dissolved in February following and no step taken therein, and many people suspect that this very necessary examination operates with some to retard and impede business. I certainly meant to recommend this inquiry to the late Assembly in the strongest terms, and as we have now no Assembly, I shall require the Treasurer to lay before me, in Council, a clear account of the produce of our funds, also the certificates that have been issued for different services, and of every account, that may be necessary to possess me with a state of the Treasury, and after that is done I shall pursue such measures, as may seem necessary for the service of His Majesty and the Province, and may be advised to by Council, of which I shall inform your Lordship."

That the Treasurer's accounts were examined and approved of at times by the deputy auditor and general and the Governor is shown by a treasury account, signed Noble Jones, Treasurer, February 26, 1767.

Audited by Gray Elliott, Dt. Aud. Gen., 6th February, and approved by James Wright, 10th of February.

On further deliberation, Mr. Habersham either found out that the accounts had been audited, or that an investigation was unnecessary, as there is no record of one having taken place— and as Noble Jones continued Treasurer until the day of his

death, which occurred three years afterwards, it would seem
reasonable to suppose that Mr. Habersham's fears were ground-
less. During Governor Wright's administration he took part
in all important matters appertaining to Georgia, and his fidelity
and absolute devotion to the Crown were unswerving.

In a card appearing in the *"Georgia Gazette"* September 7,
1774, his name appears with James Habersham, Josiah Tatnall,
and ninety-three others, criticising the meeting of the 10th of
August at Tondee's Tavern in Savannah, and protesting that
the resolutions there adopted should not be accepted as reflecting
the sentiments of the people of Georgia."

He performed his judicial duties up to the last. "Upon the
assembling of the General Court 10th of October, 1775, ten of
the jurors summoned refused to be sworn. Others "behaved in-
solently" and the conduct of business was practically obstructed.
Mr. Noble Jones, one of the associate justices, was then "lying
extremely ill." He died on the 2d of November following at
Wormsloe, and was buried near the fort, on the place he loved
so well. His remains were removed from Wormsloe to the
colonial burying-ground in Savannah, and later to Bonaventure
Cemetery, near Savannah. His death was hastened by the dissensions among the colonists; he could not sympathize with
the idea of separation from, or independence of, the mother
country, and he saw nothing but storms and troubles ahead for
his beloved Georgia. During a long life, during which he held
nearly every office in the Province, if he was found fault with
he never failed, upon investigation of the charges against him,
to rise higher in the public esteem. Notwithstanding Noble
Wymberley Jones' zealous patriotism, he was a devoted son, and,
though then first elected a member of the Continental Congress,
remained with his father at Wormsloe until his father's death.

On his tombstone in Bonaventure Cemetery is inscribed the
following:

NOBLE JONES, OF WORMSLOE, ESQ.

Senior Judge of the General Court and Acting Chief Justice of the Province of Georgia.

For twenty-one years Member and Sometimes President of His Majesty's Council.

Colonel of the first Georgia Regiment.

Died November 2, 1775.   Aged, 73—

W. J. DeRenne.

Noble Wymberley Jones.

THIS son of Colonel Noble Jones, a trusted friend and early companion of Oglethorpe, who, as military officer, surveyor, registrar, member of the Royal Council, and treasurer of the Province of Georgia, during a long life proved himself a valuable and an influential citizen, and never once wavered in his allegiance to the Crown, was born near London, England, in 1723.

Such was the respect and so great was the affection entertained for him by his distinguished and devoted son that, when first elected a member from Georgia of the Continental Congress, Noble W. Jones, in deference to the entreaties of his aged father, then sorely perplexed and trembling upon the verge of the grave, put aside for the time being this important trust, that he might, with filial love, minister to the infirmities and soothe the last hours of his dying parent.

Coming to Georgia at a tender age, he secured a cadet's appointment in Oglethorpe's regiment. Having in time studied medicine and received his degree, he was promoted to a first lieutenancy, and, with the rank and pay of surgeon, was assigned to a company of Rangers in the pay of the Crown. After a few years passed in military service, he resigned from the army, and entered upon the practice of his profession in Savannah. He rose rapidly in the public esteem, as a citizen and as a physician winning golden opinions from the community. No idle spectator of passing events, or indifferent to political preferment, he was in 1768 elected Speaker of the Lower House of Assembly of the Province of Georgia. By that body he was placed upon a committee to correspond with Dr. Benjamin

N. W. JONES.

Franklin—who had been appointed an agent "to represent, solicit, and transact the affairs of the Colony of Georgia in Great Britain"—and give such instructions as might appear necessary for the public welfare. Reelected to this position in 1770, so pronounced and influential had become his views and conduct in opposition to the objectionable and oppressive acts of Parliament and in support of American ideas, that Governor Wright, exercising the power vested in him, refused to sanction this choice, and ordered the House to select another Speaker.

Incensed at this affront offered to one who had been aptly termed a morning star of liberty in Georgia, and resenting what they deemed an unwarrantable interference with the power resting solely with them to nominate and judge of the qualifications of their own presiding officer, the members of the House passed resolutions complimentary to Dr. Jones, and declared "that the sense and approbation this House entertain of his conduct can never be lessened by any slight cast upon him in opposition to the unanimous voice of the Commons House of Assembly in particular and the Province in general." Criticising the action of the Executive, they resolved "that this rejection by the Governor of a Speaker unanimously elected, was a high breach of the privileges of the House, and tended to subvert the most valuable rights and liberties of the people and their representatives." This bold assertion the Council was pleased to stigmatize as "a most indecent and insolent denial of his Majesty's authority," and the Governor, wielding the only punitive weapon at command, dissolved the Assembly on the 22d of February, 1770.

Adhering to the preference shown on a former occasion, and resolved to rebuke the late interference on the part of the Executive, at the first session of the eighth General Assembly of the Province, convened at Savannah on the 21st of April, 1772, the Commons House perfected its organization by electing Dr.

14

Jones as its Speaker. Officially informed of this action, the Hon. James Habersham, who during the absence of Sir James Wright was occupying the gubernatorial chair, responded: "I have his Majesty's commands to put a negative upon the Speaker now elected by the Commons House, which I accordingly do; and desire that you will inform the House that I direct them to proceed to a new choice of Speaker."

Despite this inhibition, and in direct opposition to the injunction of the Executive, thrice did the House adhere to its selection; and it was only by dissolving the Assembly that the Governor was able to carry his point.

In a long letter to the Earl of Hillsborough, dated the 30th of April, 1772, Governor Habersham dwells upon the injurious effects of this dissolution of the Assembly, and yet demonstrates its necessity in obedience to existing instructions from the Crown. He also comments freely upon the conduct of Dr. Jones and his friends in "opposing the public business" under the "specious pretense of Liberty and Privilege." "My Lord," he continues, "it is very painful to me to say or even to insinuate a disrespectful word of anyone; and every person who knows me will acknowledge that it is contrary to my disposition to dip my pen in gall, but I cannot help considering Mr. Jones' conduct for some time past in opposing Public Business as very ungrateful and unworthy a good man, as his family have reaped more advantages from Government than any I know in this Province. He was several years First Lieutenant and Surgeon of a company of Rangers paid by the Crown, and in these capacities met with great indulgence. His father is the King's Treasurer, and, if I am not mistaken, reaps very considerable emoluments from it."

The truth is, while Governor Habersham was loyally seeking to carry out the instructions of the King and to support the authority of Parliament, Dr. Jones was in active sympathy with those who esteemed taxation without representation as wholly unauthorized, and who were very jealous in the maintenance of what they regarded as the reserved rights of the colonists and the privileges of provincial legislatures. Both were true men, but they viewed the situation from different standpoints. An honored servant of the Crown, Mr. Habersham was confronted with peculiar duties and stringent oaths. Dr. Jones, on the contrary, as a representative elected by the people, was free to give expression to his own and the sentiments of his constituents at an epoch when American liberty was being freely discussed and proclaimed. Of each it may be fairly said he was pure in purpose, wise in counsel, and fearless in action; enjoying in a conspicuous degree the esteem and the affection of the community. But their political paths henceforward diverged. The one clave to the Crown and shared its fortunes, while the other cast his lot with the Revolutionists, and became a favorite leader of the patriot band.

With Archibald Bulloch, John Houstoun, and John Walton, he issued the public call on the 20th of July, 1774, which convened the citizens of Georgia at the Watch House in Savannah. The resolutions then adopted and the measures there inaugurated, gathering potency and allegiance as they were discussed and comprehended, proved effective in unifying public sentiment in support of the plans suggested by the Liberty party, and paved the way for sundering the ties which bound the Province to the British Empire. Of the committees then raised to conduct the public affairs of the Colony, and to minister to the relief of the "suffering poor" of Boston, he was an active member.

Noble Wymberley Jones, Archibald Bulloch, and John Houstoun, elected delegates to the Continental Congress by a convention of patriots assembled in Savannah on the 8th of December, 1774, and again by the Provincial Congress of January, 1775, concluding very properly that, inasmuch as they had been nominated by a political convocation which in reality embraced only four of the twelve parishes then constituting the Province of Georgia, they could not justly be regarded as representatives of the entire Colony, and yet persuaded that the will of those who commissioned them should be formally made known and the mind of Georgia be fairly interpreted—on the 6th of April, 1775, addressed the following communication to the President of the Continental Congress:

"Sir:—The unworthy part which the Province of Georgia has acted in the great and general contest leaves room to expect little less than the censure or even indignation of every virtuous man in America. Although, on the one hand, we feel the justice of such a consequence with respect to the Province in general, yet, on the other, we claim an exemption from it in favour of some individuals who wished a better conduct. Permit us, therefore, in behalf of ourselves and many others, our fellow-citizens, warmly attached to the cause, to lay before the respectable body over which you preside a few facts which, we trust, will not only acquit us of supineness, but also render our conduct to be approved by all candid and dispassionate men.

"At the time the late Congress did this Province the honour to transmit to it an extract from their proceedings, enclosed in a friendly letter from the Honourable Mr. Middleton, the sense and disposition of the people in general seemed to fluctuate between liberty and convenience. In order to bring on a determination respecting the measures recommended, a few well-affected persons in Savannah, by public advertisement in the *Gazette,* requested a meeting of all the parishes and districts, by delegates or representatives, in Provincial Congress. On the day ap-

pointed for this meeting, with concern they found that only five
out of twelve parishes to which they had particularly wrote had
nominated and sent down delegates; and even some of these five
had laid their representatives under injunctions as to the form
of an association. Under these circumstances those who met saw
themselves a good deal embarrassed. However, one expedient
seemed still to present itself. The House of Assembly was then
sitting, and it was hoped there would be no doubt of a majority
in favour of American freedom. The plan, therefore, was to go
through with what business they could in Provincial Congress,
and then, with a short address, present the same to the House
of Assembly, who, it was hoped, would, by votes in a few minutes
and before prerogative should interfere, make it the act of the
whole Province. Accordingly, the Congress framed and agreed
to such an association, and did such other business as appeared
practicable with the people, and had the whole just ready to be
presented, when the Governor, either treacherously informed or
shrewdly suspecting the step, put an end to the session. What
then could the Congress do? On the one hand, truth forbid them
to call their proceedings the voice of the Province, there being
but five out of twelve parishes concerned; and on the other, they
wanted strength sufficient to enforce them on the principle of
necessity, to which all ought for a time to submit. They found
the inhabitants of Savannah not likely soon to give matters a
favourable turn. The importers were mostly against any interruption, and the consumers very much divided. There were
some of the latter virtuously for the measures; others strenu-
ously against them; but more who called themselves neutrals
than either. Thus situated, there appeared nothing before us
but the alternative of either immediately commencing a civil
war among ourselves, or else of patiently waiting for the measures to be recommended by the General Congress.

"Among a powerful people, provided with men, money, and conveniences, and by whose conduct others were to be regulated, the former would certainly be the resolution that would suggest itself to every man removed from the condition of a coward; but in a small community like that of Savannah (whose members are mostly in their first advance towards wealth and independence, destitute of even the necessaries of life within themselves, and from whose junction or silence so little would be added or lost to the general cause), the latter presented itself as the most eligible plan, and was adopted by the people. Party disputes and animosities have occasionally prevailed, and show that the spirit of freedom is not extinguished, but only restrained for a time till an opportunity shall offer for calling it forth.

"The Congress convened at Savannah did us the honour of choosing us delegates to meet your respectable body at Philadelphia on the tenth of next month. We were sensible of the honour and weight of the appointment, and would gladly have rendered our country any service our poor abilities would have admitted of; but, alas! with what face could we have appeared for a Province whose inhabitants had refused to sacrifice the most trifling advantages to the public cause, and in whose behalf we did not think we could safely pledge ourselves for the execution of anyone measure whatsoever?

"We do not mean to insinuate that those who appointed us would prove apostates or desert their opinions, but that the tide of opposition was great; that all the strength and virtue of these our friends might be sufficient for the purpose. We very early saw the difficulties that would here occur, and therefore repeatedly and constantly requested the people to proceed to the choice of other delegates in our stead; but this they refused to do. We beg, sir, you will view our reasons for not attending in a liberal point of light. Be pleased to make the most favourable representation of them to the Honorable the Members of the Congress. We believe we may take upon ourselves to say, notwithstanding all that has passed, there are still men in Georgia who, when an occasion shall require, will be ready to evince a steady, religious, and manly attachment to the liberties of America. For the consolation of these, they find themselves in the neighborhood of a Province whose virtue and magnanimity must and will do lasting honour to the cause, and in whose fate they seem disposed freely to involve their own.

"We have the honour to be, sir, your most obedient and very humble servants,

"NOBLE WYMBERLEY JONES.
"ARCHIBALD BULLOCH.
"JOHN HOUSTOUN."

The news of the affairs at Lexington and Concord reached Savannah on the 10th of May, and caused the wildest excitement. The thunders of the 19th of April aroused the Georgia parishes from their lethargy, and multiplied patriots within their borders.

The magazine at the eastern extremity of Savannah—built of brick and sunk some twelve feet under ground—contained a considerable amount of ammunition. So substantial was this structure, that Governor Wright deemed it unnecessary to post a guard for its protection. The excited Revolutionists all over the land cried aloud for powder. Impressed with the importance of securing the contents of this magazine, quietly assembling at the residence of Dr. Jones, and there hastily arranging a plan of operations, Dr. Noble W. Jones, Joseph Habersham, Edward Telfair, William Gibbons, Joseph Clay, John Milledge, and some other gentlemen—most of them members of the Council of Safety, and all zealous in the cause of American liberty—at a late hour on the night of the 11th of May, 1775, broke open the magazine and removed therefrom some six hundred pounds of powder—a portion of which was sent to Beaufort, South Carolina, for safe-keeping, and the rest was concealed in the garrets and cellars of the houses of the captors. Although Governor Wright issued a proclamation offering a reward of £150 sterling for the apprehension of the offenders, it failed to elicit any information, although the actors in the affair are said to have been well known in the community. The popular heart was too deeply stirred, and the "Sons of Liberty" were too potent to tolerate any hindrance or annoyance at the hands of Royalist informers. The tradition lives, and is generally credited, that some of the powder thus obtained was forwarded to Cambridge, and was actually expended by the patriots in the memorable battle of Bunker Hill.

On the 22d of June, 1775, in response to a call signed by Dr. Jones, Archibald Bulloch, John Houstoun, and George Walton, many of the inhabitants of the town and district of Savannah assembled at the Liberty Pole in Savannah, and elected a Council of Safety, with instructions to maintain an active correspondence with the Continental Congress, and with Councils of Safety, both in Georgia and in other Provinces, with a view to bringing about a union of Georgia with her sister colonies in the cause of freedom.

Of the Provincial Congress which assembled in Savannah on the 4th of July, 1775, Dr. Jones was a member, accredited from the "Town and District of Savannah."

In this Congress every parish was represented. Dr. Jones was of the committee then selected to frame a suitable address to the inhabitants of Georgia, advising them of the true nature of the disputes existing between Great Britain and her American Colonies, and informing them of the deliberations and conclusions of the present Congress. He was also chosen, with John Houstoun, Archibald Bulloch, Reverend Dr. Zubly, and Dr. Lyman Hall, to represent Georgia in the Continental Congress.

Georgia was now in acknowledged sympathy with her sisters, and took her place, by regular representation, in the National Assembly. Of the Council of Safety which ordered the arrest of Governor Wright, Dr. Jones was a member.

Late in 1776 the General Assembly of South Carolina adopted a resolution to the effect that a union between that State and Georgia would promote the general strength, wealth, and dignity, and insure mutual liberty, independence, and safety. Commissioners—of whom the Honorable William Henry Drayton appears to have been the chairman, as he certainly was the spokesman—were sent to Savannah to treat of the matter, and to secure Georgia's acquiescence in a project which, if carried into effect, would practically have put an end to her political existence. The members of the Council of Safety listened with patience and courtesy to the arguments and persuasions of the Carolina Commissioners, but rejected the proffered union. President Gwinnett, Dr. Jones, and all the leading Republican spirits were radically opposed to the scheme on grounds both material and constitutional; and so the effort of South Carolina to swallow up Georgia signally miscarried.

Upon the capture of Savannah in December, 1778, Dr. Jones removed to Charles-Town, South Carolina. There, upon the fall of that city in 1780, he was taken prisoner by the British and sent in captivity to St. Augustine, Florida. Exchanged in July, 1781, he went to Philadelphia, and there entered upon the practice of his profession. While a resident of that city, he was, by the General Assembly of Georgia, relected to the Continental Congress.

Shortly after its evacuation by the King's forces in the summer of 1782, Dr. Jones returned to Savannah, repaired the desolations which war had wrought in his comfortable home, and resumed his professional labors. He was a member of the committee which received and saluted President Washington with an address of welcome upon the occasion of his visit to Savannah in 1791. Over the Constitutional Convention which, at Louisville, Jefferson County, in May, 1795, amended the Constitution of Georgia, Dr. Noble Wymberley Jones presided. In 1804 he was President of the Georgia Medical Society. Preserving his intellectual and physical powers in a wonderful degree, he died in Savannah on the 9th of January, 1805, honored by the community as an accomplished gentleman, an influential citizen, a skillful physician, and a sterling patriot.

To the refined taste and liberality of his grandson, the late George Wymberley Jones De Renne, M.D., of Savannah, a gentleman of broad education (enriched by study, travel, and observation), of large wealth, exquisite culture, and thoroughly imbued with a love for Georgia and all her traditions, are we indebted, among other literary legacies, for the series of *Wormsloe Quartos,* esteemed alike for their intrinsic value, admirable manufacture, and extreme rarity.

Since his death his widow—manifesting like generous interest in everything appertaining to the early history of Georgia, and as a tribute to the memory of her husband—has borne the charge of two other beautiful and expensive Wormsloe Quartos, edited by the writer, one entitled *Acts passed by the General Assembly of the Colony of Georgia,* 1755 to 1774. *Now first printed. Wormsloe. MDCCLXXXI;* and the other, *A Journal of the Transactions of the Trustees for establishing the Colony of Georgia in America, by the Right Honorable John, Earl of Egmont, Viscount Perceval, of Canturk, Baron Perceval, of Burton, one of his Majesty's Most Privy Council in the Kingdom of Ireland, and first President of the Board of Trustees of the Colony of Georgia. Now first printed. Wormsloe. MDCCLXXXVI.* In each case the edition was limited to forty-nine copies.   C. C. JONES, JR.

Edward Langworthy.

THIS member of the Continental Congress was born in Savannah, Georgia, of obscure parentage. Left an orphan at a tender age, he was indebted for his maintenance and education to that charitable institution founded and long supported by the Reverend George Whitefield, and known as the Bethesda Orphan House. At a subsequent period he became a teacher in that school. His earliest public appearance, so far as we can ascertain, was as one of the signers of a card which was published in the *Georgia Gazette,* on the 7th of September, 1774, criticising certain patriotic resolutions adopted at a convocation of citizens held on the 10th of the preceding month, and protesting against their being accepted as reflecting the sentiments of a majority of the inhabitants of Georgia. In that card he appears as in full sympathy with the Royalists in the Province. That his political views underwent a sudden and violent change may be fairly inferred from the fact that in the following year he became the efficient Secretary of the Republican Council of Safety. In 1777 he was elected a delegate from Georgia to the Continental Congress. A similar honor was conferred upon him during the following year, when, with his confreres George Walton and Edward Telfair, he signed the Articles of Confederation. He at one time held the position of Justice of the Peace for the county of Chatham.

Not very long after the conclusion of peace between Great Britain and the United Colonies, he removed from Savannah and located in Maryland. He there formed the design of writing a history of Georgia. Of fair attainments, and possessing a personal acquaintance with many of the prominent persons and leading events appertaining to Georgia during the latter half of the eighteenth century, he was at least measurably qualified for the task. He seems to have addressed himself with energy to the collection of materials requisite for the undertaking. It would appear, from a prospectus printed in the *Georgia Gazette,* that the history was actually written, and that the manuscript was ready to be rendered into type. One of his letters lies before us, dated at Elkton, Maryland, March 1, 1791, and addressed to Seaborn Jones, Esq., Augusta, Georgia, in which Mr. Langworthy says: "Inclosed you will receive a Subscription Paper for 'A Political History of the State of Georgia,' &c., for which I must request you to take in subscriptions, and I flatter myself you will succeed therein, as the design is a well-meant attempt to rescue the patriotic exertions of our Countrymen from Oblivion and the Misrepresentation of some Writers of American History.

"What monies you will receive on this occasion you will please to pay to Mr. James Johnston, Printer at Savannah, whose receipt will be your discharge."

Suitable encouragement, however, not having been obtained, the contemplated publication was never made. Mr. Langworthy died at Elkton, Maryland, near the close of the last century, and all efforts to recover both his manuscript and the supporting documents which he had amassed have thus far proved abortive. C. C. Jones, Jr.

Daniel Marshall.

REV. DANIEL MARSHALL, founder of the first Baptist church in the State of Georgia, was born at Windsor, Vermont, of Presbyterian parentage in 1706. Being converted in early youth, and being a man of great natural ardor and holy zeal, he felt impelled to assist in converting the heathen, and went with his family to preach for three years among the Mohawk Indians, near the head of the Susquehannah river. In consequence of the Indian war, he was compelled to remove to Virginia, where, at the age of forty-eight years, he became a convert to the Baptist doctrine. Soon after being baptized into the Baptist church, he began to preach, coming through North Carolina into Georgia, where, in 1771, he settled on Kiokee creek, in what is now Columbia county, Georgia.

Although neither profoundly learned, nor very eloquent as a preacher, he was a man of pure life, unbounded faith, and fervent spirit. He possessed that earnestness and flaming ardor of zeal, connected with remarkable native strength of mind and knowledge of the scriptures. This fitted him admirably for the duties of a pioneer preacher. On his second or third visit to Georgia, he held a meeting in a grove, and while on bended knees in the opening prayer on Sunday morning, a hand was laid on his shoulder, and he heard a voice: "You are my prisoner." At this time, he was sixty-five years of age, and found himself arrested by an officer of the State, constable Cartiledge, "For preaching in the parish of St. Paul." Several years before this, the Council of Georgia, legalized the Church of England as the Church of Georgia; no other church being allowed to hold a meeting, unless by special permit. It was in violation of this law, that Mr. Marshall was arrested; although, in 1758, a special act was passed, allowing all persons "liberty of conscience" in the State of Georgia.

After a short interruption, caused by this arrest, he proceeded with the service, preaching with unusual ardor. At its conclusion, he baptized two applicants, relatives of Hugh Middleton, a prominent gentleman of South Carolina, who was present and acted as Mr. Marshall's bondsman.

Next day in Augusta, he stood his trial, and was ordered to "come into Georgia and preach no more." The answer of Mr. Marshall to this order was similar to that of St. Paul, under similar circumstances, "Whether it be right to obey God or man, judge ye," and, consistently with this just and spirited answer, Mr. Marshall continued to preach in Georgia unmolested as long as he lived. In this grove, at this point, the Kiokee Church was soon established, and is in existence till this day.

Fifteen years after this event, Kiokee Church was chartered by an act of the Legislature of Georgia.

When he moved into the State he was the only ordained Baptist minister within its bounds. There were very few Baptists in the State and no organized church. He lived to preside at the organization of the Georgia Association, in October, 1784, when there were half a dozen churches in the State, many Baptists, and a number of Baptist preachers. His grave is a few rods south of the Appling Court-house, on the side of the road to Augusta. "Memory watches the spot, but no 'false marble' utters untruths concerning this distinguished herald of salvation.

In 1837 Dr. Sherwood wrote "Daniel Marshall sleeps neither forgotten or unsung, for every child in the neighborhood of Appling can lead you to his grave." This was sixty-five years after his burial.

As a friend to the American cause, Mr. Marshall was once made a prisoner and put under a strong guard. But, obtaining leave of the officers, he commenced and supported so heavy a charge of exhortation and prayer that, like Daniel of old, while his enemies stood amazed and confounded, he was safely and honorably "delivered from this den of lions." From these incidents we not only learn the character of Mr. Marshall, but we discover also the trials and dangers amid which he and others of similar disposition maintained the Baptist cause in the early history of Georgia.

Mr. Daniel Marshall was twice married, the second time to Miss Martha Stearns, of Virginia, to whose unwearied and zealous co-operation the extraordinary success of his ministry is, in no small degree, to be ascribed. A lady of good sense, singular piety and surprising elocution, she, in countless instances, melted a whole concourse into tears by her prayers and exhortations.

Bold and independent in his methods, superior to local attachments, and undismayed by danger, Mr. Marshall was capable of the most difficult and arduous enterprises. He went from place to place, instructing, exhorting and praying for individuals, families, and congregations, whether at a muster, a race, a public market, the open field, an army, or a house of worship—wherever he was able to command attention; and the fruits of his astonishing exertions abundantly showed that he was constrained by the love of Christ.

Mr. Marshall, after all his sacrifices for the cause of Christ, was blessed by a bountiful Providence with a sufficiency of the meat that perisheth, and left behind him an estate of considerable value. This was not the result of any special efforts of his to acquire property, and still less the benefits of his arduous labors in the ministry.

R. J. MASSEY.

John Martin.

COLONEL JOHN MARTIN was the last of Georgia's Revolutionary governors. He was born about 1730, though the place and the exact date of his birth are unknown. When he was thirty-one, Mr. Martin was made a naval officer at the port of Sunbury in St. John's parish, now Liberty county. From the very beginning of Georgia's difficulties with Great Britain, Mr. Martin aligned himself with the patriots in their struggle for freedom. He was a delegate from the town and district of Savannah to the Provincial Congress which met at Savannah in July, 1775. Later he was made a member of the Council of Safety.

Mr. Martin's military career began early in January, 1776. At that time he was made first lieutenant of the seventh company of the Georgia Continental battalion, with which he served for the greater part of the Revolution. About the middle of 1776, he was promoted to the rank of captain, and in 1781, was made lieutenant-colonel of his command. His military record is without a stain and his devotion to the cause of liberty unquestioned.

In 1781, Colonel Martin, exchanging military for civil honors, represented the county of Chatham in the Georgia House of Assembly. Having been a member of the Provincial Congress and the Council of Safety, an officer of the Continental army and a member of the House of Assembly, Colonel Martin was, in January, 1782, promoted to the chief magistracy of Georgia, soon to be free from British dominion . His administration witnessed the successful termination of the Revolution and the public recognition of Georgia as a sovereign and independent state. In July, 1782, Savannah was evacuated by the British, and, before the close of Governor Martin's administration, every vestige of hostile supremacy had entirely disappeared from the commonwealth of Georgia. Lamentable, indeed, was the material condition of Georgia at this time, on account of the devastations of the Revolution. The British, assisted by the Tories and Indians, had made such inroads upon the property of the patriots, and such was the scarcity of money that it is said Governor Martin, finding it impossible to get his salary, was forced to apply to the House of Assembly for relief in order to preserve his immediate family from starvation.

At the expiration of his term as chief executive, Governor Martin was selected, in January, 1783, as one of the Georgia commissioners specially charged with the negotiation of a treaty with the Creek Indians. This task completed, he was made State Treasurer and in this capacity concluded his official public service.

Having given the best years of his life to the service of his state, Governor Martin passed away toward the close of the century, the exact date and place of his death being unknown. It is believed, however, that he was buried in Savannah.

Compiled by the Publisher.

George Matthews.

GENERAL GEORGE MATTHEWS, who figured prominently in the history of Georgia during the latter part of the eighteenth century, was a remarkable man. Qualities were united in him, which are seldom found in other men. He was short and thick with stout legs; he stood quite straight with his head thrown back, and wore a three cornered cocked hat. His features were full and bluff, his complexion florid, and his hair a light red.

To hear him speak of himself, his children, and his own personal affairs, one might think he was a puff of wind. He referred to the services which he rendered his country when quite a young man in fighting the Indians and fighting the British afterwards as superior to those of George Washington. He was never known to acknowledge but two superiors, General George Washington and the Lord Almighty. His looks plainly showed that he knew no such thing as fear. Trade with him, and he was found to be one of the shrewdest of men. He was never known to make a mistake in an investment.

His dress was quite peculiar. He wore knee breeches, fair topped boots, a shirt ruffled at bosom and wrists and his sword dangling at his side. Although very illiterate, he was a constant reader. At home and before his family, he always read aloud and pronounced very plainly the l in such words as *would could* and *should* and was certain to accentuate the *ed* in such words as drowned, returned, or learned.

He spelled coffee, *kaughphy,* he commenced congress with a *k,* spelled revenue, *ravenue,* revenge *ravange.* He was an original phonetic speller, a great disbeliever in superfluous letters. For instance, he spelled sack *sac,* and knock, *nok,* stock, *stok,* laugh, *laf.*

He possessed a wonderful memory and could repeat almost verbatim any sermon, conversation, or speech that he had ever heard, even for years thereafter. When a young man, he was for several years sheriff of Augusta county, Virginia. As sheriff it was his duty to collect the taxes. He knew every man in the county. After referring to his books, he could proceed upon his round of tax collecting and collect each man's tax from memory; and, upon his return at the end of two weeks, he would be found never to have made a mistake. After his removal to Georgia, he had been in the state only a few years before he knew the names of the owners of almost every lot of land in the state. When a, member of Congress from Georgia, a document was read before the House and was lost. Several weeks thereafter, he was known to repeat the contents of the document so correctly that the House accepted it as genuine and thereupon acted upon it.

This man was a son of an Irishman who had just immigrated to West Virginia a few years before George was born in 1737. From constant contact in his early days with wild beasts and the Indians in this frontier region, he soon became familiar with danger and endured the hardships of a rugged life. When quite a boy, he began his strenuous career by early entering into the forays then so common in resisting the marauding Indians who lived just west of the Ohio river. While yet in his teens, a neighboring family was massacred. George and two or three other boys heard the reports of the guns of the Indians and mistaking them for those of a shooting match, hurried at once to join the sport. Arriving at the scene, they found the dead bodies of the members of the family and turned to run. The Indians seeing them fired upon the boys with no other casualty than the clipping of George's que. This so aroused the spirit of the young Irishman that he set to work and collected a band of neighboring boys about his age and pursued the Indians killing nine of their number before they could get back over the river. This wonderful achievement gave him such renown that even when quite young he was put in command of a company of men, most of whom were much older than himself. On several occasions, these men did good fighting. At Point Pleasant, on the Kanawha river, they fought the Indians all day, from early morn till nearly dark, gaining little or no advantage over them. At night, the young commander conceived the plan of concealing his company in the bend of the river and attacking the Indians in the rear. This maneuver was carried out with such consummate skill that the Indians, thinking that the whites had been heavily reinforced, fled precipitately across the river. Captain Matthews and his command inflicted such heavy punishment upon them that they permanently remained upon the west side of the river. This put a stop to the marauding incursions of the Indians. In memory of the heroism displayed by this young Indian fighter, the event has long been inscribed in brilliant characters on the roll of fame. His friends and neighbors and the whole country at large gave him the very highest tokens of esteem. He was at once advanced to the rank of colonel and put in command of the ninth regiment of Virginia troops.

For nearly two years, Colonel Matthews and his regiment were stationed on the eastern shore of Virginia. In 1777, he was ordered with his command to join the army under General Washington. Our great chief knew well the value of Colonel Matthews' services, his own experience having been acquired on the frontiers of Virginia. As soon, therefore, as the contest of the Revolution assumed the shape of a war in earnest, Washington ordered Colonel Matthews to join him. He did so and took part in the battle of Brandywine. At the battle of Germantown, Colonel Matthews and his regiment attacked successfully the British troops opposed to him, pushed on to the middle of the town, and captured a regiment of the enemy. After this, in a skirmish, he was knocked down by one of the enemy, and received a severe wound with a bayonet. A British soldier, noticing some vestiges of a uniform upon Matthews, lifted his bayonet to stab him, but his commander caught the weapon and angrily demanded: "Would you murder a wounded officer? Forward, sir." Mathews, turning upon his back, asked, "To whom do I owe my life?" "If you call it an obligation, Sir, to me," said the Britisher. Matthews seeing his British uniform, curiously replied, "Well, Sir, I want you to know I scorn a life saved by a d——d Briton."

He was confined on board the British prison-ship in the harbor of New York, where he endured the most severe sufferings. Mr. Jefferson, then Governor of Virginia, in a letter to Colonel Matthews, says, "We know that the ardent spirit and hatred of tyranny which brought you into your present situation, will enable you to bear up against it, with the firmness which has distinguished you as a soldier, and look forward with pleasure to the day when events shall take place against which the wounded spirit of your enemies will find no comfort, even from reflections on the most refined of the cruelties with which they have glutted themselves." Colonel Matthews was not exchanged until toward the termination of the war, when he joined the army under General Greene, as commander of the third Virginia regiment.

While in the South, he purchased a tract of land in Georgia called the Goose Pond, on Broad river, and removed to it with his family in 1785. His high reputation in the late war made him at once the principal man in Georgia.

For sound judgment and business tact, Colonel Matthews impressed every one with whom he came in contact as a safe adviser. Through his influence, some of the best families that have ever lived in Georgia came to the state. Among those whom he induced to visit Georgia in search of suitable lands for settlement, were Francis Merriwether, Benjamin Taliaferro, P. Gilmer, John Gilmer, and many others. They visited Georgia in 1784, and were pleased with the lands in the vicinity of Goose Pond.

Francis Merriwether, John Gilmer, Benjamin Taliaferro, and at least a dozen others, with their families, at once removed to Georgia. For the next ten or fifteen years the lands on Broad river were settled by the relatives and immediate friends of these first immigrants. They formed a society of the greatest intimacy and cordiality, mutual wants making the surest foundation for the interchange of mutual kindness. An impress was made upon those people which is strong and binding up to the present period.

In 1786, Colonel Matthews was elected governor. He was the first representative of the people of Georgia in the Congress of the United States, under the present Constitution. He was again governor of Georgia in 1794 and 1795.

Having been elected governor of the state of Georgia within two years after he first settled in it, there arose great doubts in the minds of many whether the election was constitutional. The first business after the Legislature assembled, was to determine this point. While engaged in this discussion, the clerk of the House went into the executive office; the governor accosted him, saying, "What are those fellows about that they do not let me know that they are organized and ready to receive my message?" The clerk told him the members were discussing whether or not they should recognize him as governor. "By the etarnal!" exclaimed the governor, "if they don't I will cut an avenue from this office through them."

During both his administrations, Governor Matthews had the good sense to employ a school master to reduce his messages to good spelling and proper grammar.

It was during Governor Matthews' second term of service as the chief magistrate of Georgia, that the land speculators, after many years of effort, succeeded in procuring the passage by the Legislature of an operative law for the sale of the western territory of the state. This act was what has been known for over a hundred years in common parlance as the "Yazoo Fraud." Some of the largest capitalists in the South had combined to buy some five million acres of Georgia land for the sum of five hundred thousand dollars. This sale was legalized by the Legislature of the state and approved by Governor Matthews. This selling of so much of Georgia's valuable territory for so small a sum aroused great indignation and created much bitter feeling. Many members of the Legislature were openly accused of having been bribed and suspicions rested heavily upon Governor Matthews.

That bribery was extensively practiced, there was no doubt; but no act of Governor Matthews ever justified such suspicion concerning himself. As governor of the state, and believing that the sovereign power of the state was in the Legislature, and consequently the power to dispose of the public domain, he only approved the act as the state's executive, fulfilling the duties assigned to him by the law. Tradition represents Governor Matthews as opposed individually to the act, but he did not feel himself justifiable in opposing his individual opinion to the policy or propriety of the measure. Thus early in the history of the country, neither the executives of the state or of the United States had essayed to veto measures as is done at present.

Despite his revolutionary services and his high character for moral worth, being governor of the state at the time of this transaction, Governor Matthews never recovered from the odium attaching to him. In his old age, this rendered him quite unpopular. This unpopularity was keenly felt by all the members of his family. But this odium was soon outgrown by the family; and his descendants soon aspired to become the first men and women of the land. From that period, up to the present, it is remarkable that many of them have honored the highest trusts that could be reposed upon them, ranking socially among the best people in the South. Financially, in almost every instance, they were successful. The combined wealth of his children's children, is said to largely aggregate a hundred million dollars.

In this connection, it is worthy of note, that the descendants of the Merriwethers, Gilmers, Taliaferros, and others who were induced, through Governor Matthews, to remove to the vicinity of Goose Pond have shared like financial fortune. It is said that there is scarcely a family of this society of "interchange of mutual kindness" found in the nineteenth century that cannot claim its many millions of dollars.

Governor Matthews himself was a successful financier and good manager. He spent his latter days on his Goose Pond plantation gradually adding many acres to the original purchase. But he always lived in a one-room log cabin in which he and his wife slept. The girls slept upstairs in a garret. The boys occupied another log house in the yard; but, after his death, when the plantation fell to one of the sons, he improved it, erecting a magnificent house and beautifying the grounds in front.

On this place, while governor the second time, Governor Matthews is said to have planted one thousand black walnut trees. Some of those trees are living today and are well known land marks for all the region round about as the "The Governor Matthews walnuts."

Governor Matthews was married three times. All three of his wives were said to have been among the very best ladies of the land. After having been married to the second wife three or four years, she wished to go back to Virginia to visit her relatives and friends. The governor was not very willing for her to go to Virginia, but she went, however, taking the trip alone. After having remained with her friends a sufficient length of time, she wrote him to come for her as she did not wish to take the trip again alone. To this he answered that he didn't take her to Virginia nor was he going to trouble himself to go there and bring her back. After remaining separated two or more years, the Legislature of Georgia granted each a final divorce; and each remarried.

After retiring to private life, President Madison nominated him governor of Mississippi Territory. Upon sending his name to the Senate for confirmation, the President learned that there would be some opposition to Governor Matthews, whereupon, the President withdrew his name. Governor Matthews heard of this and at once proceeded to ride from Georgia to Washington City on horseback. Arriving at Washington, he hitched his horse on the grounds in front of the White House, and, walking up to the front door, gave a thundering knock. The servant, coming to the door, told the Governor that the President was quite busy. The Governor would take no denial and told the servant to say to Mr. Madison that Governor George Matthews, of Georgia, wished to see him and must see him at once. The servant carried the message, telling the President that a strange old fellow, dressed in a mighty funny suit, was at the door and wanted to see him, calling himself "Governor Matthews." The President ordered that the Governor be sent in to him at once. As soon as presented, Governor Matthews began talking to him about the appointment and the recalling of it. He said, "Sar, if you had known me, you would not have taken the nomination back; if you did not know me, you should not have nominated me to so important an office. Now, Sar, unless you can satisfy me, your station as President of the United States shall not screen you from my ravange." The President, finding that he was not to be easily placated very kindly said to him, "General Matthews, I have been wanting for two weeks, the address of your son, John. I want to commission him as Supervisor of Revenues for the State of Georgia." This pleased the old gentleman very much, whereupon, he gave the President John's address. The President then said, "Now Governor, give me the address of your second son, George, I have had a commission filled out for two weeks, appointing him Chief Justice of Mississippi, but didn't know really where to send it." This so overwhelmed the old gentleman that he and the President parted good friends.

In 1811, a class of men who called themselves patriots, obtained the ascendency in Florida. These men threw off the Spanish yoke, and declared themselves free to do what they pleased. They petitioned the United States to make Florida a portion of its territory, and Governor Matthews was appointed agent to negotiate with the constituted authorities of Florida for the annexation of the country to the United States. He made a treaty, which was, however, strongly remonstrated against by the Spanish government, and finally disavowed by the President, Mr. Madison, as not having been made with the constituted authorities of Florida, according to the terms of Governor Matthews' instructions. The disavowal of Mr. Madison enraged Governor Matthews to such a degree, that it is said he started for Washington to subject Mr. Madison to personal chastisement. He swore that he would expose the whole affair to the world. His high state of excitement, added to the fatigue and exposure he had undergone, brought on a fever while on his way to Washington to execute his threat, of which he died in Augusta, Georgia, March, 1812.

R. J. MASSEY.

Hugh M. Ball

Hugh McCall.

I T is a matter of much regret that Georgia's first historian, who with such commendable efforts rescued from oblivion many of the early traditions of our State, should himself have left such scanty material for his own biographer. The life of this modest and worthy man has been too long neglected, and the reader must be content with only a brief sketch from the fragments gathered from various sources.

In the old Colonial Cemetery at Savannah, upon a plain marble slab level with the ground, may be read the following inscription:

"Sacred to the memory of
HUGH McCALL,
Brevet Major in the U. States army.
Born in N. Carolina
Feb. 17, 1767,
died
June 10, 1824.

He served the U. S. in various capacities 30 years; the last 20 years under severe bodily suffering, but with usefulness to himself, his country and his friends."

It is singular that so accurate a historian as Colonel C. C. Jones in his published address before the Georgia Historical Society in 1881, refers to Hugh McCall, the historian, as an "officer in the army of the Revolution." As the subject of this sketch was only eight years old at the beginning of that memorable struggle, Colonel Jones obviously confounds the name of the historian with that of his father, James McCall, or of his uncle Hugh McCall, both of whom rendered valuable service in the Revolution.

The following sketch of the McCall family was written in 1829 by Thomas McCall, Esq., a brother of the historian, who lived on a plantation on the Oconee river near Dublin in Laurens county, Ga.

"The family of which I am a descendant were Scots, and in Scotland lived in the neighborhood of the family of Calhoun, properly Calquhun. The time of their migration is not known, but the McCall, Harris, and Calhoun families passed over from Scotland in the same ship to the northeast of Ireland, where they settled and remained two entire generations, when the three families migrated to Pennsylvania, where my grandfather James McCall, was married to Jenet Harris, the elder daughter of James Harris, and settled, as a farmer, on Canacocheque creek, where my father James McCall, Agnes, Hugh and Rachel were born, the former on the 11th of August, 1741. The three families removed from Conachocheque to New river, or little Kenhoway, in the western part of Virginia, where they remained for a number of years, and where Thomas McCall, Wm. McCall, and Jane (afterward married to Robert Harris) were born. The three families were driven away by the Indians after several of the Calhouns were killed. James Harris, my great grandfather, remained on New river, and there died at the advanced age of 110 years. His children were Janet McCall Robertson, Isabell, Martha, and Wylly. James McCall, Robert Robertson and James Wylly, settled in Mecklenburg county, North Carolina, where my father, James McCall, married Elizabeth, daughter of Thomas McCall, second cousin of my grandfather James McCall. John William and Patrick Calhoun removed into South Carolina and gave name to Calhoun's settlement on Little river, a branch of Long Cane. My grandfather James' family married in Mecklenburg, viz., my father James to Elizabeth McCall, Agnes to Elias Alexander, Rachel to

Thomas McCall, son of Francis, a distant relation, not much liked by the family—ran away; Thomas married Jane, daughter of Samuel Harris; William married Elizabeth, daughter of Matthew Stewart; and Jane married Robert, son of John Harris. My maternal grandmother was Margaret Greenfield—had two sisters, Esther and ————, the former married Andrew Elliott and the latter married James Barr. My grandfather James had a brother Thomas, who settled at Wilmingotn in Delaware, and I think another brother William, of whom I know nothing. James Harris, my great-granfather, was related to the family of Livingstons, which went from Scotland to Holland, removed from Holland to New York (New Netherlands) and there remained. My grandfather, Thomas McCall, had children; viz., Elizabeth my mother, Margaret, Jane, Martha, and Ann and Mary who died in youth. Margaret married Thomas Harrison and had a number of children; Jane married John Luckie and had a number of children; Martha married Samuel Nelson and had several children. I know not what became of her or them. None of my family were men of letters except Thomas my uncle, who when at college changed his name to Thomas Harris McCaule. His posterity, Laird, Melinda Penelope, Leroy, Thomas 1st, and 2nd, and Jane, all died without issue, except Melinda, who married William Pinder and has two living children, viz., Thomas and Jane who married Captain J. M. Russell, and later married Captain Phillips of Manchester, England, had a daughter (Melinda) and died. My father's decendants were Thomas, Hugh, Janet, Margaret, James, Harris, Elizabeth and William —all dead but Thomas, Janet and Margaret. Thomas married Henrietta Fall in 1787, and their issue were Eliza Henrietta, died young; Selina Mary Ann, married to Virgil H. Vivien who has many children in Florida; Louisa Freeman, married to George Gaines, has three children, and resides in Decatur county; Thomas William and James, both dead; and youngest still-born. He, in 1798, married Elizabeth Mary Ann Smith, by whom he had Sarah Georgiana, married to Colonel Spivey; Elizabeth Smith married to Doctor Thomas Moore; Harriet Moore, married to Major Mizell; Margaret, died young; Janet Harris married Ira Stanley; Margaret Sanders, married Jeremiah H. Yopp, Esq.

Patrick Calhoun, father of John C. Calhoun, Vice-President of the United States, paid us a visit in 1794 or 93, and gave his benediction to three of my oldest children, and said to me: "This is the fifth generation of your family that I have had by the hand and have intimately known," and mentioned to me several of the above circumstances.

My father was an advisor in what was called the Regulation in North Carolina about the year 1768 or '69, and that was the real beginning of the American Revolution. He, in 1771 or 1772, removed into the Calhoun settlement, South Carolina, and became an active officer in the Revolution. He was captain of minute men under the government in 1774, and rose in rank to that of colonel, and died of small-pox and a wound after having been in seventeen engagements against the enemy. Died in April, 1781.

I was born 19th of March, 1764, old style, which was properly at the time 19th or 30th of March, 1765, new style, uncertain which day, as those old folks, all farmers, were not very learned and adhered to the old style and the old year for a number of years after the beginning of the year was altered from 25th of March to 1st of January."

From these facts it appears that while Major Hugh McCall, the historian, was himself too young to take an active part in the Revolution, he lived amid the stirring scenes of that great struggle, and upon his youthful memory were indelibly stamped the dramatic records and traditions which he so faithfully describes.

But little is known of his early life, but when quite a young man he became interested in military affairs, and for a long time he was connected with the United States army. On May 12th, 1794, he was ensign of the 3rd sub-legion, and May, 1796, he became first lieutenant. He was made deputy paymaster-general January 31st, 1800, and August of the same year, he was advanced to the position of captain. On the reorganization of the army, in 1802, he was retained in the second infantry, and on July 10th, 1812, he was breveted major. On July 15th, 1815, he was mustered out of service. On March 31st, 1818, he became military store-keeper at Savannah and in May, 1821, he served in the same capacity at Charleston, South Carolina. For eighteen months he lived at Point Peter. From 1806 to 1823, he was the jailer of Savannah, and it was during this period that he wrote his History of Georgia. Many years before his death, his health failed and he became an invalid. He suffered much bodily pain, and when not actually confined to his bed, he had to use a roller chair to move about his room.

This was not an age of books and official records, and the experiences and traditions of those who actually took part in the War of the Revolution were fast fading from memory. It was fortunate, indeed, for Georgia's early history that Major Hugh McCall, at this crisis, though suffering from a painful disease, and in the face of great difficulties, undertook to rescue from oblivion the history of his State, and fix in imperishable record the deeds of her distinguished sons. From his own notes and experiences, and from the lips of many of the chief actors of the scenes he portrays, his materials were taken, and with wonderful patience and fortitude he prepared for the press the first volume of the History of Georgia, which was published in 1811. In the preface he says: "The occurrences of a new country, when dressed in their best attire are not very engaging, and it is to be expected that many interesting facts have escaped the author's notice, owing to the limited scope of his researches, in consequence of his affliction under a portion of disease and decrepitude almost without a parallel in the history of human life."

In 1816, he published the second volume of his History of Georgia, thus bringing down the record of the State to that date.

While his History of Georgia is not free from legitimate criticism as to style and historic treatment, still it is of inestimable value in the preservation of many of the important facts upon which are based the writings of later historians. He did not attempt a finished production, but he collected the material for the future historian, and in estimating the value of his work we must bear in mind what Jared Sparks says of it: "The work has its merits, but its author labored under disadvantages, and his materials were scanty."

Major McCall was never married, and his will, which is of record in the office of the Ordinary in Savannah, shows that he lived in moderate circumstances. After a lingering illness and years of bodily suffering, he died in Savannah June 10th, 1824, and was buried in the Old Colonial Cemetery, now in the midst of the city.

The only likeness of him in existence is an oil portrait in possession of the Georgia Historical Society at Savannah, from which the accompanying engraving is made.

As the years go by, his valuable work is more and more appreciated, and for all time he will be known and honored as Georgia's first historian.   OTIS ASHMORE.

John McIntosh.

JOHN McINTOSH was born in McIntosh county and was the son of General John M. McIntosh. When quite a young man, he was appointed captain, commanding the third company of the battalion, ordered February 16, 1776, to be made for the protection and defense of the colony of Georgia. Of this battalion, his uncle, Lachlan McIntosh, was colonel, commanding. In an address to the Provincial Congress of Georgia, the battalion was required to subscribe to an oath in the following words: "We bind ourselves upon the words of soldiers and men of honor, at all times, to obey and carry into effect, as far as in us lies, the object and commands of the present or any future Congress or Council of Safety of this province as if the same should be issued by us, provided, nevertheless, that the same do not contradict or interfere with the orders of the general Congress of the United States."

For the signing and carrying out of this promise, Colonel McIntosh was disqualified by Great Britain in such a way that, in the event of their recovering possession of Georgia, he would have been imprisoned, probably for life, and debarred from enjoying any of the rights of a citizen. Colonel McIntosh saw much service during the Revolutionary War. He had command of the fort at Sunbury when the British officer, Colonel Fuser, demanded immediate surrender. The correspondence between these two officers follows:

Sir:—You cannot be ignorant that four armies are in motion to reduce this Province. One is already under the guns of your fort and may be joined, when I think proper, by Colonel Prevost,

16

who is now at the Midway Meeting-house. The resistance you can, or intend to make, will only bring destruction upon this country. On the contrary, if you will deliver me the fort that you command, lay down your arms, and remain neutral until the fate of America is determined, you shall, as well as all of the inhabitants of this parish, remain in peaceable possession of your property. Your answer, which I expect in an hour's time, will determine the fate of this country, whether it is to be laid in ashes, or remain as above proposed.

I am, Sir,

Your most obedient, etc., L. V. FUSER,

Colonel 60th Regiment, and Commander of His Majesty's Troops in Georgia, on His Majesty's Service.

P. S.—Since this letter was closed, some of your people have been firing scattering shots about the line. I am to inform you that if a stop is not put to such irregular proceedings, I shall burn a house for every shot so fired.

Colonel McIntosh promptly responded:

FORT MORRIS, November 25th, 1778.

SIR:—We acknowledge we are not ignorant that your army is in motion to endeavor to reduce this State. We believe it entirely chimerical that Colonel Prevost is at the Meeting-house; but should it be so, we are in no degree apprehensive of danger from a juncture of his army with yours. We have no property compared with the object we contend for that we value a rush; and would rather perish in a vigorous defense than accept your proposals. We, Sir, are fighting the battles of America, and therefore disdain to remain neutral till its fate is determined. As to surrendering the fort, receive this laconic reply: Come and take it. Major Lane, whom I send with this letter, is directed to satisfy you with respect to the irregular, loose firing mentioned on the back of your letter.

I have the honor to be, Sir,

Your most obedient servant,

John McIntosh,
Colonel of Continental Troops.

Fuser did not take it.

The Legislature of Georgia, in acknowledgment of the conspicuous gallantry of Colonel McIntosh on this occasion, voted him a sword with the words "Come and Take It" engraved on it.

At the battle of Brier Creek, the manner in which he displayed his bravery will always entitle Colonel McIntosh to the highest rank as a soldier.

He stood his ground until almost every man was killed. Upon surrendering his sword, a British officer attempted to kill him. He was saved only by the interference of Sir Æneas McIntosh of the British army.

In the early part of the Revolutionary War, Colonel McIntosh was operating in South Carolina as lieutenant. Here he met a Miss Sarah Swinburn. It was a case of mutual love at first sight. At the same time, a young Pole, Captain Elholm, was also in love with her. The rivals had a duel with swords for her hand. Colonel McIntosh won the prize. After the duel, Colonel McIntosh, all bleeding and disfigured, was nursed back to life and strength by his affianced. They soon married and lived a long and happy life together. He continued in active service until the close of the war.

After a treaty of peace had been declared between England and the United States, Colonel McIntosh, hearing such glowing reports of Florida was induced to settle on St. John's river. Florida, at that time, was a province of Spain, and prominent Americans, going there were regarded with more or less suspicion by the Spanish authorities. The Captain General of the State in St. Augustine ordered Colonel McIntosh seized and had him confined in Moro Castle, Havana. During this time, his wife unfortunately became blind. Notwithstanding this infirmity, she put forth every energy of which she was capable for his release; even writing letters, guided by the hand of an assistant.

As Colonel McIntosh had voluntarily placed himself under the Spanish government, no interposition in his behalf by the United States could be made. But the private influence of General Washington and of the most distinguished men of the country, many of whom had served with him during the war, was exerted in his behalf, mainly through the active correspondence and ceaseless efforts of Mrs. McIntosh. In her addresses to the functionary of the Spanish government, she endeavored to propitiate him by a persuasive and flattering style; but meeting with dissappointment, and wearied by procrastination, and the neglect of prevaricating officials, she had recourse to a more energetic manner, through letters to her husband, which she knew could not fail to fall into the hands of the Captain General. In a little less than a year, Colonel McIntosh was released, without trial, confronted by no accuser or testimony of any kind, since no formal charge had ever been preferred against him.

Chafed by the injustice and rigor of his confinement, Colonel McIntosh left Florida immediately, not, however, without some acknowledgment of his gratitude for Spanish hospitality. He, in company with a few faithful followers, who had also suffered imprisonment by the Spaniards, destroyed a small fort on the St. John's, opposite Jacksonville, then called the Cow Ford, and burned several galleys in the river, as they passed into Georgia. The late Colonel Abner Hammond of Milledgeville was a fellow prisoner with Colonel McIntosh in the Moro Castle and was released at the same time.

Colonel McIntosh's family was informed of his release and of his arrival in Florida from Cuba just before he reached home. This release from the injustice and tyranny of the execrable Spanish government seemed like a resurrection from the dead. Mrs. McIntosh sprang from her seat, and with clasped hands expressed the emotions of her long and sorely bruised heart in a flood of grateful tears. The tumultuous burst of joy by the family and servants around her was too much for her delicate health, and she sank to the floor oppressed by the overpowering sensation of the moment; and when she awoke to consciousness, she found herself in the arms of her husband, whose fate she had long deplored.

Mrs. McIntosh died among her friends on St. Simon's Island, and was buried in the old family cemetery.

In 1812, Colonel McIntosh again entered the service of his country and served through the war of 1812. He died in his native county, McIntosh, on his plantation in 1826. He belonged to that illustrious family, some of whom have held commissions in every war in which the country has been engaged from 1776 to 1900.

R. J. MASSEY.

Lachlan McIntosh.

MAJOR-GENERAL LACHLAN McINTOSH was born at Borlam, not far from Inverness, in Scotland, in the year 1727. He was the second son of John More McIntosh, who was the head of the Borlam branch of the clan McIntosh. The kindred houses of Moy and Borlam had been the chiefs of the warlike clan "Chatan" for many ages; they had mingled in all the feuds that divided Scotland for centuries, and though not decorated with courtly titles, claimed for themselves a distinction in the ancient wars of their country beyond all others of the northern clans. But the glory of the house of Borlam was destined to sink in the Rebellion of 1715. John More McIntosh, the father of General Lachlan McIntosh, was born in the year 1701. He was not fourteen years old at the period of the Rebellion, and was therefore too young to command his clan in battle; but his uncle, Willian McIntosh, had gained experience and acquired renown in foreign service, and, as he then administered the affairs of his nephew, he led that portion of the clan McIntosh that was immediately connected with the house of Borlam, to join the Pretender of that day, who made him a brigadier general. William McIntosh crossed the frith of Forth in open boats at night, surprised, and defeated the English near Edinburgh. He distinguished himself during the whole contest; but when finally the collected forces of the Pretender were assembled at Preston, they were surrounded, and he was taken prisoner. His fall brought down ruin upon his nephew and the house of Borlam. The property of his family was confiscated; too young himself to suffer in person, he was stripped of every thing, and, from having been

Engraved by Hoppner Meyer from a Painting by J.B. Longacre after an original Portrait.

GENERAL LACHLAN McINTOSH.

Lachr. McIntosh

rich, became poor. From that memorable time to 1736, John More McIntosh lingered in obscurity upon what had been his own property. He married, however, and had several children, naming his eldest son William after his unhappy uncle, then a prisoner in the tower; and his second son, Lachlan, after his own father, who had died a few years before the Rebellion of 1715. It is not to be wondered then that the invitation of General Oglethorpe, who was himself more than suspected of participating in the political feelings of the family, to emigrate to America, should have been welcomed at Inverness by one then living in poverty, but who had not forgotten that the time was when the sound of his own bugle would have rallied a thousand kinsmen around him for war to the knife.

John McIntosh, with his family, and one hundred and thirty Highlanders who followed his fortune, arrived in Georgia with General Oglethorpe, in February, 1736, and was immediately settled upon the Altamaha at a point they named New Inverness, now Darien. The eastern costume of the highland clansman, his cap and plume, his kilt and plaid, soon became very dear to the red men of the woods as they mingled together in their sports and hunted together in the woods of Georgia.

More McIntosh, who had first been appointed civil commandant of New Inverness, was later instructed to enroll a hundred of his Highlanders as the light infantry of General Oglethorpe's regiment.

In 1740, General Oglethorpe invaded Florida by water and took post upon an island opposite St. Augustine. Captain McIntosh, with his Highlanders and a few auxiliary Indians, marched by land. When within a few miles of St. Augustine, he was joined by some militia from Carolina and placed under the command of Colonel Palmer.

He allowed himself to be surprised at Fort Moosa, by almost

the whole Spanish garrison. There were many breaches in the walls of the fort, and the first notice that Captain McIntosh had of the advance of the Spaniards was the rush of a regiment of Spanish grenadiers. His Highlanders rallied around him, but he and thirty-six of his men fell wounded or dead at the first charge. This surprise, in truth, led to the failure of Oglethorpe's expedition. The General having no officer to exchange for Captain McIntosh, the Spaniards sent him prisoner to Spain, where he was detained many years. When he finally returned, it was with a broken constitution, soon to die and leave his children to such destiny as might await them.

Lachlan McIntosh was thirteen years of age when his father was wounded and taken prisoner at St. Augustine. General Oglethorpe, placed Lachlan and his elder brother in his regiment as cadets, and would no doubt, in due season, have procured commissions for them; but just as he was leaving Georgia to meet rumors of the invasion of England by the Pretender, the two young brothers were found hid away in the hold of another vessel; for they too had heard the rumors of another attempt of the ancient house of Stuart to vindicate their rights against the Brunswick family, and were anxious to regain or perish in the attempt of re-establishing their own house. General Oglethorpe ordered the two lads to his own cabin; he spoke to them of the friendship he entertained for their father, of the kindness he entertained for them, of the hopelessness of every attempt of the house of Stuart, of their folly in engaging in this wild and desperate struggle, of his own duty as an officer of the house of Brunswick; but if they would go ashore, be hereafter quiet, and keep their own secret, he would forget all that had passed. He received their pledge, and they never again saw him.

The means of education in Georgia at that period were very limited, yet Lachlan McIntosh and his brothers were well instructed in English under their mother's care, and after they were received under the patronage of General Oglethorpe, were instructed in mathematics, and other branches necessary for their future military course. But when General Oglethorpe left Georgia, all hope, and perhaps all wish, for remaining longer attached to his regiment, ceased in the young men. William became an active and successful agriculturist, and Lachlan, in search of a wider field of enterprise, went to Charleston, South Carolina, where his father's gallantry and his father's misfortunes, drew to him the attentions of many; and his fine, manly appearance, his calm, firm temper, his acquirements for his opportunity, procured for him the acquaintance, and then the warm friendship of Henry Laurens, the most distinguished and most respectable merchant at that time in Charleston, afterwards President of Congress, and first minister from the United States to Holland. Mr. Laurens took young McIntosh into his counting-house and into his family. In association with this enlightened and respectable gentleman, Mr. McIntosh had an opportunity of studying men and books, and of filling up the blanks in his education. From some repugnance to commerce, arising probably from his early military propensities, he did not adopt the pursuit of his friend and patron, but after spending some years in Charleston, he returned to his friends still residing on the Altamaha. Here he married and engaged in the profession of a general land surveyor. His talents particularly qualified him for this course, as well as his education and his disposition, and, therefore, he soon obtained independence and the promise of fortune, in the acquirement of extensive bodies of what were then deemed valuable lands. But when he had been engaged for some years in these pursuits, Georgia became involved in a dispute with Carolina about the right of soil of the lands between the Altamaha and St. Mary's rivers. The first charter of Georgia to the trustees had taken out of the ancient limits of Carolina the territory between these two rivers; she still claimed all that was beyond the Altamaha, therefore, as belonging to Carolina, and as the Indian claim to this land was extinguished, she gave grants to individuals for portions of the soil. Subsequent to that period, the chartered limits of Georgia had been extended to St. Mary's.

Governor Wright was a native of South Carolina, and had been attorney-general of that province, before he was appointed governor of Georgia. Both officially and personally he differed with the high authorities of South Carolina, and, in his administration of the government of Georgia, exhibited on every occasion great bitterness of feeling against his native province. Mr. McIntosh, from his long residence in Charleston, and from his many friendships there, was the person to whom they looked, and with whom they advised, upon the many occasions in which they considered themselves unjustly treated. This circumstance was really the cause of, or afforded Governor Wright the pretence for, a long but deliberate opposition to the views and interests of Mr. McIntosh; and thus he was gradually prepared and schooled by a petty persecution for the event that was approaching, long before the time had arrived for the separation of England and her American colonies.

Every eye in Geogia was turned to General McIntosh, as the future leader of whatever force Georgia might bring to the struggle for independence; and although living in solitude, and at a distance from Savannah, which had then become the populous and important and wealthy portion of the province; yet the Elberts, the Habershams, the Harrises, of that day, gallant and good men, felt no reluctance in yielding to him the first rank. When, therefore, a revolutionary government was organized, and an order for raising a regiment in Georgia was adopted,

Lachlan McIntosh was made colonel commandant; and again, soon after, when the order was extended to four regiments, he was immediately appointed brigadier-general commandant, to take rank from September, 1776.

But about this time, unhappily for Georgia, and unhappily for General McIntosh, the enlightened and patriotic president of the council, Archibald Bulloch, died, and was succeeded by a disappointed, ambitious, and restless man. Button Gwinnett was placed at the head of the civil power.

Georgia was at the extremity of the colonies; her people were more divided in sentiment upon the subject of independence than in the older provinces, for she had passed the last from the bosom of the mother country, and, in the convulsive struggle of parties as equally divided, there was more of venom than elsewhere. Division of opinion soon began to show itself in the state administration. General McIntosh had been bred in a soldier's tent; he had been taught in his youth that it was honorable and just, because it was necessary, to kill his enemy in the field, with arms in his hands; but he could not reconcile it to his feelings to hunt him down like the wolf of the woods, nor permit this to be done when he could prevent it. This desire on his part to repress unnecessary cruelty, or impolitic suspicion, soon led to some bickerings with the head of the civil government. Although he had brought his troops into good military discipline, and into a high state of military feeling; and although he had turned aside, without material injury to Georgia, a strong invading force from Florida, and was himself wounded on the occasion; although his brother, his nephew, and his sons, all held rank under him, and had gained praise at this early period, wherever opportunity had been afforded them; yet still there had been no great occasion to win renown for himself. The enemy was elsewhere engaged, and Georgia had temporary repose; and,

but for the unquiet man at the head of the government, would
have had time to prepare and strengthen herself against the
evil day that was to arrive. This man had ventured to offer
himself to the command of the troops, in opposition to General McIntosh, and was rejected, and when unhappily, upon
the death of Mr. Bulloch, he succeeded to civil power, he inter-
meddled with the discipline of the troops, irritated the angry
passions of the people, and finally pointed suspicion and in-
stituted a cruel persecution against an honorable gentleman, a
near and dear relation of General McIntosh. The elder brother
of General McIntosh, William, had been appointed to recruit
and command a regiment of cavalry, and which he, in a great
measure, armed and equipped at his own expense; but upon this
attack of the civil power upon his relative, he indignantly threw
up his command. General McIntosh, more calm, waited until
Gwinnett ceased to be governor, when he told him sternly his
opinion of his actions. Gwinnett challenged him; they met
with pistols at eight feet; both fired; both were wounded, Gwinnett mortally. But all feud did not die with him, and Georgia,
being free from foreign enemies, General McIntosh applied
through his friend, Colonel Henry Laurens, to be ordered to
join the central army under General Washington. This was
readily granted, with permission to carry his staff with him.
He soon won the confidence of the commander-in-chief, and was
placed for a long time in his front, while watching the superior
forces under General Howe in Philadelphia. He remained in
this delicate and important position until his services were required elsewhere.

The Indians on the north-western frontier, from New York
to Virginia, had been brought into action by England. General
Schuyler was doing all he could to mitigate the sufferings of the
people to the west of New York, but on the Ohio there was no

unity of action in defense. In this situation, and under these circumstances, Congress instructed General Washington to indicate an officer to undertake the difficult command. There were no laurels to be gleaned in a defensive war in an Indian field, and Congress could not spare men for an offensive war with the Indians, when her capitals, Philadelphia and New York, were' in quiet possession of the enemy. General Washington knew by experience, what unwearied watchfulness was necessary, even for self-preservation, in a war of this kind, and the officer in command was to march with a few hundred men over the same hills, and through the same valleys, for the same point, where Braddock and his troops were met, and had been destroyed; he was to encounter the same ruthless enemy, with feeble means, in the infancy of American power, before whom, many years after, a Harmar and a St. Clair were to fall.

General Washington reluctantly called upon General McIntosh to undertake this difficult and dangerous command; and it was only the deepest sense of public duty and obedience to the will of the commander-in-chief, whom he revered as a soldier and loved as a man, that made him consent to accept it.

General McIntosh had been instructed by Congress to take command of the western districts of Virginia and Pennsylvania, but he was transferred to the Southern Army at the request of General Washington as set forth in the following letter:

"May 11, 1779. Brigadier General McIntosh will have the honor of delivering you this. The war in Georgia, being the State to which he belongs, makes him desirous of serving in the southern army. I know not whether the arrangements Congress have in contemplation may make it convenient to employ him there; but I take the liberty to recommend him as a gentleman, whose knowledge of service and of the country promises to make him useful. I beg leave to add, that General McIntosh's conduct, while he acted immediately under my observation, was such as to acquire my esteem and confidence, and I have had no reason since to alter my good opinion of him."

General McIntosh was deeply sensible of the difficulties, which the time and the condition of the American troops afforded to success; but was too much interested in his country, his family, and his friends, not to desire to mingle his efforts with theirs for deliverance, if deliverance was possible.

The British troops were in quiet possession of Savannah, under General Prevost, and had an imposing force threatening Charleston under Colonel Maitland.

When General McIntosh joined General Lincoln in Charleston, they made every preparation that their feeble means afforded for the invasion of Georgia, whenever the French fleet should arrive on the coast. General McIntosh marched to Augusta, and took command of the advance of the American troops. He proceeded from thence down to Savannah, which he reached about the 10th of September, cutting off some small British parties and driving in all the British outposts. In expectation of being joined by the French, he marched to Beauley, where they expected to effect a landing.

From the 12th to the 14th the French were landing. On the 15th, General Lincoln joined them. By a fatality, the British commandant had been apprised of the approach of the French fleet as early as the 3rd of September; the dispatched vessels from which had made their first appearance off Tybee Island, instead of Charleston; and the British troops had been most diligently engaged in improving their fortifications from that time; still, upon the 15th and 16th their works were incomplete, and not more than thirty or forty guns mounted; but what was more important still, Colonel Maitland, with the elite of the British troops, had not arrived from Carolina. General McIntosh, who had learned all this, pressed for an immediate attack; but Count d'Estaing, the commanding officer, believed he was sure of his game, and would not listen to the proposition. He coolly summoned General Prevost to surrender; General Prevost demanded time for reflection and consultation, which was granted. Colonel Moncrief, the most distinguished engineer of his day, was engaged, with a thousand men, white and black, strengthening the British post. Colonel Maitland arrived on the night of the 17th, with eight hundred veterans, to man the works; and General Prevost then sneeringly refused to surrender. What was practicable and easy on the 15th and 16th, became impossible on the 17th and 18th, when one hundred and fifty cannon had been mounted, and 2,800 veteran troops manned the trenches.

From that time to the 8th of October, the allied troops had been wasting away under the influence of the climate; and Count d'Estaing became sensible that he could no longer trust his ships upon the open coast, exposed to tempest, and to the attack of the enemy. Stung with disappointment at reflections upon the past, he determined, before his retreat, to lead the American and French Army to a desperate attack upon the British lines. At the rising of the sun on the 9th of October, the allied troops were led on by their officers; they succeeded in planting their standards on several points of the works; but the British cannon were pouring a fire upon their flanks that swept them off in masses. They were compelled at length to retire, leaving one thousand out of four thousand on the field. The French troops and French fleet went to sea, and General Lincoln and General McIntosh had to recoil upon Charleston, where they were soon themselves to be beseiged by an overwhelming force under General Clinton; and where after a long and gallant defence, and after doing all that human prudence and human courage could accomplish, they were compelled to surrender. General McIntosh was detained for a long time a prisoner of war; and here, in a great measure, closes his military life, for he never again took any command.

When General McIntosh was finally released, he retired with his family to Virginia, carrying with him a high testimonial from the officers that had served with him, and under him, at the siege of Charleston, belonging to the Virginia line; which constituted the most efficient part of the force of the southern army.

General McIntosh remained in Virginia with his family until the British troops were driven from Savannah. When he returned to Georgia, he found his personal property had all been wasted, and his real estate diminished in value; and from that time to the close of his life, he lived in a great measure in retirement, and in some degree of poverty. His two gallant sons, William and Lachlan, who had followed him to the field, died at an early period of life, leaving no children behind them. His younger children had suffered much from his long absence in the public service. General McIntosh died in Savannah in the year 1806, in the 79th year of his age.

Adopted from National Portrait Gallery.

Engraved by J. C. Buttre from a Daguerreotype.

Wm. McAllister

OF GEORGIA.

Engd. expressly for this work.

Rev. William McWhir.

FOR at least thirty-five years of the first part of the nineteenth century, Sunbury, Liberty County, Georgia, was
the educational center, not only of the whole State, but
that of the surrounding Southern States. The Academy at this
point was established by an act of the legislature assented to the
first of February, 1788. To a board of commissioners, or a
majority of them, authority was given to sell at public sale and
upon previous notice of thirty days in one of the State gazettes,
any confiscated property within the county of Liberty, to the
amount of 1,000 pounds, equivalent to $5,000. When realized,
this sum was to be expended by them in the construction of a
building, suitable for academy purposes, and salaries of teachers.
So strict was this act, that each commissioner was required to
execute a bond in favor of the Governor of Georgia, in a penalty
of 1,000 pounds, conditioned on the faithful performance of the
trust. This board of commissioners, in 1803, was increased to
seven. Two years thereafter, however, a return to the original
number of five was directed.

The legislature of Georgia in full session, in 1811, directed a
conveyance to these commissioners, for the sole use and benefit
of this Academy, of one-third of a tract of land adjoining Sunbury, known as the distillery tract; this tract had already been
confiscated and had become the property of the State. By means
of this confiscation and appropriation, Sunbury Academy became the possessor of quite a sum of money. At this time and
for many years thereafter, this academy was the only institution
of the kind in the State which had enjoyed like appropriations.

17

This was a prime factor in placing it far above any similar institution in the South.

In 1793, Dr. McWhir first came to the town as principal of the Academy. Sunbury was then in a prosperous condition, and had been for many years. For the first fifty years of the existence of the town, in point of shipping and commerce, Sunbury was the only rival the city of Savannah had ever known in Georgia. The first Masonic Lodge ever organized in the State of Georgia held its first meeting under one of the grand old moss-covered live oaks so abundant in that section.

In addition to this, the people of Liberty County strictly adhering to the rigid Puritanical practices and principles of their forefathers, lived up to the right standard of piety, and believed in placing education second only to religion. In the employment of their teachers and ministers, they looked closely, not only through the South and North, but even in England, Ireland, and Scotland, to find men of the right stamp.

From the very outset the trustees of Sunbury Academy conducted its affairs with great prudence and skill; and, for many years, this institution attracted pupils in great number, not only from all parts of Georgia, but from other states. The teacher, whose name was for the longest period and most notably associated with the management of this Academy, and who did more than all others to establish a standard of scholarship and maintain rules of study and rigid discipline, was Rev. Dr. Wm. McWhir. For at least two generations, great was the obligation conferred upon the sons of Southern Georgia by this learned teacher, competent instructor, and forceful disciplinarian.

A native of Ireland, born in 1769, a graduate of Belfast College, and licensed to preach by the Presbytery of that city, he came to America in 1783, settling in Alexandria, Va. Here, for ten years, he was principal of the academy of which General

Washington was a trustee. He often enjoyed the hospitality of General Washington at Mt. Vernon. Once while he was dining with the family, the General, as was his custom, asked the usual blessing. Mrs. Washington, somewhat surprised that he had not invited Dr. McWhir, said, "You forgot that we had a clergyman at the table with us to-day." "No, Madam," said he, "I did not forget. I desired clergymen, as well as all others, to see that I am not a graceless man."

Dr. McWhir moved to Sunbury in 1793. Here he became principal of the Academy, which position he held for nearly thirty years. An uncompromising observer of prescribed regulations, and a firm believer in the virtue of the rod, he was a terror to all laggards and delinquents, but a generous instructor to the studious and ambitious. The average attendance of his school was about seventy. Two generations sat at his feet. Fathers and sons in turn responded to his nod and feared his frown.

So impartial was he in the support of whatever was just and of good report, and so competent and thorough as a teacher, that for at least a full generation his numerous pupils found in him their mentor, guide, and helper in the thorny paths of knowledge. The evening of his days was spent at the residence of his old pupils from whom he always received a cordial welcome. This welcome, however, was recognized by him as genuine and agreeable when accompanied by a generous supply of buttermilk and a good glass of wine. The latter might be dispensed with; but a failure to provide the buttermilk was an unpardonable breach of hospitality, and in his eyes, materially impaired the comfort of his sojourn and the tranquility of the venerable guest.

As a Greek and Latin scholar, Dr. McWhir is said to have been without a rival, not only in the South, but in the whole United States, for at least twenty-five or thirty years of his active life.

At the age of sixty, he returned to his native Ireland, also visiting England and Scotland.

About the years 1823-24, he visited Florida, preached at St. Augustine and Mandarin and in the vicinity, and founded a church at Mandarin, the first Presbyterian church ever organized in Florida; and it was mainly through his efforts that the church at St. Augustine was founded. Dr. McWhir never had a regular pastoral charge; nevertheless, he continued to his death a member of the presbytery, within the bounds of which he lived, and was frequently in Synod, and a commissioner of the general assembly of the church. The church found in him a willing contributor, and considering his means, which never were large, few men ever gave more liberally to religious and benevolent objects. Until wthin the last ten or fifteen years of his life, he preached occasionally, chiefly in destitute places, and at his decease was probably the oldest Presbyterian minister in the United States. At the age of nearly ninety, Dr. McWhir was a voluntary colporter of the American Tract Society, and did not give up the work until he was too feeble to labor.

In the cause of education, Dr. McWhir was a leader, not only in Georgia, but throughout the whole South. As a teacher, his chief merits were thoroughness of instruction and the most exact discipline, such as would in these days be esteemed too rigorous. He never enjoyed much reputation as a preacher, owing, no doubt, to the want of ready eloquence, and the almost entire absence of the faculty of the mind called imagination. *Nature and education seemed to have fitted him for the school-room.* Among his pupils, may be ranked some of the most eminent men in the State. At least four governors, six congressmen, fifty preachers, and as many teachers were trained by this noble old man at Sunbury Academy during his administration.

When Dr. McWhir retired from the Academy, although old and feeble, he devoted himself entirely to the improvement of the moral condition of the people of Liberty County and other portions of Southern Georgia. He continued actively in good works even to the day of his death. In 1853, at the age of ninety-four, he died greatly regretted and very much beloved by the thousands who had in former years in some capacity become his beneficiaries.

In 1815, Dr. McWhir married Mrs. Baker, widow of John Baker, a Colonel in the Liberty Guards during the Revolutionary War. The Bakers were among the very first settlers in Liberty County, and, in his many ministrations and acts of benevolence, this good woman was to Dr. McWhir truly a helpmeet.   R. J. MASSEY.

John Milledge.

THE State oftentimes neglects, if it does not altogether forget, its duty to eminent patriotic and useful citizens, who have rendered unselfish service for the general good. As a people, we are indebted not so much to the public men who have constructed wisely and well the institutions of our government, as to those who gave us fundamental principles and policies, wisely conceived and heroically executed, from which later generations have been enabled to evolve a government without compare among the nations of the world.

We are too prone to believe our development as a people is measured by the advance of our civilization and, in only limited sense, dependent upon the wisdom and heroism of those who gave us the policies and possibilities of free government through the sacrifices and blood of the Revolution. The spirit of the Fourth of July is dying out at the South and, in this, we are descrediting ourselves while we dishonor the heroes of the past whose services and blood made it possible for us to be a free and independent people.

Prominent among the many whom the State has, seemingly, forgotten is Governor John Milledge. So far, no material tribute has been paid him except giving his name to a central city of the State.

John Milledge was born in Savannah in 1757. His ancestors came to Georgia with General Oglethorpe. His father, John Milledge, was a trusted friend of Oglethorpe and this relation sustained by the father gave the son opportunities that might have been denied him if born of parents of less prominence and distinction. Whilst the opportunities for education were greatly limited, young Milledge took advantage of such as he could make avail, added to his personal efforts.

After his primary education was completed in such colonial schools as were open, he was taken into the office of the King's Attorney to study law. He was thus engaged at the beginning of the Revolution. His young life had just opened with the darkened prospects of these times. He had obtained all the education possible for a young man of his day. He was socially intimate with the leading spirits and officials of the colony. He moved in the best circles that were then known. He had chosen the leading profession that promised prominence in financial and social success. He had associated himself with the leading Counsel of the King. When the question came as to his personal advancement or the redemption of the oppressed, he did not hesitate a moment, but, obeying his patriotic impulses, he promptly laid down his personal ambitions for the righteous claims of an abused people, which found in him an undaunted and inspiring advocate and defender. In the very first bold, revolutionary act on Georgia soil, young Milledge was a prominent party. Daring and dangerous as it was, his heroism was sufficient for the venture and he won.

May 11, 1775, John Milledge, then only eighteen years of age, together with Joseph Habersham and a small band of noble young fellows, surrounded the Royal Magazine and successfully appropriated a large quantity of gunpowder and applied it to the purposes of the war. The authorities were highly incensed and because of the audacity and success of this daring achievement, Governor Wright offered a large reward for the arrest of all parties implicated in so disloyal and damaging an attack upon his resources for defense.

This expressed threat of summary and speedy punishment did not daunt the young spirits that had put their lives upon the altar of Liberty. Milledge and his party made good their escape, having made secure the valuable seizure they had made. Some few weeks thereafter they appeared at the executive mansion and, more daring than before, actually captured the royal governor and imprisoned him in his own home and held captive Chief Justice Stokes at the same time, thus overturning the King's government in the colony.

When it is remembered these daring deeds were executed before the sentiment of the people was fully set in sympathy with the aggressive policies of this little band of young patriots, it is to be seen that they were impelled by an intrepid heroism born from above and supported by a bravery equal to the demands and possibilities of the Republic they conceived and helped to make possible through the freedom of the oppressed.

Part of the powder seized was sent to Boston and distributed to the Continental Army, and part was used in the battle of Bunker Hill that took place something more than one month following.

These daring transactions, wisely planned and successfully executed, when Mr. Milledge was but a youngster and before the general sentiment of the colony was openly committed to the policy of the Revolution, show the material of which the boy was made and upon which the sturdy character and the high purpose and public life of the man was builded.

From this time forward he identified himself with the cause of the Revolution. In December, 1778, he was at the defense of Savannah. When the city fell into the hands of the enemy, he evaded pursuit by crossing over into South Carolina. He was accompanied, in this escape, by Captain James Jackson. Jackson was about the same age as Milledge, having been born in England September 21, 1857. Upon his arrival at Savannah at fifteen years of age, he found the times exciting and the people speaking their sentiments freely in regard to the differences between Great Britain and her colonies. Jackson soon laid aside his law books, as did Milledge, and he allied himself to those who had resolved no longer to wear the chains of slavery. Young as he was, he gained distinction and was elected Lieutenant and later Captain. This latter position he resigned because he felt that he had not been justly treated by his Colonel.

As these two young heroes, ragged and barefoot, were making their escape into South Carolina, after the attack upon Savannah, they were apprehended as spies by some American soldiers and condemned to be executed. The gallows was actually prepared, and, but for the timely arrival of Major Peter Deveaux, an American officer, who had accidentally heard of their trouble, these two young patriots would have met an ignominious death. This event seemed a marked interposition of Providence in the light of the history of these two boys, who became distinguished citizens of the State. These young soldiers, after their deliverance from death, joined themselves to the command of General Moultrie.

Mr. Milledge was present and took active part in the unsuccessful attempt made by the combined forces under Count D'Estaing and General Lincoln to recover Savannah from the British. At the seige of Augusta and throughout the whole of the Revolutionary conflict, few made more costly sacrifices in herioc daring than he.

Mr. Milledge's civic life really began in 1780, when he was made Attorney-General of Georgia. This position he held less than two years, but with credit to himself and special service to the State. He, subsequently, became a member of the legislature and served several sessions, increasing in favor with the people because of his patriotic devotion to the common good.

In 1792, Mr. Milledge was elected to the second Congress to

succeed Anthony Wayne, whose seat had been declared vacant. In this position he served from November 22, 1792, to March 2, 1793.

He was elected to the fourth, fifth, and seventh Congresses. He resigned his seat in Congress in 1802 to become Governor of the State. This position he held until 1806, when he was elected to the United States Senate, to fill the vacancy occasioned by the death of James Jackson, his patriot companion, when they were boys in the hands of the American forces and about to be executed as spies and were miraculously rescued by the order of Major Peter Deveaux.

In all these positions, Governor Milledge was conspicuous because of his patriotic devotion to the State and the people. He studied diligently and intelligently the needs of the commonwealth and he considered no effort too strenuous and no sacrifice too exacting for him to endure for the well being of those he was so often called to serve. He won, as he deserved, the confidence and admiration of all the people, because of his military and his civic service.

The generous character of the man is best exemplified by his notable benefaction to the State University as the foundation of higher education in the State.

In 1784, the Legislature passed an act providing for the laying out of certain lands, now included in the counties of Hancock, Oglethorpe, Greene, Clark, Jackson and Franklin, and in a part of what is now the State of South Carolina. This territory covered 40,000 acres and was set aside for the endowment of a college or seminary of learning. In 1785, a bill was enacted to complete the establishment of a "public seat of learning."

February 3, 1786, an act was passed requiring the trustees to meet and proceed to the transaction of the business for which they had been appointed. The first meeting was held in Augusta, February 13, 1786. There were present Abraham Baldwin, William Few, William Glascock, John Habersham, Nathan Brownson, Hugh Lawson, and Benjamin Taliaferro.

Abraham Baldwin was chosen President of the University and, as such, continued until the institution went into active operation in 1801.

The work of the trustees for the next fourteen years consisted in the management of their lands, with a view to accumulating a fund necessary to the maintenance of the institution.

November 28, 1800, the trustees were directed to name a location for the college. That body held a meeting and after repeated balloting decided upon Jackson County as the favored place. A committee was appointed, consisting of John Milledge, Abraham Baldwin, George Walton, John Twiggs, and Hugh Lawson, and requested to visit that section and select a site for the buildings.

This committee met at Billup's Tavern in June, 1801, on the Lexington road and made tours of inspection to various localities. The committee examined tracts belonging to the University as well as tracts owned by private individuals. Upon taking the ballot to determine the location, the vote was unanimous in favor of a place owned by Daniel Easely, and this was chosen for the seat of the University of Georgia. The tract consisted of 633 acres.

Mr. Milledge asked the privilege of paying for the lands out of his own private funds and he made the whole body a donation to the trustees for the uses of the University. The forty thousand acres granted by the State to the University yielded, finally, one hundred thousand dollars and this amount is still held as a permanent fund for this institution. The donation by Governor

Milledge brought, first and last, thirty thousand dollars and sustained the University at sundry times, when in dire distress. For this timely and munificent generosity, the University has called the Chair of Ancient Languages "The Milledge Chair of Ancient Languages."

The State, until the end of time, will be due this splendid citizen a debt of gratitude that can not be paid short of a statue in bronze, perpetuating his "encouragement of religion and learning as an object of great importance to any community, tending to the prosperity, happiness and advantage of the same."

President Meigs of the University, in a letter addressed to Governor Milledge, May 11, 1808, says:

"Your institution has taken strong root and will flourish; and I feel some degree of pride in reflecting that a century hence, when this nascent village shall embosom a thousand of the Georgia youths, pursuing the paths of science, it will now and then be said you gave this land and I was on the forlorn hope."

Although the State had donated forty thousand acres of land for the benefits of the University, it could not be availed as it was not suitably located for the purposes and it was valueless because of the fact that there was much land in the State and but few people to purchase. When the grant was made it was estimated that the whole forty thousand acres would bring, in the markets, about fifty rifles and as many saddle horses.

The land donated by Governor Milledge became valuable, not only as the seat of the University, but through the sale of lots for the location of the city of Athens.

In 1809, Senator Milledge resigned his place in the United States Senate and returned to the life of a private citizen, having used with dignity and great practical benefit the highest honors in the gift of the people.

In recognition of the general esteem and his commanding influence as a statesman and a leader, he was honored with the position of President *pro tem* of the Senate. He was holding this place when his resignation was tendered.

It is impossible within the limits here allowed to give worthy sketch of so distinguished a citizen. The details of his service in the varied places assigned him by the popular choice deserve to be known not simply in honor of his memory, but for the pride of the State.

Governor Milledge died February 9, 1818, at what was then called "The Sand Hills" near Augusta, now known as Summerville.   W. J. NORTHEN.

James Oglethorpe.

THERE has been considerable discussion among Georgia historians and biographers as to whether General Oglethorpe's Christian name was James or James Edward. The name is written James Edward in his will and in the English encyclopedias. This was probably his baptismal name, but in his letters from Georgia and all mention of him in the accounts of that time, he is written James.

He came of a very old family in England. His grandfather had been a member of the Court of Charles I, and adhered to him in his war against Parliament and paid a heavy fine for his devotion. His father, Sir Theophilus, was a soldier under James II., and went into banishment with him. Just before the abdication of James II., James Oglethorpe, the seventh child and fourth son was born. Although the chronicle says the father went into exile, it adds that he returned to England and purchased a handsome estate in Surrey.

At sixteen, as the fourth son, he entered the University at Oxford, and a few years afterwards, when he was twenty-two, entered the British army as ensign and was soon made Lieutenant of the Queen's Life Guards. Going abroad, he enlisted under Prince Eugene and finally became his aid de camp. His soldier life was largely spent on the continent, where he saw some very stirring campaigns. His older brothers died and he became the heir to the estate in Surrey, and shortly afterwards was elected to the British Parliament, of which body he remained a member for thirty-two years. He was a high churchman and a Jacobite, and when Bishop Atterbury was being tried for conspiracy to bring in the Stuarts again, he made his maiden

GEN: OGLETHORPE.

speech in defense of the Prelate. It was not a successful plea, for the Bishop was banished and died in exile. He was an active member of the House of Commons, a Deputy Governor of the Royal African Society, and a gentleman of high position and independent means, and withal, a man of genuine piety. The condition of things in England was very much to be deplored. Business was depressed and there was much distress and many were in debt, and the laws for the imprisonment of debtors were rigidly enforced. The good soldier had his heart touched by certain cases of suffering, and he conceived the plan of providing means to alleviate and prevent such. It was the same plan so largely used in England now, but projected on a much broader scale, and with wiser provisions, if they had been practicable. He would establish a colony in America, which should be a refuge for poor people. They were not to be servants, but proprietors; not to work five years for their passage, but to have it paid. They were to have small farms which they could not sell. No strong liquors were to be allowed. No African slaves should be introduced. A clergyman and a schoolmaster should go with the colonists. Provision should be made for their sustenance for twelve months, and he himself, without any compensation, would go with them, govern the colony, and establish it. It was a beautiful scheme and twenty-one nobles, gentlemen, and merchants united with him in securing a charter and a grant from Parliament. This was easily done. He did not go into prisons and pay insolvent debtors out, as far as any records show. He simply invited those who were willing to go to the wilds and serve the colony for one year, for their maintenance, to go with him. Thirty-five families, counting a few gentlemen who were in reduced circumstances, and sundry mechanics and poor farmers took shipping in the latter part of the year 1732, for their homes in the new world, with the philanthropist in charge.

One familiar with the geography of eastern Georgia, and the condition of things on the frontier, can but be amused at the utter ignorance of these well meaning Englishmen as to what these conditions were. It belongs more to history than to this short sketch to go into the full story.

The colonists reached hospitable Carolina January 13, 1733, and secured some generous help from well-to-do planters, and with the aid and advice of these old settlers, chose the bluff on which Savannah now stands as the location for the colony. They landed here February 12, 1733, and Mr. Oglethorpe spent the night near where the city hall now stands on Bay street. The spot has been marked with a marble seat, which bears the following inscription, "On this spot one hundred and seventy-three years ago James Oglethorpe, the founder of the colony, pitched his tent and here rested. Erected by the Georgia Society of the Colonial Dames of America on the 12th of February, A. D. 1906." They pitched their tents and began to build their cabins. Mr. Bryan, Mr. Bell, and Mr. St. Julien sent over their axemen and sawyers to aid them and soon their little cabins dotted the forest.

Mr. Oglethorpe was very active and kind to the emigrants. He shared their humble fare and had the same kind of shelter, a small cabin 15 x 16. He aided the Salzburghers in choosing a section of the poorest land, in what is now Effingham county, for a settlement; and the Highlanders from Scotland he located in the swamps of the Altamaha at Darien. He established a fort on the Ogeechee called Fort Argyle. He met the Indians and made good terms with them, and greatly elated at the success of his venture, after a little over a year in the village of Savannah, he took shipping for England again. His report to the trustees was a very glowing one. The new colony was flourishing, and it was to be an ideal one. He had been somewhat unfortunate in his efforts to secure a clergyman. Mr. Herbert had gone back to England an invalid, and Mr. Quincey was a failure, and when Mr. Oglethorpe was prospecting for a new rector he heard of young John Wesley, who he thought would suit this mission work, so he invited Mr. Wesley and his brother, Charles, and two friends and associates, Mr. Delamotte and Mr. Ingham, all of whom had belonged to the Holy Club, to cooperate with them. They willingly consented and, in the month of October, 1735, with two hundred emigrants, the two small ships sailed for Georgia.

Mr. Oglethorpe had decided on a settlement near the Spaniards. So, leaving a large part of the emigration at Savannah, he went with the other part to St. Simon's Island, where he established the town of Frederica, which was afterwards his home while he remained in Georgia. He had no "bed of roses" in establishing the colony. Those who came with him were by no means in full sympathy with his altruistic views. There was much sickness, and no little want and discontent; but the sanguine founder did not lose heart. He extended the boundary of his settlements and established a fort near the falls of the Savannah River, which he called Fort Augusta, and placed a small garrison there. He found the Spaniards a menace, and so returned to England to represent the true condition of things to Parliament and get authority to raise a regiment and secure such military supplies as he thought might be demanded in the near future. He was successful in his endeavors and set to work to recruit a regiment. After enlisting several hundred recruits, securing munitions of war, and being appointed General and Commander-in-Chief, he returned to Georgia. He saw plainly the necessity of a closer alliance with the Indians, in case of trouble with the Spaniards, and he determined on a journey to Cowetatown, the headquarters of the Creek nation, which was

18

near what is now Columbus. He had a long journey of over three hundred miles through an unbroken wilderness before him. One who knows the difficulties of a way which led across swamps and deep creeks and unfordable rivers, where there was to be found no habitation, save now and then a small Indian town, can but appreciate the noble spirit of Oglethorpe and his scorn of privation and perils. He started on his journey on a trail which led from the far west to Charleston. Beginning his journey westward in the lower part of Screven county, he went in a straight course through what is now Jefferson, Twiggs, Jones, Bibb, Houston, Macon, Taylor, and Muscogee counties. There were no dangers save from exposure and wild beasts, as the country was almost entirely unsettled, except by a few friendly Indians. He crossed the Ogeechee, the Oconee, the Ocmulgee, and the Flint and rested on the banks of the Chattahoochee.

He made a cordial agreement with the Indians, and, by the same route returned to Augusta, where he met the Chickasaws and Creeks, and also made a treaty with them. He had turned over the management of affairs in Savannah to Mr. William Stephens and to his subalterns at Frederica while he attended to military affairs.

As he expected, the troubles in Spain ultimated in war, and with his regiment and some Carolina troops and an Indian contingent, he invaded Florida, expecting to take the Spanish stronghold at St. Augustine. There is no discount on General Oglethorpe's courage and endurance, but his best friends would hardly have regarded him as an able commander, and his effort to capture the Spanish fort was a sad failure, and the whole campaign ended ingloriously.

The Spaniards now took the aggressive and moved on St. Simon's, and met disaster in their turn. Of course, as is always the case, the failure of his military measures was ascribed to his incompetency, and a court martial resulted, in which the General was acquitted. This was in 1744,—just twelve years from the time he made his first expedition to Georgia. The affairs in the new colony had by no means prospered. The General said the people were to blame; the people said the General's visionary scheme was the cause of failure. History tells in full of the measures of the malcontents and the efforts of the friends of Oglethorpe to refute their charges. One thing was certain,—the colony was not successful. Rum could not be excluded; silk culture did not pay; wine making was a failure; and fifty acres of poor pine land in a wild forest was but a pitiful inducement to an emigrant. Savannah was dilapidated, and poverty and want were seen everywhere. So the General decided to let others lead the forlorn hope, and he found solace in his family and his homes in London and in Surrey. He never returned to Georgia.

Although his family had been Jacobites, and he had begun life with that party, he was now a Hanoverian, and when Charles Edward raised a revolt in England, he mustered a troop of four companies and went as a volunteer into the field. He had been made a Major-General of the Militia. He was not successful as a commander, and was again court-martialed and acquitted. In consideration, however, of his devotion and high character he was given the complimentary position of a Brigadier without command, and was known as General Oglethorpe while he lived, and was when he died the oldest general officer of the staff.

The story so often told of his being offered the position of Commander-in-Chief in the American War, and his noted reply, is doubtless a fabrication, for he was over ninety years old when the war began.

He was a quiet country gentleman with a town house in

London. He had a good fortune of his own, and married an heiress. He spent his time in the company of the learned and good, and in his library. He had no children and his estate descended to his nephew, a Frenchman.

He was one of the few men of whom history tells, who founded a colony from which he aimed to secure no personal return, and who gave years of trying labor to bring to success plans, which, while impracticable and visionary, were of the loftiest kind. While he was not one of the world's great men he was what is better, a pure, good man, who laid foundations upon which others built with greater success. GEO. G. SMITH.

Henry Parker.

HENRY PARKER, the second president of the colony of Georgia, was a native of England, though we have no record of the exact place or date of his birth. He was one of the pioneers of Georgia, for, as early as 1734, he held the office of Bailiff in Savannah, which was regarded at that time as quite dignified and honorable. Bailiffs then acted as magistrates, and, when on the bench, wore a purple gown edged with fur.

Soon after coming to Georgia, Mr. Parker received a grant and made a settlement on the Isle of Hope. In 1741, the province of Georgia was divided into the two counties of Savannah and Frederica. William Stephens was made president of the former. His assistants were Henry Parker, Thomas Jones, John Fallowfield, and Samuel Mercer. No president of Frederica was appointed, and, later, to avoid the erection of separate governments, the whole colony was placed under the administration of Stephens and his assistants.

On the departure of General Oglethorpe from Georgia, Mr. Stephens was promoted to the presidency of the colony. When his age and physical infirmities rendered him incapable of longer discharging the duties of his office, Mr. Parker was, on the 19th of March, 1750, appointed vice-president and attended to the duties of the president, although Colonel Stephens continued to hold the office until April 8th, 1751. He then resigned and Mr. Parker succeeded to the presidency of the colony.

About this time, the Trustees were brought to see the importance of a colonial assembly to deal with local affairs. Accordingly an assembly was authorized. Mr. Parker issued writs of election and on January 15th, 1751, sixteen delegates, representing the different parishes in proportion to population, assembled in Savannah. Their meeting being announced to the vice-president, they were invited to an audience at the Council Chamber, where the objects of their meeting were suggested in an address by Mr. Parker.

Francis Harris was chosen Speaker and the vice-president was requested to form a special court the next day for the purpose of administering the oaths of allegiance, supremacy and abjuration to the members. This being the first assembly in Georgia, the names of its members will not be out of place here. They were Francis Harris, Speaker, John Milledge, William Francis, William Russell, George Catagan, David Douglas, Christian Reidlesperger, Theobald Keiffer, William Ewen, Charles Watson, Patrick Houstoun, Peter Morrell, Joseph Summers, John Barnard, Audley Maxwell, John McIntosh, B.

After the organization, the house sent Mr. Parker the following address:

Assembly Room, 25th of January, 1751.

Sir,—We the deputies of the several districts, in General Assembly met, desire to return you our sincere thanks for your speech to us; and we assure you, we shall endeavor, with all concord and unanimity to go through the business appointed for us to do; and we also beg leave to embrace this opportunity of heartily congratulating you on your being appointed Vice-President of the Province, which we look upon as no more than a just reward for your long and faithful services in it; and we have no doubt but the same steadiness, justice and candour which have formerly guided you in the execution of other offices, will direct and govern you in this.

Francis Harris, Speaker.

Henry Parker, Esquire, Vice-President of the Colony of Georgia.

The Vice-President returned the following answer:

MR. SPEAKER AND GENTLEMEN OF THE ASSEMBLY,—I heartily thank you for your kind and flattering address, and will always make it my study and endeavor to promote anything which may tend to the service and advantage of the Colony.

HENRY PARKER,
Vice-President of the Colony of Georgia.

A feeling of sympathy and co-operation seems to have existed between Mr. Parker and the Assembly, as almost every request made by these representatives of the people was either granted or referred to the Trustees.

The Indians became troublesome during his administration and the Bosomworth Claims demanded attention. He seems to have been a prudent man and continued to administer the affairs of the colony till the time of his death in 1754.

Compiled by the Publisher.

William Pierce.

WILLIAM PIERCE, a soldier of the Revolution, was born in Georgia about 1740. He was a delicate child and was given country air rather than the crowded schoolroom. He was ambitious and full of energy and early entered the army in defence of his country, at the call to arms against Great Britain. He was a modest and unassuming gentleman, polite and courteous. General Greene admired him and made him an Aid de Camp. He was in the battle of Eutaws and for his bravery the American Congress voted him a sword. Before the close of the Revolution, he had risen to the rank of major in the Continental Army.

After the close of the war, he returned to Savannah and engaged in mercantile pursuits as the head of the house of William Pierce & Co. Overtaken by misfortune, the firm went into liquidation.

In 1786 and 1787, along with William Few, Abraham Baldwin, and William Houstoun, he represented Georgia in the old Congress which met in Philadelphia. He took his seat May 31st and assisted in the revision of the Federal Constitution. It was a source of much regret to him that business called him to New York and that he was not present to sign the Constitution. On September 28th, 1787, he enclosed a copy of the Constitution to St. George Tucker, Esq., and wrote, "You will probably be surprised at not finding my name affixed to it; and will no doubt be desirous of having a reason for it. Know then, sir, that I was absent in New York on a piece of business so necessary that it became unavoidable. I approve of its principles and would have signed it with all my heart had I been present.

To say, however, that I consider it perfect would be to make an acknowledgment immediately opposed to my judgment. Perhaps it is the only one which will suit our present situation. The wisdom of the Convention was equal to something greater; but a variety of local circumstances, the inequality of States, and the dissonant interests of the different parts of the Union made it impossible to give it any other shape or form."

On the 4th of July, 1789, when the Society of the Cincinnati at Savannah celebrated its anniversary at Hamilton's Long Room, he pronounced the oration which was most favorably received, and he was elected Vice-President, General Anthony Wayne, being elected President. This was a great compliment as there were others present who were his superiors in rank in the Continental Army. A grand dinner was served and the first toast was: The President-General of the Society of the Union. The thirteenth and last toast was: May North Carolina and Rhode Island, by speedy adoption of the Federal Constitution, complete the number of the Thirteen United States.

Major Pierce died at Savannah on the 10th of December, 1789, and the following tribute to his memory appeared in the Georgia Gazette, Tuesday, December 24th, 1789: "To speak of the dead is no uncommon thing; however, a friend can not refrain from paying the last tribute to the name of Major William Pierce, who died last Thursday week universally regretted. He, at an early period of the contest between America and Great Britain, took a decided part in favor of his country, which he loved to his last moments; for we may say that when the hand of death was over him, he was a candidate to become its servant. He was particularly noticed by that gallant officer, General Greene, who honored him with his friendship and most secret confidence. Congress, in respect to his services at the battle of Eutaws, made him a compliment of an elegant sword as a token of their approbation of his conduct. He had the honor to represent Chatham County in the General Assembly; and was sent as a delegate from this State to Congress at a time when deliberation and great judgment were necessary; which duties he discharged to the satisfaction of his country.

Though born with a delicate constitution, he had, till lately, enjoyed a firm, uninterrupted state of health, which, however, was from the fatigues of the war, diversities of climes and elements, at length undermined and destroyed. His manners were polite and obliging, his reasoning precise, his diction perspicuous and elegant. His love of truth was not tainted by the desire of popularity, nor his modesty impaired by the favor of those in power; for he was of no party but the general good of his country. His way of thinking had preserved him from pursuits of selfishness and sordid intrigues; his character appeared worthy of the favors of fortune; but alas! he stood the hardest tests of misfortune; a sincere and occasionally an active friend; always an agreeable companion. The Society of the Cincinnati honored him as their Vice-President, and by whom he was attended as mourners to the tomb. An affectionate and endearing husband, kind master and all that was worth possessing in a domestic situation, he supported a lingering disease and beheld the slow approaches of death with philosophical calmness and serenity; and I am told by a friend who visited him at that solemn period, when he took leave of his wife and friends, his soul seemed, as it were, already received in the blissful mansions of the blessed—to make use of his own words which were the last he uttered, Farewell! Farewell all! Now dies the happy man."　　　　WM. BERRIEN BURROUGHS, M.D.

John Reynolds.

AFTER the surrender of their charter by the Trustees to the Crown, the Lords Commissioners for Trade and Plantations were directed to lay before the Privy Council a plan of government for the Colony of Georgia, which they accordingly did on the 5th of March, 1754. The plan recommended was aproved, and Captain John Reynolds was appointed by the King of England Governor of Georgia, with the title of "Captain-General and Governor-in-Chief of His Majesty's Province of Georgia, and Vice-Admiral of the same." A few days after the date of his commission, (6th of August, 1754), he embarked for the colony, and on the 29th of October of the same year landed at Savannah.

A new system of government now commenced, entirely different from that which existed under the supervision of the Trustees, but similar to that which prevailed in the other colonies. The Governor had authority to call an Assembly, to pass laws, to erect courts of judicature, to grant lands, etc., etc. A Council of twelve persons was also appointed to advise and assist the Governor. Officers were also appointed to collect the customs and duties, to manage the quit-rents and grants of land, besides others, such as Secretary, Provost-Marshal, and Attorney-General. The seal of the Colony was changed, and the following persons appointed Councillors: Patrick Graham, Sir Patrick Houstoun, Bart., James Habersham, Alexander Kellett, William Clifton, Noble Jones, Pickering Robinson, Francis Harris, Jonathan Bryan, William Russell, James Habersham, Secretary of the Province; William Clifton, Attorney- General; Alexander Kellett, Provost-Marshall; William Russell, Naval

Officer; Thomas Young, William Brahm, Surveyors; Sir Patrick Houstoun, Bart., Register of Grants.

One among the first acts of Governor Reynolds was to secure the friendship of the Indians, for which purpose he wrote letters to the head men of the Upper and Lower Creeks, assuring them of his amicable feelings, and promising some tokens of his Majesty's regard. The establishing of proper courts of judicature being of great importance to the prosperity of the Province, Governor Reynolds, as early as circumstances would permit, brought this subject before the Council, and on the 12th of December, a General Court was established besides a Court of Chancery, a Court of Oyer and Terminer and a Court of Admiralty.

After the arrangement of the Courts, the Governor called a General Assembly to meet in Savannah on the 7th of January, 1755, and accordingly the first Legislature of Georgia, consisting of three branches, the Governor, Council, and Commons met upon the day appointed. With the exception of some interruptions originating with Edmund Gray, a pretended Quaker, one of the members of the Assembly, business was conducted with harmony. Twelve acts were passed and received the assent of the Governor. After the adjournment of the Assembly, Reynolds made a tour through the southern parts of the Province. It was on this tour that he laid out a town on the Ogeechee River, which he named Hardwick. In a letter addressed to the Board of Trade, he expressed the opinion, "that Hardwick will become a fit place for the seat of government." The necessity of having the southern boundaries clearly defined struck the Governor as highly important, and he proposed to the Council in England to extend his authority to thirty degrees, twenty minutes north latitude, and thence in a straight line westward to the Pacific, but no definite action was taken upon the subject. In his efforts to protect the colony by proper military defences, the Governor exhibited much zeal, and sent to the Board of Trade a representation upon the subject. Wishing to maintain peaceful relations with the Indians, he resolved, accompanied by some of the Council, to meet them at Augusta. A day was appointed, but the Indians failing to attend, he returned to Savannah, leaving William Little as his agent to deliver his speeches and presents. It was just about this time that two transports from Nova Scotia, with four hundred French Papists, arrived at Savannah. It was one of the express conditions on which Georgia was settled that no Papist should be allowed in it, and consequently the Governor was placed in an awkward position. These new comers brought letters to Reynolds from Lieutenant-Governor Lawrence, of Nova Scotia, acquainting him, "that for the better security of that province, and in consequence of a resolution of his Council, he had sent these people to Georgia, and he did not doubt of his concurrence." To the honor of the Governor, he treated them with kindness. The season of the year not admitting of their going North, and their provisions being nearly exhausted, they were distributed about the Province in small parties and maintained at the public expense until the following spring, when the greater part of them left.

In 1756, misunderstanding began between the Assembly and the Governor. This arose from the Assembly refusing to admit to their seats, three new members, on acount of which, it was adjourned from the fifth to the twelfth of February, 1756. So determined was the Assembly to disregard the instruction of the Governor, that they ordered a message of adjournment, sent by him, to lie on the table, confined the Speaker to his chair, forced him to sign a paper, while some private members seized upon the minutes, made such alterations as they pleased, and refused to deliver them to his written order. Of these proceedings, he complained to the Board of Trade. With the Council, also, the Governor had difficulties. In a letter to the Board of Trade, he informs them "that a great majority of the Council have all along appeared to be extremely greedy of power, and would fain have all things determined by vote, desiring even his official correspondence with the Board of Trade to pass under their approval." Representations were made to the Board of Trade, that a sad decline of the colony had taken place, which was attributed to the Governor and to William Little, his secretary. This man had served with Reynolds in the navy as a surgeon, and had accompanied him to Georgia and by him was advanced to some of the most responsible posts. In consequence of this conduct, he became very unpopular, and in September, 1755, all the Council, except one, presented to the Governor a memorial in which they charged Little with forgery, illegal commitments, and arbitrary conduct, and desired his removal from office. The Governor refused to remove him. Various representations were sent to England against the Governor and Little. And although active measures were taken to contradict these representations, the Lords of Trade felt it to be their duty to attend to the complaints, and accordingly, Reynolds was recalled. On the 17th of February, 1757, the Governor received a letter from the Board of Trade, dated 5th of August, 1756, signifying His Majesty's pleasure "that he should return to England, to the end that an account of the present situation, and circumstances of the Province, and of his conduct in the administration of the government there might be laid before His Majesty, for his further directions, and to resign the government of the Colony into the hands of Henry Ellis, Esquire." Immediately upon receipt of this letter, Governor Reynolds resigned and in a few days embarked for England, having previously furnished himself with such necessary documents and papers as he thought would enable him to obey the commands of His Majesty. The vessel in which he embarked was taken by a French privateer, and carried into the port of Bayonne, from whence he procured passage home, having been stripped by the enemy of his Journal, papers, and everything of value belonging to him. On the 17th of July, 1757, he arrived in London, and it was not until the 6th of March, of the next year that the Board of Trade furnished him with a statement of complaint. To these complaints he responded, but the Board of Trade was not satisfied with his explanations. He now resumed his rank in the navy. He was finally made Rear-Admiral of the Blue and died in January, 1776.

White's Historical Collections.

Robert Sallette.

LIBERTY County has given to the state and nation many prominent men, but the story of none of their lives surpasses in romantic interest that of Robert Sallette. It is known that his family was connected with the Midway congregation, but it is impossible, at this distance from his day, to give either the date of his birth or his death.

Tradition has preserved many stories of his brave deeds. The following will serve to illustrate his personal courage and his fidelity to the cause of liberty:

Robert Sallette was distinguished by his opposition to the Tories. It is not known with certainty to what particular command he was attached. He appears to have been a sort of roving character, doing things in his own way. The Tories stood very much in dread of him, and well they might, for never had they a more formidable foe. On one occasion a Tory who possessed considerable property, offered a reward of one hundred guineas to any person, who would bring him Sallette's head. This was made known to our hero who provided himself with a bag, in which he placed a pumkin, and proceeded to the house of the Tory, and told him that, having understood that he had offered one hundred guineas for Sallette's head, he had it with him in the bag and that he was ready to deliver it, provided the money was first counted out for him. The Tory believing that the bag contained Sallette's head, laid down the money, upon which Sallette pulled off his hat and placing his hand upon his head said, "Here is Sallette's head." This answer so frightened the Tory that he immediately took to his heels, but a well-directed shot from Sallette brought him to the ground.

On one occasion, Sallette and Mr. Andrew Walthour who with some others, were the advance guard of the American Army, met the advance of the British, when a smart skirmish took place and the British guard was driven back. In the skirmish a very large man of the British was killed. Noticing a pair of boots on the feet of the dead man, Bob resolved to possess them and was pulling them off while his comrades were hallooing to him to leave for he would be killed; but he answered, "I must have the boots for I want them for little John Way."

He was known to leave the American Army during battle, get into the rear of the enemy and kill many of them before he was discovered.

On a certain day he dressed himself in British uniform, dined with a party of the enemy and, whilst the toasting and drinking were going on, suddenly drew his sword, killed his right and left-hand man, sprung upon his horse without having time to throw the bridle over his neck and rode off amidst the fire of his pursuers. His motto was never to forgive a Tory; and if one was liberated, he would follow and, if possible, take his life.

Andrew Walthour, Sallette and another man were once riding a small trail late in the evening near to Fraser's old mill seat, when they met three men. Mr. Walthour, being in front, said to Sallette, "I will pass the first and second man, and as soon as I am opposite the third sieze his gun, and you can do the same." In this way the three men were disarmed. "Dismount, gentlemen," said Sallette, addressing himself to the leader, "what is your name?" He replied, giving a fictitious name. "Where is your camp?" asked Sallette. "We are from over the river," replied the Tory. He then inquired where they had crossed and was told that they had crossed at Beard's on the Altamaha, where Sallette knew the Whigs were most numerous. Sallette replied, "That is a lie." Then asking the second man the same question and receiving the same answer, he turned to the third and repeating his questions, received like answers. "If you do not tell me the truth," said he, "I will cut off your head." The fellow replied as at first and was shot down by Sallette. The others promised, if he would spare their lives, they would conduct him to their camp. Their lives were spared and with the aid of his prisoners, he captured a large party of Tories.

Compiled from *White's Collections.*

James Screven.

GENERAL JAMES SCREVEN was the second son of James and Mary Screven, of James Island, South Carolina. His grandfather was Samuel Screven, who married a daughter of James Witter, all of whom were of James Island. His great-grandfather was the Rev. William Screven, who from having his settlement in South Carolina named "Somerton," is inferred to have been the "William Screven of Somerton," who according to Ivimey's History of the English Baptists "was one of twenty persons, ministers and laymen, in behalf of the whole," who signed in 1656, " A Confession of Faith of Several Churches in the County of Somerset, and the counties near adjacent." It is a fact, however, that Mr. Screven owned two adjoining tracts of land in South Carolina at the head waters of the western branch of the Cooper River, the locality being called Wampee and near Pineopolis. One tract he purchased on June 23rd, 1698, and the other was granted to him January 11, 1700, which are respectively known, in 1907, as "Somerton" and "Somerset."

Mr. Screven is first mentioned in the province of Maine in a record of his purchase November 15th, 1673, of ten acres of land at Kittery, Maine; the second record is that of July 23rd, 1674, when he married at Kittery, Bridget Cutt, a daughter of Robert Cutt, one of the three brothers, who were prominent among the early settlers of New Hampshire. Mr. Screven also served on the grand jury in 1678 and 1680, and as a deputy from Kittery at the general assembly held at York June 30th, 1681.

In Septemebr 1682, Mr. Screven was the elder of a Baptist

church at Kittery, when a covenant was signed by himself and others. He met with so much opposition and hardship, on account of his religious faith that he agreed to move out of the province. This move is said to have taken place, 1683-1685, to Somerton on the Cooper River, some miles above Charleston, South Carolina.

Mr. Screven was the first preacher of the "First Baptist Church" at Charleston. His memoir by the Rev. H. S. Burrage of Maine, was written for the Maine Historical Society and it is also to be found in "Two Centuries of the First Baptist Church in South Carolina." He died at Georgtown, South Carolina, October 10th, 1713, aged eighty-four years. His wife, Mrs. Bridget Screven, survived him.

Mary Screven, the mother of General James Screven, was born October 9th, 1717, according to Mrs. Poyas' "Carolina in the Olden Times," and she is said to have died about 1758. She was the niece of Edward Hyrne of "Cape Fear Barony, Hyrneham, North Carolina?" Her father was Thomas Smith, born 1670, in England and died in South Carolina in 1738; and her mother was Mary (Hyrne) Smith, whose will was dated in 1776, she dying in 1777, aged 80 years, according to Mrs. Poyas. Thomas Smith was the oldest son of Landgrave and Governor Thomas Smith, who was born in England and died in South Carolina in his forty-sixth year, his will being dated June 26th, 1692. The Warrant Book of the province of South Carolina for the years 1672-1694, perhaps fixes the arrival of Governor Thomas Smith, his first wife Barbara, and their sons, Thomas and George, as they were entered in the Secretary of State's office, July 10th, 1684, for a grant of 650 acres of land, the warrant being dated January 20th, 1684-5.

General Screven married Mary Odingsells, a daughter of Charles Odingsells, of Edisto Island, South Carolina. According to the records, Mrs. Screven was a member, in 1771, of the

Midway Church in Liberty County, Georgia. General Screven moved into the province of Georgia prior to September the 11th, 1769, for a South Carolina record of that date is, that James Screven, "formerly of James Island, now of Georgia, and Mary, his wife," conveyed to William Royal a tract of land in the southwest part of that island.

The grants of land in Georgia to General Screven were, June 12, 1700, 300 acres in St. David's Parish; August 4th, 1772, 100 acres in St. John's Parish; and January 19th, 1772, 200 acres in St. Paul's Parish.

The political life of General Screven began at Savannah, when, on June 27th, 1774, he was one of a committee of thirty-one members selected "at a meeting of a respectable number of freeholders and inhabitants of the province assembled at the watchhouse in Savannah to prepare resolutions similar to those adopted by the Northern colonies, expressive of the sentiments and determination of this province." He was also a member from St. John's Parish of the Provincial Congress, which met at Savannah, July 1775, at which a number of resolutions were adopted and five persons were elected to "represent the province in the Continental Congress."

General Screven was a member of the Council of Safety from May 23rd, 1776, until October 10th, 1776, when he may have resigned on account of his military duties. He also took the oath on May 23rd, 1776, as one of the three Justices of the Quorum, and on July 22nd, 1776, he was one of thirteen persons who were "recommended and approved of as magistrates for the parish of St. John's." On January 9th, 1776, he was commissioned captain of a company of rangers, afterwards known as the St. John's Rangers.

Captain Screven and his company of rangers were at Savannah March 2nd, 1776, when a British fleet attempted to capture and carry away vessels which were loaded with rice, etc. The authorities directed the dismantling of these vessels by Captain Rice. Not knowing that the British were on board, Captain Rice was captured. Captain Demere, of St. Andrew's Parish, and Lieutenant Daniel Roberts, of the St. John's Rangers, were sent under a flag of truce to apply for Rice's release, but they too were detained. Cannon fire was opened upon the British, when they proposed to treat with two trustworthy officers if sent over. Captain Screven and Captain Baker of the St. John's riflemen were selected. With twelve men of the St. John's Rangers, these officers were conveyed by boat to the vessel and demanded the return of the detained officers and Captain Rice. Captain Baker fired at some one on board the vessel, who used an insulting remark, when the British returned the fire and continued to do so until the boat's party was out of range, one man being wounded. Fire was then opened between the Yamacraw Bluff battery and the British troops on the merchant vessels, lasting about four hours. One of the vessels was set on fire and turned loose from its moorings by volunteers. The flames on this vessel spread to others. Two vessels escaped damage by the fire. The British soldiers on these two were ordered ashore and detained prisoners of Captain Screven in the country. For this event refer to Jones' Hist. of Ga., Vol. II, pp. 226-227.

At a meeting of the Council of Safety, June 21st, 1776, it was "ordered that his Excellency, the President, do issue orders to Colonel Screven in order to draught part of the militia to bring the cannon from Frederica." On July 2nd, 1776, he is "ordered to support Lieutenant-Colonel McIntosh with a sufficient number of his men to make a stand against the troops of Indians;" on July 30th, 1776, "ordered that Colonel McIntosh, Colonel Screven, Captain Baker, and Captain Woodriffe be recommended to go as volunteers to East Florida, and that his Excellency do issue orders accordingly."

In referring to Colonel and Brigadier General Samuel Elbert's

Order Book, April 8th, 1777, Colonel Screven is mentioned as
"President of the last general court martial;" on June 21st,
1777, he is "Colonel of the third regiment of Continental
troops;" on January 27th, 1778, "Colonel James Screven, commanding at Savannah;" on March 17th, 1778, Brigade Orders
Headquarters, Savannah, "James Screven, Colonel, Commandant;" therefore acting Brigadier-General; and on May 25th,
1778, Camp at Fort Howe, "the following promotions have
taken place in the Georgia Brigade, ...Lieutenant-
Colonel Stirk of the second battalion, Colonel of the third vice
Screven, resigned 21st of March." Up to the latter date, from
January 2nd, 1776, Colonel Screven had been actively employed
on duty at points from the Savannah to the Satilla River.

It is not known when Colonel Screven was commissioned a
Brigadier-General. It probably occurred soon after his resignation of the Colonel's commission, May 25th, 1778. Histories give an account in the experience as General Screven,
upon the approach of Lieutenant-Colonel Prevost and his troops
of one hundred regulars and three hundred refugees and Indians
under McGirth from East Florida towards Midway Church.
Colonel Prevost after entering the Georgia settlements on
November 19th, 1778, encountered the first resistance, Friday,
November 20th, by Colonel John Baker and some mounted
militia at the point where the Savannah and Darien road crosses
the Bulltown swamp in Liberty County. The Americans retreated, Colonel Baker, Captain Cooper and William Gould-
ing being wounded. The next resistance, Saturday, November
21st, was at North Newport Bridge, afterwards called Rice-
borough Bridge. Meanwhile, Colonel John White had concentrated one hundred Continentals and militia with artillery, "at
Midway meeting house," and "thrown up a slight breastwork
across the road at the head of the causeway over which the enemy
must advance. On the morning of November 22nd, Colonel

White was joined by General Screven with twenty militia men. It was resolved to abandon their position and occupy a new one a mile and a half south of the meeting house where the road was skirted by a thick wood in which it was thought an ambuscade might be advantageously laid. McGirth being well acquainted with the country and knowing the ground held by Colonel White, suggested to Prevost the expediency of placing a party in ambush at the very point selected by the Americans for a similar purpose."

"The contending parties arrived upon the ground almost simultaneously and firing immediately commenced. Early in the action the gallant General Screven, renowned for his patriotism and beloved for his virtues, received a severe wound, fell into the hands of the enemy, and was by them killed while a prisoner and suffering from a mortal hurt." Jones' Hist. of Ga., Vol. II, p. 306.

Ramsay's "History of the Revolution of South Carolina" says that "General Screven received a wound from a musket ball, in consequence of which he fell from his horse. After he fell, several of the British came up, and upbraiding him with the manner in which Captain Moore of Browne's Rangers had been killed, discharged their pieces at him."

Judge Charlton in his Life of General James Jackson, after referring to Dr. Ramsay's statement, says: "My notes and memoirs afford me an account somewhat different. They inform me that the General was on foot reconnoitering in a thicket on the left flank of the enemy's position on Spencer's Hill. On this spot an ambuscade had been formed and he fell in the midst of it."

Benjamin Baker in "Published Records of Midway Church," says: "Sabbath morning, 22nd. Our party retreated yesterday to the meeting-house, where a recruit of some hundreds joined them with some artillery, and some of our party crossed the swamp, and coming near a thicket where they expected an ambuscade might probably be, Colonel James Screven and one more went forward to examine, the Colonel and one Continental officer and Mr. Judah Lewis were shot down. The Colonel had three wounds, the other two were killed. A flag was sent and brought off the Colonel. Monday, 23rd. We hear the Colonel still lives."

McCall relates that Colonel White sent a flag to Colonel Prevost by Major John Habersham requesting permission to furnish General Screven with such medical aid as his situation might require. The American Doctors were permitted to attend him, but his wounds were found to be of such a nature that they could not save him.

The following extracts are from letters of Colonel J. White and Lieutenant-Colonel J. Prevost:

CAMP MIDWAY, November 22nd, 1778.

SIR:—General Screven and Mr. Strother having been missing since the skirmish with your troops, I have sent Major John Habersham to know whether they have fallen, or are prisoners in your hands; and if in the former case to request that their corpse may be permitted to be brought in for interment.

I am Sir, with proper respect, etc.,

J. WHITE, C. C.

Lieutenant-Colonel J. Prevost, Commander of the King's Troops.

The reply of Colonel Prevost is:

"ST. JOHN'S PARISH, November 22nd, 1778.

SIR:—I had the honor of yours relating to Brigadier-General Screven and Mr. Strother. The former I am happy to inform you is likely to do well from the report of the Surgeon, the other I believe, is dead,—I shall give directions for his burial.

P. S.—Brigadier-General Screven being desirous to return, I was glad to send him when he could meet with proper assistance. I am really unhappy to hear from him that one of the rangers shot him after he was already disabled. Captain Muttac whom I send with him with eight men, has orders to deliver him safe in your camp, and to return immediately. I beg he may not be detained . Your flag was detained no longer than to give attendance to the General."

Tradition adds to the facts already narrated that General Screven was taken from the Midway Church Vestry-House to the dwelling of the patriot John Winn, Sr., which was about two miles eastward of the church and thence to the dwelling of the patriot John Elliott, Sr., which was about six miles from Screven's Hill. The burial place of General Screven in Midway burial ground is said to be in its northeast corner and under the northern wall, about two feet from a grave marked by a marble headstone, upon which is this inscription: "This stone marks the spot where by the side of her renowned brother, General James Screven, are deposited the remains of Mrs. Elizabeth Lee, etc."

There is a tradition that General Screven's widow, soon after his death, died while on the way to her relatives in South Carolina. One of their sons, Rev. Charles O. Screven, in a letter now extant and dated Sunbury, November 13th, 1826, states: "While my father was endeavoring with others to repress the progress of an overpowering enemy, in which he fell a victim, his dwelling and furniture, with the exception of a few valuable papers, rescued by his family, were entirely consumed by the enemy as soon as they came to it."

On September 20th, 1781, Congress passed a resolution requesting the Georgia Legislature at the expense of the general government to erect a monument to General Screven costing not more than $500.00. The resolution was not carried into effect but an interesting paper is here produced.

HOUSE OF ASSEMBLY, February 20th, 1784.

Whereas, the late General James Screven, served as Colonel in the Georgia line of the Continental Army for a considerable time and afterwards distinguished himself by repeated exertions as a militia officer, against the Common Enemy, and at last fell bravely fighting for his country,

Therefore Resolved, that his two only surviving daughters, viz: Hester and Mary, be entitled to a grant of one thousand acres of land each. To be run and surveyed on some part of lands reserved for the officers of the army.

Extract from Minutes. JOHN WILKINSON, C. G. A."

On December 14th, 1793, Screven County was laid out from Burke and Effingham and named in honor of General James Screven. In 1899, by direction of the President of the United States, the name of the fortifications and military reservation on Tybee Island was changed to Fort Screven also in honor of General Screven.

Thus have the virtues of this citizen of Georgia been honored by his neighbors of the parish of St. John, by historians, by the state of his adoption and by the United States.

T. F. SCREVEN.

William Stephens.

WILLIAM STEPHENS was the son of Sir William Stephens, Baronet, Lieutenant-Governor of the Isle of Wight, at which place the subject of this sketch was born, January 28th, 1671, O. S. When a boy he was remarkable for his amiable disposition. The rudiments of education he obtained at Winchester School, from which he was sent to King's College, Cambridge; and after his graduation, he was entered at the Middle Temple, in London, although he was never called to the Bar.

In his twenty-fifth year, he married a daughter of Sir Richard Newdigate. About a year after his marriage, he represented the town of Newport in Parliament. At this time, he held several offices, was highly esteemed among his neighbors, and was often called to decide their differences. In 1712, he was appointed a Commissioner of the Victualling. After this, Colonel Horsey made him an offer to go to South Carolina to survey a barony of land. Upon his arrival in Charlestown, he was received very courteously. Here he became acquainted with General Oglethorpe, at whose recommendation, in August, 1737, he was appointed Secretary to the Trustees in Georgia, and arrived in Savannah the following November. His office was to take a general oversight of affairs. In religion he was opposed to Wesley and Whitfield and often commented on their doings and preaching with great severity. In 1741, he was made President of the County of Savannah, and in 1743, President of the whole Colony. He was over seventy years when he entered upon this office; and the infirmities of age, hastened upon him by private misfortunes and domestic bereavements, soon incapacitated him for his duties. He was called upon in 1750, by his assistants, who frankly stated the difficulties under which they labored, resulting from his age and incapacity. The venerable President immediately comprehended their intentions and told them to proceed without him; "that he would soon retire into the country where he should be at liberty to mind the more weighty things of a future state; not doubting but the Trustees would enable him to end his few remaining days without care and anxiety." He died in August, 1753, at the age of four score years.

Colonel Stephens kept a journal which commences on the 20th of October, 1737, and comes down to October 28th, 1741. Of this Journal the Rev. Thaddeus Mason Harris, in his Biography of General Oglethorpe, thus speaks: "It gives a minute account of everything which occurred, and bears throughout the marks of correctness, ingenuousness, and frankness in the narrative of transactions and events, and of integrity, strict justice, and unflinching fidelity in the discharge of his very responsible office. As exhibiting 'the form and pressure of the times,' it is of essential importance to the historian of Georgia, and happily, it was printed, making three octavo volumes. But the work is exceedingly rare, especially the third volume. A complete set is among the Ebeling books in Harvard College Library." In the library of the Georgia Historical Society there is a book called "The Castle Builders; or the History of William Stephens"—a very rare work, written by his son.

[Stephens Journal was published in 1906, by the State of Georgia as the fourth volume of the Colonial Records of Georgia.] *White's Historical Collections.*

Daniel Stewart.

N O history of Georgia would be complete without the name of Daniel Stewart, the soldier, patriot, and Christian gentleman. He was born in St. John's Parish on the 20th of October, 1761, and received only a limited education. At the early age of 15, he shouldered his musket in defense of home and liberty. A few months later, while standing guard on a very cold night at St. Mary's, Georgia, Colonel Baker, while making his rounds, perceived his youth, and taking off his own cloak, wrapped it around him.

Stewart afterwards joined Captain Youngblood's company and was wounded by a sabre and captured at Pocataligo, South Carolina. He was carried to the Prison Ship in Charleston, from which he made his escape through the port holes one stormy night with eight others. He was pulled through by his companions and, being a large man, was seriously injured.

He belonged to the famous commands of Sumter and Marion, and suffered during the remainder of the war from the injury to his shoulders, which he received when pulled through the port holes of the British man-of-war; but he remained actively in the service to the end. When the war had ceased, and he had returned to his home, he was again called into service to command a regiment against the Indians, who were robbing the settlers along the coast of cattle and horses, pillaging houses, and murdering families. His territory extended from the Savannah river to Florida, and no man connected with our early history more richly deserves the thanks of his people than this noble Christian soldier and patriot. He was ever ready to serve his country and state and frequently represented his county in the legislature. He was a presidential elector and voted for President Madison.

When General Washington visited Savannah, in 1791, he was placed on a committee of the Midway Church and Society, formerly St. John's Parish, to carry General Washington an address. After expressing their attachment for General Washington in person, the communication reads: "To the troops stationed on our frontiers by your order, and to the treaty lately concluded with the Creek nation under your auspices, we are indebted, under providence, for our present tranquility. The hatchet is now buried, and we smoke with our Indian neighbors the calumet of peace. This, while it affords a happy presage of our future protection, gives at the same time, a recent proof of how justly you have earned in your civil, as well as military capacity, the glorious title of Father of your Country. With the laurel then, be pleased to accept the civic wreath from a grateful people." General Washington replied in his modest language, and ended his communication with this sentence: "A knowledge of your happiness will lighten the cares of my station, and be among the most pleasing of their rewards."

On his return home after the Revolutionary War, he found that his Tranquil Plantation, which was his home place, and is situated one and a half miles from Riceboro, had been occupied by General Prevost, commanding the British troops in the South, and his officers; and on the wall of the sitting-room, he found, branded on the boards: "This house was the home of a nest of rebels." This brand remained on the wall until a few years before our Confederate war, when Dr. Samuel Way, who owned the property, destroyed it while making repairs. The British, hearing that a pot of gold had been buried on this plantation spent much time in digging but without success. This historic home was destroyed by Federal troops during the war between the states, and now only the chimneys remain.

> " The garden with its arbor gone,
>   And gone the orchard green;
> A shattered chimney stands alone,
>   Possessor of the scene."

In 1797, the court-house and jail of Liberty County were moved from Sunbury to Riceboro. General Stewart, assisted by Henry Wood and Thomas Stevens had laid out a town there.

In the second war with Great Britain, in 1812, General Stewart again took the field to meet the foes of his country, and the office of Brigadier-General of cavalry was created and given to him.

In General Stewart's private life, his virtues were most conspicuous. He was a devoted husband and father, a useful citizen, a most merciful master, and an honored member of the Midway Church. He died May, 1820, at the age of 68, and his sacred dust rests in the Midway Church-yard.

In recognition of his military services, Georgia has perpetuated his name by calling one of her counties Stewart after him. His daughter, Martha, called Patsie, first married U. S. Senator, John Elliott, and after his death, she married James S. Bulloch. Mattie, daughter of this alliance, married Theodore Roosevelt, Sr., whose son, Theodore Roosevelt, is now President of the United States. This makes General Stewart the great-grandfather of the President.

WM. BERRIEN BURROUGHS, M.D.

Samuel Stirk.

M R. STIRK is believed to have been a native of Savannah, Georgia. He there resided and was a practitioner of law when he first attracted public notice.

Of the Executive Council chosen in 1777—when John Adam Treutlen, defeating Button Gwinnett, was elected first Republican Governor of Georgia—Benjamin Andrew was complimented with the Presidency, and Samuel Stirk was appointed Clerk.

By the Assembly convened in August he was, on the 16th of August, 1781, elected a Delegate from Georgia to the Continental Congress. By the same Legislature he was honored with the position of Attorney-General of Georgia, and to this office he was re-elected in January, 1783. Simultaneously with this latter appointment, he was named as a Commissioner on the part of the State to negotiate with Governor Patrick Tonyn, of East Florida, for the accommodation of all differences and the prevention of further disturbances along the line of the river St. Mary.

Among the Justices of Chatham County his name appears in 1786, and also in 1789. During the last-mentioned years he was President of the Board of Wardens of Savannah.

In 1778 and 1779, he was in the military service of the State and Confederation; and, with the rank of Lieutenant-Colonel, participated in the ill-starred expedition launched by President Gwinnett against East Florida.   C. C. JONES, JR.

Josiah Tattnall.

TATTNALL COUNTY commemorates a name which has been an important one in Georgia history. The first of the name in Georgia, Josiah Tattnall, came from Charleston, South Carolina, in 1762, and settled at Bonaventure, in Christ church parish, now Chatham county. His picture, now in the possession of his great-grand son, Captain John R. F. Tattnall of Savannah, bespeaks the English gentleman of that period. While he was a staunch Loyalist and could not bring himself to take up arms against the mother country, he was, at the same time, opposed to the oppressive measures of Great Britain. On his refusal to take up arms, at the outbreak of the Revolution, he was compelled to leave Georgia and his estates were confiscated by the patriot government.

His son, Josiah Tattnall, the subject of this sketch, was born on his grandfather, Colonel Mullryne's place, Bonaventure, below Savannah, in 1764. Though only eleven years old at the beginning of hostilities with England, he was loyal to his native colony. In January, 1776, he was carried by his father to Nassau, New Providence, Bohamia Islands, and shortly afterwards to England. Here he was entered at Eaton School under the direct personal supervision of his father.

The atmosphere of the schoolroom, however, did not eradicate from young Tattnall's brave heart the desire to return to his native Georgia. To preclude, what he thought would be, the possibility of such a course, his father transferred him to a British man-of-war, bound for India, and the captain of which was his personal friend, with the hope that the lad might with this association be estranged from his allegiance to the cause of American freedom. Though favored with the patronage of the captain and assured of rapid promotion if he remained in the service, he never swerved from his determination to return to Georgia at the first opportunity. Even while under the British flag, our young patriot was not careful to conceal his sentiments. As a result of his outspoken sympathy for the cause of American liberty, he, at one time, had a quarrel and fought a duel in which he wounded his antagonist.

The vessell's destination having been changed to the American Coast, put in at Port Royal, South Carolina, and without the knowledge of his father, young Tattnall procured a little money from his godfather, a Mr. Elliott, a resident of South Carolina, and made his way back to his native state. Thus it happened, that at the age of 18, near the close of the Revolution, Mr. Tattnall found himself on the north bank of the Savannah river, homeless and penniless. Undaunted, he traveled alone on foot through the country to Purysburg, in South Carolina. There he crossed to the Georgia side. Still pressing forward, he joined the troops under General Anthony Wayne at Ebenezer. This was in 1782, and the war was practically at an end. It was through no fault of his that Mr. Tattnall had failed to take part in the great struggle.

Upon the evacuation of Savannah by the British, in July, 1782, Mr. Tattnall was placed in command of the White Bluff District. In 1787, our subject, now a captain at the head of a detachment of light infantry, participated in the successful expedition under Colonel James Gunn against the fortified camp of a body of insurrectionary slaves on Abercorn Creek. These black brigands had received some military training and experience from the British during the siege of Savannah. Being armed, several hundred in number and urged on by their vengeful leaders, their murders and depredations had gone unpunished till this time.

In 1788 and again in 1793, he organized detachments of militia which were sent from Chatham into the counties of Bryan, Liberty, and McIntosh, where the Creek Indians had become troublesome. In 1792, he was advanced to the captaincy of the Chatham Artillery and the following year was promoted colonel of the first Georgia Regiment. His crowning military honor was conferred on him in 1801, when he was made Brigadier-General of the first brigade of the first division of the Georgia state militia.

General Tattnall's civil life was quite as honorable and successful as his military career. He was frequently in the Georgia legislature which then met at Louisville. In 1796, he assisted in passing the act rescinding the Yazoo Fraud of the previous session. In February, 1796, he was by that body elected to the United States Senate to succeed General James Jackson, resigned. He took his seat April 12th, 1796.

On the expiration of his term in 1799, he retired to private life. Such was his popularity, however, that in 1801, he was elected Governor of Georgia. Thus in less than twenty years, this great son of Georgia, whom we saw homeless and penniless on the banks of the Savannah had represented his State in the United States Senate and was now called to her chief magistracy. As a further mark of the state's appreciation of his public services, the decree of banishment against his father was repealed and he was invited to return to Georgia. He did not avail himself of the invitation, however, and died in England.

After serving the state a year as chief magistrate, Governor Tattnall's health failed so completely that he was compelled to resign his office in November, 1802. He repaired to the

Bahama Islands, hoping that the change would benefit his failing constitution; but it was too late. After languishing for a year and a half, he died at Nassau, New Providence.

His dying request was that his body should be removed to his native state. The Hon. Nathaniel Hall, of Nassau, to whom the management of his affairs was committed, complied with his last wishes, and accompanied his remains to Georgia and deposited them in the family burial ground at Bonaventure.

No picture of him has been preserved.

JOHN R. F. TATTNALL.

Edward Telfair.

ONE of the most accomplished and successful of Georgia's distinguished men was Edward Telfair. A zealous patriot of the Revolution, twice governor of his state, a representative in the national Congress, and a man of wealth, ability and influence, he was one of the most prominent figures of his times. He was born in Scotland in 1735, on the farm of Town Head, the ancestral estate of the Telfairs, and he received his English education at the grammar school of Kirkcudbright. He afterwards received a thorough commercial training, which was the basis of much of his subsequent success in managing the affairs of state entrusted to him, and in the accumulation of a large private fortune. At the age of twenty-three he came to America as the representative of a business house, and for a time he lived in Virginia. From this state, he removed to Halifax, North Carolina, and afterwards, in 1766, he settled in Savannah, Georgia. Here he soon established a successful business, and became well known for his honesty, thrift, and ability.

When the storm of the Revolution began to gather upon the political horizon, Mr. Telfair promptly took sides with the patriots, and became one of the most prominent men in their councils at this critical period. On July 27th, 1774, he was placed upon a committee to draw up resolutions assuring the other colonies of Georgia's determination to resist the unjust acts of Great Britain. He was also on a committee to solicit and forward supplies for the relief of the suffering patriots in Boston during the operation of the infamous Boston Port Bill.

On December 8th, 1774, he was elected as a delegate to the

Provincial Congress, which assembled on the 18th, of the following January.

On the 10th of May, 1775, the news of the battle of Lexington reached Savannah, and created the profoundest excitement. Impressed with the importance of securing at once every means of military defense possible, Edward Telfair, Dr. Noble W. Jones, Joseph Habersham, William Gibbons, Joseph Clay, John Milledge, and some others, most of whom were members of the Council of Safety, on the night of May 11th, broke open the powder magazine in Savannah and took therefrom about six hundred pounds of powder. This powder was concealed till needed, and a tradition states that a portion of it was sent to Massachusetts and used in the battle of Bunker Hill.

Mr. Telfair was elected a member of the Council of Safety June 21st, 1775, and in the Provincial Congress, which met in Savannah, July 4th, 1775, he took his seat as a delegate from the "Town and District of Savannah." He served on important committees of this congress, and on December 11th, he was reelected as a member of the Council of Safety by that body.

In February, 1778, he was chosen as a delegate from Georgia to the Continental Congress, and, with the exception of one leave of absence, he remained a member of this distinguished body until January, 1783. In May, 1785, he was again reelected to this congress, but it is probable that he did not take his seat. His business training rendered his services specially valuable in the domain of finance, and his sound judgment was much respected in the Continental Congress. His name is affixed to the "Articles of Confederation."

On January 9th, 1786, he became Governor of Georgia, and he discharged the duties of the Chief Magistracy with great ability and dignity. The finances of the state at that time were in an embarrassing condition, and Governor Telfair devoted much of his great business skill to this situation.

He was a prominent member of the State Convention which ratified the Constitution of the United States in 1789.

On November 9th, 1789, Mr. Telfair was again called to the office of Chief Executive of the state, being the first governor elected under the new constitution. It was during his second administration that President George Washington visited Georgia, and in May, 1791, Governor Telfair in the most gracious manner welcomed and entertained this distinguished visitor at his home in Augusta, at that time the capital of the state.

The following letter from General Washington addressed to Governor Telfair upon his departure shows his appreciation for the honors and courtesies bestowed upon him:

"Augusta, 20th May, 1791.

To His Excellency Edward Telfair,

Governor of Georgia:

Sir,—Obeying the impulse of a heartfelt gratitude, I express with particular pleasure my sense of obligations which your Excellency's goodness and the kind regard of your citizens have conferred upon me. I shall always retain a most pleasing remembrance of the polite and hospitable attentions which I have received in my tour through the state of Georgia, and during my stay at the residence of your government.

"The manner in which you are pleased to recognize my public services, and to regard my private felicity, excites my sensibilty and claims my grateful acknowledgements. Your Excellency will do justice to the sentiments which influence my wishes by believing that they are sincerely offered for your personal happiness and the prosperity of the state over which you preside.   George Washington."

When Governor Telfair retired from his official position in 1793, he returned to Savannah where the remainder of his life was spent in the management of his extensive private business, in works of charity, and in the counsels of public bodies on important occasions. Here on September 19th, 1807, at the age of seventy-two years he died, and was buried with every honor due to his long and useful life. His body was interred in the family vault in the old Colonial Cemetery in Savannah, and many years afterwards the remains were removed to Bonaventure cemetery, where they now repose.

The will of Governor Telfair contains the following clause: "I do hereby require and direct my said executors to cause my remains to be placed in a rough wooden coffin with common nails in it, with black crape only for such as may incline to mourn."

Governor Telfair married on May 18th, 1774, Miss Sallie Gibbons, daughter of William Gibbons, Esq. Their children were Josiah G., Thomas, Alexander, Mary, and Margaret. Thomas was a member of congress from 1813 to 1817. Margaret married W. B. Hodgson, of Savannah.

A large portion of the Telfair estate was finally distributed by Miss Mary Telfair and Mrs. Hodgson in public benefactions. Among these are the Telfair Academy of Arts and Sciences, the Telfair Hospital, the library building of the Georgia Historical Society now used as a public library, the Mary Telfair Home for aged women, Bethesda Orphan Home, and the Independence Presbyterian Church,—all in Savannah.

By these generous bequests and by the name of a county in Georgia the memory of the Telfair family is fitly perpetuated by the grateful people of the state.

OTIS ASHMORE.

Tomo-chi-chi.

TOMO-CHI-CHI, the Indian warrior, was the friend and protector of the infant colony of Georgia. Words are inadequate to express the debt of gratitude that Georgia owes to this brave, wise red man. Without his aid and friendship, General Oglethorpe's little colony would have been annihilated or driven from the Savannah river. Whereas, with it, this isolated little band of one hundred and thirty souls has grown to be a great state with two and a half million people.

Early historians tell us of the great brutality and murderous deeds of this cruel, cunning, and relentless race; in the present age, we learn more of their valor, eloquence, and good laws. Few men of Tomo-chi--chi's day possessed his wisdom, discretion, and farsightedness. After a brief conversation with General Oglethorpe, he realized the power of the white race, and explained to his tribe that an association with the English meant the uplifting and improvement of the Indian nations. His pledges of good-will were always met with fidelity.

We first find his name mentioned in Charleston, South Carolina, July 8th, 1721, when he represented the town of Pallachucolas, one of the Lower Creek towns. He was one of the contracting parties in the "Articles of Friendship and Commerce" between General Johnson of South Carolina, representing King George, II., and the different tribes constituting the Lower and Upper Creek towns. His name on the records is spelled *To-Mee-Chey.*

He stood high in his connections; the King of the Etiahitas was his brother, and Ouee-Kachumpa, the Mico of the Oconas, in his conversation with General Oglethorpe, claimed him as his cousin, and always spoke of him as a good man, who had been a great warrior.

Having had some disagreement with his tribe, he left them and, with some disaffected warriors of the Yamasee and Lower Creek Indians, settled on the highland of Yamacraw near the present city of Savannah. Here General Oglethorpe first met him after he landed on that memorable 12th of February, 1733, as a single representative of the "Trustees for establishing the Colony of Georgia in America." We are told that he lost no time in seeking a personal interview with this Mico of the Yamacraws at his headquarters at Yamacraw Town, but a short distance from where General Oglethorpe landed. He is spoken of as a man of commanding presence, marked character, great influence, undaunted courage, natural ability, and wonderful military knowledge in the rude arts of war.

On the 18th of May, 1773, with Mr. Wiggan as an interpreter, General Oglethorpe met at Savannah representatives of all the tribes of the Lower Creek nations, consisting of their Micos, head warriors, and war captains. These eight tribes claimed all the land from the Savannah river to St. Augustine, and up the Flint river which falls into the Gulf of Mexico. All the Lower Creeks speak the same language. Being seated, Ouee-Kachumpa, from the tribe of the Oconas and cousin to Tomo-chi-chi, a very tall old man, and with graceful action and good voice said: "He that gave the English breath gave his people breath also; that he gave the English more wisdom and had sent them to enlighten his people and their families; therefore his tribe and all the others would give the English all the land that they did not use themselves; that they had consulted together and had sent their head men with skins, which was their wealth." He then stopped. The head men from each tribe brought buckskins, and eight bundles from the eight tribes were laid at General Oglethorpe's feet.

Tomo-chi-chi then came in with the Indians of Yamacraw, and bowing very low, said: "I was a banished man and came here to look for good land near the tombs of my ancestors, and the Trustees sent people here. I feared you would drive us away, but you have been good to us and gave us food and will instruct our children. We will love your people and with them we will live and die." He sat down, and the Yahou-Lakee, Mico of the Coweta tribe, stood up and said: "We came twenty-five days' journey to see you. You have comforted the banished and gathered them that were scattered like little birds by the eagle." Then he spoke about the abatement of the price of goods and agreed upon the articles of a treaty. Tomo-chi-chi invited them to his town, where they passed the night in feasting and dancing. On the 21st of May, 1733, the treaty was signed. To each Indian chief a laced coat and laced hat and a shirt were given; to each warrior, a gun and a mantle of duffel; and to all the others, coarse cloth for clothing, gun-powder, kegs of bullets, tobacco, eight kegs of rum, and many other things were given to carry home to their different tribes.

General Oglethorpe says, that in Tomo-chi-chi's first set speech to him Tomo-chi-chi gave him a buffalo skin painted on the inside with the head and feathers of an eagle, saying, "Here is a little present. The eagle signifies speed and the buffalo strength. The English are as swift as the bird and as strong as the beast, since, like the first, they flew from the uttermost parts of the earth, over vast seas, and, like the second, nothing could withstand them. The feathers of the eagle are soft and signify love; the buffalo skin is warm and signifies protection, therefore, I hope you will love and protect our little families."

The most unmatched letter that ever adorned the Georgia office in Westminster was written by a Cherokee chief upon a neatly dressed skin of a young buffalo; it was the admiration of fifty chiefs. The unique epistle expressed the grateful acknowledgment that the Indians felt for the kindness shown to Tomo-chi-chi and his friends, and also their admiration of the grandeur and greatness of their King George and of his power, wealth, and influence. Upon its receipt, a resolution was passed that this hieroglyphic painting be framed and hung in a conspicuous place.

In April, 1734, General Oglethorpe returned to England and carried with him Tomo-chi-chi, Lanauka, his wife, Tooma-Howi, his nephew and adopted son, and other Indian kings. They accepted the hospitality of General Oglethorpe at his own country seat and visited many places of interest. On August 1st, Sir Clement Cotterell conducted the Indians to Kensington Palace, where they were presented to the king. They were conveyed in three of the king's coaches, each drawn by six horses. A most interesting account of this visit and the speeches that were made, is given in the "Gentlemen's Magazine." Tomo-chi-chi was greatly impressed with the power, greatness, and wealth of the English Empire; nothing escaped his attention. He expressed surprise that short-lived people should build such substantial houses. His return trip was made in the *Prince of Wales,* and on the 27th of December, 1734, they cast anchor at Savannah Bluff. The value of the presents that they brought home was over two thousand dollars.

In March, 1735, Tomo-chi-chi, with forty warriors, waited upon General Oglethorpe at Frederica and insisted that they show him the precise boundary lines dividing the lands the Creeks had ceded to the English and separating them from the Spanish domains. Arriving at the south end of Wasso Island, they encamped that night, and Tooma-Howi, holding in his hand a self-repeating watch, which the Duke of Cumberland had given him, changed the name of the Island to Cumberland, saying, "We will remember him at all times." The island still bears that name. This brave nephew of Tomo-chi-chi was with General Oglethorpe in his expedition against St. Augustine. Later he made an attack to the very walls of this ancient city and captured Don Romaulda, captain of the Spanish horse and nephew of the Spanish governor. Later still we find him in the battle of Bloody Marsh where Captain Mageleto shot him in the right arm. He drew his pistol with his left hand and shot the captain dead.

Tomo-chi-chi died at his own town four miles from Savannah, October 10th, 1739, aged ninety-seven years. He desired that his body be buried among his friends, the English. General Oglethorpe and all the people of the town met the body at Savannah Bluff. The pallbearers were General Oglethorpe, Colonel Stephens, Colonel Montaigut, Mr. Carteret, Mr. Lemon, and Mr. Maxwell. Great respect was shown at his funeral; minute guns were fired from the battery. He was buried in Wright's Square.

The Colonial Dames of Georgia have erected a boulder to his memory made from North Georgia rock. It stands between the Court House and the Post Office and Custom House in Savannah and bears the following inscription: "In memory of Tomo-chi-chi, the Mico of the Yamacraws, the companion of Oglethorpe and the friend and ally of the Colony of Georgia. This stone has been here placed by the Georgia Society of the Colonial Dames of America.—1739-1899.

WM. BERRIEN BURROUGHS, M.D.

John Adam Treutlen.

JOHN ADAM TREUTLEN was the first Governor of the State of Georgia. There is but little information available with reference to him that is sufficiently well authenticated to be called history. He was an official member of the church of the Salzburgers at Ebernezer before the war of the Revolution began, as his name appears among the twelve deacons of that church during the pastorates of Rabenhorst and Tribner. He was a citizen of that part of Effingham county which was then St. Matthews' parish and his home was about eight miles above Ebenezer, in the immediate neighborhood of Sister's Ferry. His identification with the Ebenezar congregation is the only indication that he was a Salzburger unless it be his name, which has a German sound. Other evidences, such as the personal characteristics of his descendants, point toward English origin, though there is no documentary evidence to this effect. Nothing is definitely known of his history prior to the Revolution. The records of his youth, the time of his arrival in Georgia, and his activities as a private citizen have all been lost to the historian. His subsequent history has fared but little better; for, while he was a conspicuous figure among the Georgia patriots and was called to the chief magistracy of the State during the most eventful period of her history, there has been no one to record the date, place, and manner of his death. The fact that he took his place as a member of the Provincial Congress of 1775, among such men as Walton, Habersham, Bryant, Telfair, Houstoun, Clay, Cuthbert, and McIntosh and was later selected from among these as Governor of the new state, on whom, from the very nature of the case, it was necessary to confer almost arbitrary power, would indicate that he was a man of unquestioned patriotism and unusual powers. His executive council consisted of the following: Jonathan Bryan, John Houstoun, Thomas Chisholm, William Holzendorf, John Fulton, John Jones, John Walton, William Few, Arthur Fort, John Coleman, Benjamin Andrews, and William Peacock.

During his administration, an effort was made on the part of South Carolina to induce Georgia to surrender her individuality and become a part of the former. Many citizens of Georgia had become interested in the project through the commissioners of South Carolina, one of the most prominent of which was a Mr. Drayton. It required great firmness on the part of the Governor to meet the emergency, but his courage and energy were equal to the occasion. On the 14th of July, 1777, the Council requested the Governor to offer a reward for the apprehension of Mr. Drayton and those associated with him. Next day, he responded with the following Proclamation:

GEORGIA.

By his Honour John Adam Treutlen, Esquire, Captain-General, Governour, and Commander-in-Chief in and over the said State.

A PROCLAMATION.

Whereas it hath been represented unto me, that William Henry Drayton, Esq., of the State of South Carolina, and divers other persons, whose names are yet unknown, are unlawfully endeavoring to poison the minds of the good people of this State against the Government thereof, and for that purpose are, by letters, petitions, and otherwise, daily exciting animosities among the inhabitants, under the pretence of redressing imaginary grievances, which by the said William Henry Drayton it is said this State labours under, the better to effect, under such specious pretences, an union between the states of Georgia and South Carolina, all of which are contrary to the Articles of Confederation, entered into, ratified, and confirmed by this State as a cement of union be-tween the same and the other United and Independent States of America, and also against the resolution of the Convention of this State in that case made and entered into: Therefore, that such pernicious practices may be put to an end, and which, if not in due time prevented, may be of the most dangerous conse-quences, I have, by and with the advice and consent of the Executive Council of this State, thought fit to issue this Procla-mation, hereby offering a reward of One Hundred Pounds, law-ful money of the said State, to be paid to any person or persons who shall apprehend the said William Henry Drayton, or any other person or persons aiding or abetting him in such unlawful practices, upon his or their conviction: And I do hereby strictly charge and require all magistrates and other persons to be vigi-lant and active in suppressing the same, and to take all lawful ways and means for the discovering and apprehending of such offender or offenders, so that he or they may be brought to con-dign punishment.

Given under my Hand and Seal in the Council Chamber at Savannah, this fifteenth day of July, one thousand seven hun-dred and seventy-seven.

JOHN ADAM TREUTLEN.

By His Honour's Command,
    JAMES WHITFIELD, *Secretary.*
    GOD SAVE THE CONGRESS."

On the expiration of his term, January 8th, 1778, he suddenly passes out of Georgia's history to appear no more. Neither his patriotism nor his courage has ever been questioned, and the only satisfactory explanation that has ever been made of his disappearance from subsequent history is a family tradition that he was murdered by Tories. According to this tradition, on a visit to Orangeburgh district, South Carolina, where he had near relatives, he was followed by brutal Tories and murdered in the most horrible manner. He was, it is said, tied to a tree and hacked to pieces with swords in the presence of his family. His body, or what remained of it, was buried, either by the Tories or by his own people at some place, where either from not knowing at first, or from being forgotten amid the troubles of the time, was placed where no one now living knows. Governor Truetlen having in this sad way departed from the scene of action, and it being so long before the close of the war, and having no son or other descendant in the State in public life, he was neglected and forgotten. Georgia to this day owes him the debt of some appropriate recognition. Effingham county records show that the estate of John A. Treutlen—presumably the Governor—was settled in 1784.

Numerous descendants of Governor Treutlen are to be found in Georgia, South Carolina, and Alabama.

A. B. CALDWELL.

John Twiggs.

TWIGGS COUNTY, GEORGIA, is named for one of the bravest soldiers of the Revolution, General John Twiggs, who lived and died in Richmond county. He came to Georgia from Maryland with the family of John Emanuel, whose daughter he married, thus becoming the brother-in-law of Governor David Emanuel. He was of good English ancestry and was a mill-wright by trade.

He early enlisted with the patriot forces. In 1779, after the fall of Savannah, he joined his forces with those of Colonels William and Benjamin Few, the combined forces numbering about two hundred and fifty. They fell upon and, with small loss, defeated four hundred mounted men under Colonel Brown, who was marching to join some Tories under Colonel Thomas in Burke county. Expecting that the enemy would be reenforced and would retaliate, Colonel Twiggs very wisely retired and awaited another opportunity to strike a decisive blow for his country. He did not have to wait long, for Major Harry Sharp and two other Tory leaders from South Carolina, raising a partisan corps, greatly distressed the almost unprotected people of Burke and the neighboring counties. Closely observing the movements of the enemy, till they were seen to encamp in a position favorable for attack, Colonel Twiggs and Captain Joshua Inman rushed to the attack and completely routed them. After the battle of Kettle Creek, Colonels Twiggs, McIntosh, and Hammond surprised seventy British regulars at Herbert and killed or captured the whole detachment.

After General Lincoln's defeat and the consequent confusion of the Americans, Colonel Twiggs and his compatriots, Clarke and Dooly, kept the field and whenever an opportunity offered struck a blow for home and native land.

In 1780, the notorious McGirth and his Tories were laying waste Southeast Georgia. Twiggs and Pickens formed a post on the Ogeechee, which served as a rallying point for the Americans. A body of British troops under Captain Conklin, leaving Savannah before daylight on April 4th, reached the American camp about ten o'clock, but were driven from the field.

His defeat of the grenadiers under Captain Muller at Hickory Hill on the Ogeechee and the rout by him of the party of McGirth, infused new courage into the few remaining faithful patriots.

In 1781, he had attained the rank of General and joined the forces of General Greene, with which he moved southward. He dispersed the Indians and Tory bands at the Big Shoals on the Oconee and for some months gave peace to that section, which had known no peace for so long.

In November, 1783, John Twiggs, Elijah Clarke, Edward Telfair, Andrew Burns, and William Glascock, were appointed a Commission by the state; and made a treaty at Augusta with the Creek Indians, by which the state obtained much new territory. The counties of Washington and Franklin were cut from this territory.

He was also a member of the commission to select a site for the State University somewhere within the bounds of what was then Jackson county.

In the unfortunate stand which General Clarke took after the Revolution, General Twiggs was made intermediary, with General Irwin, between Governor Matthews and General Clarke. His report follows: "I proceeded to the unauthorized settlements on the southwest side of the Oconee River and in the presence of General Elijah Clarke and his party I read the letter from the

War Department to your Excellency, together with Judge Walton's charge to the grand jury of Richmond county and the law opinion of the Solicitor and Attorney-General. After a full explanation of the papers above recited, I entered into a friendly conference with E. Clarke and his adherents, pointing out to them the danger of their enterprise, without the sanction of the State. Notwithstanding all the arguments which could be advanced, they still persisted in their undertaking. Lastly, finding nothing could be done with them, I ordered them to remove within the temporary line between us and the Creek Indians. General Clarke called on his officers to collect the opinion of their men, which they did and gave me for answer that they should maintain their ground at the risk of their lives."

On the expiration of Governor Matthews' term, November 6th, 1795, there was an interregnum till January 2, 1796. Being at that time the oldest Major-General in the State, he was requested to so far assume authority as to convene the Legislature, but after consultation with General James Jackson, he declined to do so.

General Twiggs passed away about the close of the century, leaving behind the heritage of a good name and a family whose members have been an honor to the State.

A. B. CALDWELL.

George Walton.

OF the three signers of the Declaration of Independence from Georgia, the oldest, Lyman Hall, was born in Connecticut and was fifty-two years of age when independence was declared. The next, Button Gwinnett, was born in England about the time Oglethorpe came to Georgia, and was forty-four years of age when he signed the declaration. The youngest of the three was George Walton, who was born in Virginia in 1749 and who was twenty-seven years of age when he signed that great document which made the United States free and independent. Thus we see that not one of the three signers was by birth a Georgian, yet all were most loyal and patriotic citizens.

George Walton was born in Prince Edward County, Virginia, in 1749. He became an orphan when he was a very young child and his guardian did not care to be burdened with bringing him up. While he was a young boy, he was given to a carpenter as an apprentice, was put to hard work, and not allowed to go to school. But young Walton was not to be deterred by this fact from getting an education, so at the end of a hard day's work he would light a fire of shavings or fat pine in the shop and lie down by it and study. What books he read we do not know, but we may be sure they were good books of an improving kind and that he was not throwing away his time on useless literature. The good carpenter seeing him thus occupied, and finding that he did not waste his nights in sport and idleness, allowed him to keep the money he earned, and helped him all he could. He borrowed books from his friends and neighbors and studied all his spare time, until the carpenter relieved him of his apprenticeship and told him he might go where he chose.

He decided to come to Georgia, which was then a new and prosperous colony. By private conveyance he made his way to Savannah when he was twenty years of age and began to practice law. Savannah was then a small town of a few thousand people, while all Georgia was full of Indians, with a white settlement here and there along the rivers or on the coast.

He was received into the law office of Henry Young and studied with the same earnestness that he had always shown, and in a short time was ready for admission to the bar. He attracted attention at once from everybody, for he was a good looking young man, fair in complexion with light hair, rather small in stature, but with great earnestness and dignity of manner. He had in his face the look of a student who was well bred and ambitious, and without any of the bad habits that beset the youth of that day. He came promptly into a good practice of the law, and was employed, in a case of considerable importance by Edward Telfair, who was a citizen of means and afterwards governor of Georgia.

About this time the American colonies were having their disputes with England. The mother country was insisting upon some very oppressive and foolish measures. The British Parliament passed a bill prohibiting any commerce with the town of Boston, another bill that the representatives of the Provincial Council of Massachusetts should no longer be elected by the people but should be appointed by the crown, another that the Royal Governor should have the power of nominating and removing all judges, sheriffs, and other important officers, that the sheriffs should nominate the judges, that no town meeting of the people should be held for any purpose except upon written permission of the Royal Governor, and also that all persons accused of murder or any criminal offense might be sent to England for trial instead of being tried in the colony where the offense was committed. All these measures excited the indignation of the people in America, for they thought them to be oppressive and depriving the people of their just rights.

The people of Georgia were as indignant as any of the colonists at those coercive measures against the northern colonists and a public meeting was held in Savannah at Tondee's Tavern, in August, 1774, and resolutions were passed condemning the act of Parliament and expressing the sympathy of the people of Savannah for the people of Boston and Massachusetts. George Walton was among the most prominent persons and speakers present at this meeting. He was a member of the committee to prepare resolutions and entered earnestly into the proceedings to defend the colonists against the mother country.

Affairs continued to grow more alarming and the following year in June, 1775, a call, signed by George Walton, Noble W. Jones, Archibald Bulloch, and John Houstoun was issued asking the people to meet at the Liberty Pole at ten o'clock in the morning, to take measures to bring about a union of Georgia with her sister colonies in the cause of freedom. The meeting was held, a Council of Safety was organized, of which George Walton was a member, the Union Flag was raised at the Liberty Pole and patriotic speeches were made.

In July, 1775, a congress of representatives from all over Georgia was held in Savannah. Every parish was represented, and measures were adopted putting Georgia in active sympathy and cooperation with all her sister colonies. This Congress has been called "Georgia's first secession Convention," for it declared that the colony was no longer bound by the acts of England, since the mother country was acting unjustly and oppressively. George Walton was present and stood shoulder to shoulder with the ablest and most fearless of the men of that day. Though he was then only twenty-six years of age, yet he was recognized as one of the most able, learned, and patriotic representatives of the convention. Indeed, so able was he that he was selected to prepare a written account of the proceedings and purposes of the Congress to be printed and distributed among the people of Georgia. This address was a model of its kind and its influence was far reaching in bringing all the citizens of the State to an understanding of the true state of affairs. In December, 1775, George Walton became president of the Council of Safety and practically had charge of the colony. The Royal Governor Wright was taken prisoner but escaped, and there was no one left to dispute the authority of the Liberty Boys. The crisis of the American Revolution was rapidly approaching. The colonists were resolved upon justice or freedom. The British Parliament was bent upon stubborn measures that disturbed and inflamed the people of America and the breach between the colonists and the mother country became greater every day .

A Continental Congress, of delegates from every colony was meeting in Philadelphia to agree upon what was best to be done for the common good. George Walton was sent as a delegate to this Congress in 1776. In the meantime war had begun and several battles had been fought. The Revolution was on and the country was aroused. After much discussion and effort at reconciliation it was decided that independence was the only proper course and so July 4th, 1776, a declaration of independence was written by Thomas Jefferson and was signed by all the delegates. The delegates from Georgia who signed this great paper were Lyman Hall, Button Gwinnett, and George Walton. The effect of the Declaration of Independence was to make the American colonies free and independent states. This deepened the war already in progress, brought out all the soldiers of the colonies under George Washington, the great commander, and the happy result was the defeat of the British armies everywhere and the establishment of a great country known as The United States of America.

George Walton was busy all the time. He had thrown himself with great eagerness into the affairs of the colonists. It took a long time to go by stage coach, or on horseback from Savannah to Philadelphia, but he was constantly travelling back and forth, making speeches and encouraging the patriots. In 1777, he was married to Dorothy Camber, a young and beautiful girl to whom he remained devotedly attached all his life. In 1779, after services in the field as a soldier, he was made Governor of Georgia. Then he went back to Philadelphia as a member of the Congress where he stayed until October, 1781. There was no member of the Congress more active or capable than he. He was a member of the Treasury Board, the Committee on Naval Affairs, made treaties with the Indians, and took a great interest in the financial affairs of the young government. In 1778, with Edward Telfair and Edward Langworthy, he signed the Articles of Confederation, which was a provisional constitution of the United States. Thus we see that the young patriot from Georgia had a reputation and a power that extended beyond the limits of his own state.

All of his history however was not confined to legislative actions. In December, 1778, he laid aside his state affairs and became a colonel in the first regiment of Foot Militia for the defence of Georgia. The British were then pressing upon the Southern coast intent upon the capture of Savannah. Colonel Walton with one hundred men was posted on the South common to guard the approach to Great Ogeechee Ferry. General Robert Howe was in command of the American forces and Colonel

Walton had warned him that there was a pass through the swamp by means of which the enemy could attack them in the rear, but General Howe paid no attention to this. The result was that this path was left unguarded, and guided by a negro the enemy found their way to the rear of the American forces and fell upon them with great disaster. Colonel Walton sustained the shock of the enemy with bravery, but he was shot in the thigh, the bone being broken, and falling from his horse was captured by the British. The enemy entered Savannah and held that city captive. Colonel Walton was taken prisoner to Sunbury, where he was well cared for by the British surgeons, until he recovered. His leg healed but he never regained the complete use of it, for he limped thereafter to the end of his life. At last he was exchanged for a British captain of the Navy, and proceeded to Augusta which was then used as the capital of the State. It was soon after his return to Augusta that he was made Governor of Georgia, but the State was so overrun by the British and so little organization was possible among the forces in Georgia that a governor had little to do.

Peace came to the colonists in 1782, and the British forces withdrew from Savannah. America was free and the States were independent. George Walton now turned again to his chosen profession and began to practice law. In 1783, he was made Chief Justice of Georgia, with duty to hold court in each of the eight counties then composing the State. This obliged him to ride by private conveyance or on horseback a great deal of his time, over bad roads in all sorts of weather, to hold court at the various county seats, but he performed his duty faithfully and for seven years was a beloved judge in all parts of Georgia.

In 1789, he was again made Governor of Georgia for a term of one year. During his administration the State remodeled her own constitution. Augusta was still used as the capital, and it was here that George Walton had his home. While he was Governor he received the copy of the Constitution of the United States which had been framed by the delegates from all the states.

In 1791, George Washington visited Augusta and was received by the people with great demonstration of joy and affection. Judge Walton was Chairman of the Committee on reception and presented President Washington with a complimentary address on behalf of the people. The days were spent in parades, public meetings, and entertainments for the beloved guest, for the great Virginian had proven himself to be one of the notable men of all history.

In 1795 and 1796, George Walton was sent as senator to the Congress of the United States. He was prominently interested in education, and was one of the first trustees of the University of Georgia, giving valuable services in forming plans for higher education in the State. For many years and up to the time of his death he was judge of The Middle Circuit of Georgia, embracing the counties of Richmond, Columbia, Jefferson, Screven, Burke, Montgomery, Washington, and Warren.

During the latter part of his life, his home was in Augusta, at a beautiful country place, named "Meadow Garden," the house of which is still standing and dedicated to memorial purposes by the Daughters of the Revolution. A visit to the place will be full of pleasure to any one interested in revolutionary history of the city of Augusta. It was at this home, February 2, 1804, that Judge Walton was taken suddenly ill and died in the fifty-fifth year of his life. He was buried with distinguished honors at Rosney, a burial ground several miles from Augusta. Here his body rested until 1848, when it was reinterred, being brought to Augusta and placed under the monument on Greene Street, in front of the court-house. The body of Lyman Hall was placed there at the same time. The grave of Button Gwinnett could not be located so that only two of the signers of the declaration rest under this stately memorial.

Few men in the United States have received as many honors as George Walton. He was six times elected a representative to Congress, twice Governor of Georgia, once a senator of the United States, four times judge of the Superior Court, once the Chief Justice of the State. He was a commissioner to treat with the Indians, often in the State legislature, member of nearly every important committee on public affairs during his life. His name occurs in the State's annals for over thirty years of eventful and formative history.

He was the grandfather of Octavia Walton, who as Madame LeVert, attained prominence in the social and literary world. She inherited her grandfather's taste for reading and study, illustrating the noblest qualities of her distinguished ancestor.

George Walton was comely in appearance, grave, and dignified. He was a student by nature and loved to spend his hours in his library. He has left us an honored name on the roll of our great statesmen, and his example should inspire us to a greater zeal in discharge of the duties that fall to us as citizens of our great State.

LAWTON B. EVANS.

John Walton.

WITH regard to this member of the old Congress we have been able to gather but little information. A brother of the Honorable George Walton, he was born in Virginia about 1738. To the Provincial Congress which assembled at Savannah on the 4th of July, 1775, he was a Delegate representing the Parish of St. Paul. On the 20th of July of the previous year, in association with Noble W. Jones, Achibald Bulloch, and John Houstoun, he signed the public call which convoked the liberty-loving citizens of Georgia, under the eye and in defiance of the protest of the Royal Governor. Of the Executive Council, chosen when John Adam Treutlen was elected first Republican Governor, he was a member. By the General Assembly of Georgia, Mr. Walton was, on the 26th of February, 1778, commissioned as a Delegate to the Continental Congress.

His home was then at New Savannah, situated in the county of Richmond, on the Savannah River, not many miles below the town of Augusta. Here he owned and cultivated a plantation, the principal market crop of which was indigo. As we write, one of his letters lies before us, written from this place, dated on the 21st of January, 1777, and addressed to the Honorable Edward Telfair. In this communication Mr. Walton advises that gentleman of a shipment of indigo he had recently made to him, and bespeaks his best efforts in effecting advantageous sale of the consignment.

For a number of years Mr. Walton held the office of Surveyor of Richmond County. He died at New Savannah in 1783.

His will is now on file in the Ordinary's office in Augusta. It is dated the 11th of June, 1778, and was admitted to probate on the 24th of June, 1783. George Walton, William Glascock, and Britton Dawson were named as executors. He left a considerable estate, consisting of lands and negroes. The maiden name of his wife was Elizabeth Claiborne. Several children were born of this marriage, and their descendants may be found in Georgia to the present day.   C. C. JONES, JR.

Anthony Wayne.

GENERAL ANTHONY WAYNE, or "Mad Anthony" as he was popularly called on account of the impetuosity of his charges, like a number of great men whom Georgia delights to honor, was not a native of the state. His daring and skilful work in Georgia after the surrender of Lord Cornwallis and his subsequent residence in the state entitle him to a place among these sketches.

He was born in Eastown, Chester County, Pennsylvania, January 1, 1745. His grandfather was a native of England, but lived in Ireland before emigrating to America. His father was Isaac Wayne, a native of Pennsylvania and a well-to-do farmer who represented Chester County in the state legislature several times. He was also prominent among the forces operating against the Indians, who at that time were very troublesome in Pennsylvania.

Young Anthony was sent to school to his uncle and passed from there to the Philadelphia Academy. It is said that the love of military amusements interfered somewhat with his education although he was very successful in his mathematical studies. After leaving school at the age of eighteen, he became a surveyor.

In 1773, he was selected as a representative to the General Assembly where he took a firm stand against the demands of Great Britain. He had long desired a military command, and the Revolutionary War furnished him the opportunity of gratifying his wish. He raised a regiment of volunteers of which he was elected colonel, and afterwards received the appointment of colonel from Congress. He accompanied General

Ant.y Wayne

Thompson to Canada and displayed his military talènts at the battle of Three Rivers. On the 21st of February, he was appointed Brigadier-General and, in the following May joined the army of Washington. He shared in the perils and glories of Brandywine, Germantown, Monmouth, and Stony Point. For the action at Stony Point, the first United States Congress voted General Wayne a gold medal and with it thanks "for his brave, prudent, and soldier-like conduct in the well conducted attack on Stony Point." A similar testimonial was voted him by the General Assembly of his native state.

After the capture of Cornwallis, in which he displayed bravery bordering on rashness, he was sent with seven hundred troops to conduct the war in Georgia. Headley in "Washington and His Generals" gives the following account of his work in Georgia: "The enemy outnumbered him three to one; yet he boldly took the field, and kept it in spite of every effort made against him.

"Fearless, untiring, and indefatigable, he made up in activity and promptness what he lacked in strength; and driving his enemy from one post to another—now hanging on his flanks, and now falling furiously on him in front—he pressed every advantage with such vigor, that in five weeks he had wrested the entire state from his grasp, with the exception of Savannah. But a strange spectacle met his gaze as he advanced. The British, in order to distress him, gathered together, as they fell back, all the provisions and forage, and set fire to them; so that as he slowly moved down the river, all along its winding course, as far as the eye could reach—from the shores and islands, fires were blazing and vast volumes of smoke ascending; rendering the scene at once fearful and picturesque.

"During these five weeks of almost constant marching and fighting, Wayne exhibited a patience and fortitude equal to his intrepidity, and imparted a portion of his spirit to his brave

22

troops, who cheerfully marched wherever he led, and never in the whole time once took off their clothes to rest. In speaking of the difficult task assigned him, in a letter to Greene, he says: 'The duty we have done in Georgia was more difficult than that imposed upon the children of Israel; they had only to make bricks without straw, but we have had provision, forage and almost every other apparatus of war, to procure without money; boats, bridges, etc., to build without materials, except those taken from the stump; and what was more difficult than all, to make Whigs out of Tories. But this we have effected, and have wrested the country out of the hands of the enemy, with the exception only of the town of Savannah. *How to keep it without some additional force is a matter worthy of consideration.*' True enough, worthy of serious 'consideration,' especially how, with a few hundred cavalry and infantry, to blockade this same town of Savannah, containing more than two thousand troops."

"Receiving, however, a small reinforcement, he kept the field and every advantage he had gained. In the meantime, the British commander had induced the Choctaws and Creeks to join him as allies, and they were far on their way before Wayne got word of it. Immediately putting his troops in motion, he fell furiously upon the former, just as they were approaching Savannah and routed them completely. Hearing of this catastrophe, the British commander sent out a strong party of horse and foot to protect the Creeks, now also marching up. Wayne, knowing of a defile across a swamp, over which the detachment must pass, took with him only one company of infantry and a few dragoons and set out for it with all the speed he was master of. Remembering Stony Point he had all the flints knocked out of the muskets, telling his men to rely solely on the bayonet and sabre. The gallant little band pushed rapidly and noiselessly forward, and reached the defile at midmight, when to their surprise they found the enemy already entering it. It was starlight, and Wayne could see by the glittering of the bayonets and sabres, that he was outnumbered two to one; but there was no time for hesitation, and instantly ordering the charge, he poured his enthusiastic troops with such impetuosity on the astonished column, that it broke and fled."

"The Creeks heard of this disaster, but did not prevent their intrepid chieftain from pressing on. Leaving, however, the open country, he kept to the woods and marched so warily that Wayne could get no tidings of him. Stealing thus cautiously through the swamps and forests, he at length, one evening, found himself within a short distance of Wayne's camp. Waiting till all were wrapt in slumber, these stealthy warriors crawled up to the sentinels and dispatched them so silently that the alarm was not given. They then advanced directly upon the camp, and suddenly screaming out their terrific war-whoop, rushed to the attack. With a single bound they swept over the artillery, driving the guard in affright before them, while that thrilling war-cry brought every sleeper to his feet. The men rushed for their arms, but all was terror and confusion. Wayne, however, whom no terror could unbalance, was himself in a moment, and rallying his men like magic, and ordering them not to fire, neither dragoons nor infantry, but trust to their swords and bayonets, led them fiercely against the shouting savages. A tall chief threw himself before him, whom he, with a single stroke of his sword, cut to the earth; but the undaunted warrior lifted with a dying effort his rifle and discharged it at him. His gallant steed sunk dead in his footsteps, but Wayne, springing to his feet, pressed forward on foot amid his men. After a short conflict the savages were routed, and fled leaving their dead chief and thirty warriors behind them. Being now close on Savannah, it occurred to him that the attack was designed to be a combined one, and that the firing of the Indians would be the signal of a sally from the town. Instantly, while everything was in confusion, and the midnight was blazing with musketry and echoing with the war-whoop, he dispatched a company to fall on the English pickets, in order to convey the impression that he had won the battle, and was ready to meet them. A short time after this the British evacuated Savannah, and Wayne rejoined Greene."

Later he occupied Charleston, South Carolina, when that city was evacuated. Peace followed, and broken in health by long exposure he returned to his native state and was elected a member of the legislature. He also served in the convention ratifying the Constitution of the United States in 1785.

In 1786, he removed to Georgia and settled upon a large tract of land which Georgia had confiscated and granted to him "as a recompense for valuable military services in her behalf." He was soon elected a delegate to the Convention of 1787, which made the Constitution of Georgia. In 1791, he was elected one of the three congressmen from Georgia. He served in this capacity from October 1791 to 21st of March, 1792, when his seat was contested by General James Jackson and declared by Congress to be vacant. He was compelled to sell his Georgia property on account of financial embarrassment, but in the transaction lost both land and money.

His military character, however, was established and when President Washington wanted a safe but vigorous man to send against the Indians, he selected Wayne. In the role of Indian fighter he covered himself with glory and when he died at the age of fifty-one, he held the rank of commander-in-chief of the American Army. He now lies buried at his native place, and over his remains stands a monument reared by his brave companions in arms. Georgia has honored him by naming one of her counties for him. R. J. MASSEY.

George Wells.

U NDER the Constitution of 1775, the president of the
executive council succeeded to the chief magistracy of
the state, in case of the death or inability of the governor. Accordingly when Governor Richard Howley left
Georgia in February, 1780, to take his seat in the Continental
Congress at Philadelphia, George Wells who was president of
the council succeeded him as Governor. He bears the distinction of having been Governor of Georgia for the shortest time of
anyone who has ever held the office.

In that day, personal differences were not settled in news-
paper interviews but on the "field of honor" as the meeting
ground of duelists has been called.

Immediately after becoming Governor, Mr. Wells and General James Jackson had a personal difficulty which resulted in
a duel. The Governor fell at the hand of his antagonist, February 17, 1780, having enjoyed the honor of being Governor only
three or four days. He was succeeded by Stephen Heard.

A. B. CALDWELL.

John Wereat.

JOHN WEREAT, the third Governor of the State of Georgia, Chief Justice of the commonwealth, and president of the convention which ratified the Constitution of the United States, was born about 1730, and it is believed was a native of England, where, it is supposed, he was educated for the bar. There is no authentic record as to when he arrived in Georgia, but at the outbreak of the Revolution, he was a citizen of St. Andrew's parish.

Mr. Wereat was an early and zealous advocate of colonial rights. We first hear of him officially in July, 1775, when he represented his parish in the Provincial Congress which met in Savannah. At the next session of the same body, January, 1776, he was further honored by being made speaker. Evans says: "When Savannah fell, Governor Houstoun and the Council withdrew to Augusta and summoned the General Assembly to meet them in January to elect a Governor. But ten days later Colonel Campbell's troops occupied Augusta, and the State officers sought refuge in the Carolinas. Consequently there was no meeting of the Assembly. The State was without a regular Governor and Council. After Augusta was abandoned by the British, the legislature met there, but did not have a quorum. The few members present elected a new executive council. John Wereat was elected President of the Council and acted as Governor." This was on the 6th of August, 1779, and on the 4th of the following November, Mr. Wereat issued a proclamation which shows so clearly the unsettled state of affairs at that time that it is inserted here in full.

"AUGUSTA, in the State of Georgia, November 4, 1779.

Whereas, from the invasion of the State by the enemy, in December last, the absence of many of the members elected to represent the different counties in the House of Representatives for the present year, with unavoidable causes, several ineffectual attempts have been made to convene a legal House of Representatives; and whereas, it is essential to the welfare and happiness of the State that a legal and constitutional House of Assembly should be convened: We, therefore, earnestly recommend to such of the citizens of this State as have preserved their fidelity to the cause of America, and were inhabitants of the counties of Chatham, Liberty, Glynn, Camden, and Effingham prior to the reduction of these counties by the British forces, to repair to such place within this State as to them shall appear most safe and convenient, on the first Tuesday in December next, that being the day appointed by the Constitution for a general election throughout the State, in order to elect persons to represent those counties in the General Assembly for the ensuing year, that a full, free, and equal representation may be had to proceed on business of the utmost importance to the community; and it is the opinion of this board that this town would be the most eligible in the present situation of affairs, for the meeting of the General Assembly, which will be the first Tuesday in January next, agreeably to the Constitution of the State.

By order of the Board.   JOHN WEREAT, President."

George Walton denounced the election as illegal and organized at Augusta a General Assembly which elected him Governor. Thus it happened that for more than a month, Georgia had two acting Governors, neither legally chosen. Both were displaced by the General Assembly which met on January 4th, 1780, and elected Richard Howley Governor.

In 1781, John Wereat was elected Chief Justice of Georgia with a salary of three hundred pounds per annum. It was then the duty of the Chief Justice to preside at the Superior Courts of all the several counties, and the terms were so arranged as to permit his presence. In each county, he was aided by the assistant justices, selected for the county.

Much of Georgia had been laid waste by the contending armies, and in 1782, Judge Wereat who had removed to Augusta, did much to alleviate the want and suffering of his fellow citizens by the free use of his boats and negroes in conveying rice and other provisions up the river to the famishing people.

In the following year, he was appointed commissioner on the part of the State to negotiate with Governor Patrick Tonyn, of East Florida, for the accommodation of all differences and the prevention of disturbances along the line of St. Mary's River.

He was a delegate from Richmond County to the Convention, which met in December, 1787, and which, on the 2nd of January, 1788, ratified the Constitution of the United States. He was further honored by being made president of that convention, composed, as it was, of the leading patriots of Georgia.

In 1794, Judge Wereat moved from Augusta to Bryan County, where, four years later, he passed away.

Compiled by Publisher.

From an Original Painting in the possession of the Family.

C Wesley

Charles Wesley.

CHARLES WESLEY, ranking with Watts among the foremost of the world's great writers of sacred poetry. was born at Epworth, Lincolnshire, England, December 18th, 1707. He was a brother of Rev. John Wesley and Samuel Wesley, Jr., and son of Rev. Samuel Wesley, himself a writer of hymns. He was educated at Christ Church, one of the colleges of the University of Oxford, and, as he observed very carefully the method of study prescribed at the University, this gave him, so he tells us, "the harmless nickname of Methodist." The name appears to have had, at first, no religious significance.

When John Wesley, who was fellow of Lincoln College and who had taken holy orders in 1728, went, in 1729, to perform his duties at Oxford, he found an association of students of which his brother Charles was a member. Their habit was to meet on Sunday evenings to read the Scriptures and on other evenings to read secular literature. These habits won for them various nicknames such as "The Holy Club," "Bible Moths," "Sacramentarians," and "Methodists.' John Wesley joined this society which gradually became exclusively religious in its object, its members fasting frequently, spending much time in meditation and prayer and visiting the sick and those who were in prison.

In 1735, Charles Wesley was ordained a priest of the Church of England and accompanied his brother John to Georgia for the purpose of assisting in ministerial duties among the colonists and of preaching to the Indians. While in Georgia, he concerted with General Oglethorpe a scheme for an orphanage near

Savannah, and this plan was subsequently put into execution by Rev. Whitefield. On St. Simon's Island, near Frederica, the favorite residence of General Oglethorpe, stands what is left of the Wesley Oak, beneath whose shade the brothers officiated on more than one occasion. Having returned to England in 1736, he became unlicensed curate of St. Mary's, Islington, where he remained till 1739. From 1739 to 1756, he was an itinerant preacher. He resided for some years at Bristol and Bath and in 1771, went to London, where he labored much in all religious work, and where, after a career of great usefulness he died March 29th, 1788. He is said to have written six thousand five hundred hymns of which about five hundred are in general use. The choicest of them being found in the books of sacred songs of all Christian denominations.

JOSEPH T. DERRY.

John Wesley

John Wesley,

THIS great man, who introduced the great religious movement, known as Methodism, began his ministerial life as a rector in Georgia. He had been a curate of his father's at Epworth and Wroote and had been a tutor at the University of Oxford where he had a fellowship. He had not had sole charge of a flock, until he came to Savannah with Mr. Oglethorpe in 1735. When he landed in Savannah, he was thirty-three years old. He was not a Catholic in his religious views, but he was a High Churchman of the highest rank. When he came to America, near where Christ Church in Savannah now stands, there was a little board tabernacle, which served the villagers for a church. Mr. Oglethorpe had built for the former rector a two-room parsonage on what were then outskirts of the village not far from the taberancle.

Here, the two celibates, Mr. Delamotte and Mr. Wesley fixed their home. The community was but a small one. Little cottages, 14 x 18, which dotted the pine forest were mainly the homes of the people, although there were several which were more pretentious. The community was a mixed one. While there was only one church recognized and only one minister, there were a number of different religious communions. There were German Moravians, German Lutherans, Dissenters, Scotch Presbyterians, and Episcopalians. The Rector of the parish had charge of sundry small settlements nearby. Mr. Wesley's journal gives us the best insight into the condition of things at that time. He begins his journal in October, 1735. Bejamin Ingham, Charles Delamotte and the brothers, Charles and John Wesley, were the religious band which had taken shipping in

England as missionaries. They were devotees of the sternest order. They left off flesh and wine and lived on bread and rice. There were some good Germans on board who wished to learn English and the missionaries desired to learn German, so there was a mutual exchange of instruction. They rose at four and spent an hour in prayer, then read the Bible and the fathers till seven. After that they gave three hours to German. Then they met together for religious talk, dined at one and till four taught those they had taken in charge. At four they had a lecture and prayer, or catechised the children, then spent an hour in private prayer. Next there was a meeting of the passengers after which they joined the Germans and at eight had another religious assembly and went to bed at nine.

Mr. Wesley had already begun his work and had baptized a Quaker and his family, and, on the way out, had instructed several penitents. He was sadly troubled, however, because he was not willing to die before God said he must. Not content with giving up wine and meat the ascetics now gave up supper.

After riding the waves from October till February, nearly four months, they anchored at Cockspur Island and for the first time John Wesley trod Georgia soil. On that little bank of sand, the weary passengers knelt and he thanked God for their safe passage. Mr. Spaugenberg, the German Moravian had reached Savannah in a previous ship and when Mr. Oglethorpe, who had gone to Savannah by a small boat, returned, he brought Mr. Spaugenberg with him. The young Rector asked the older German for some religious advice and out of that advice came Methodism.

Tomo-chi-chi, as Mr. Wesley writes it, with his wife and children came down to meet the new comers. He had been to England and was glad to meet the immigrants. Mr. Wesley began his religious work by baptising a baby in Savannah by immersion.

On reaching Savannah, he found the little parsonage ready for him, and at once began his regular work with high hopes. His brother, Charles, had gone before him to Frederica and he made a journey there. The trip was made in a flat boat and Mr. Wesley narrowly escaped drowning but reached St. Simon's Island where he spent a few days and then returned to Savannah.

It will be remembered that he had not come to Georgia to preach to the white people, but to establish an Indian mission. The door to the work among the Indians not yet being open, he became a regular rector not from choice but from necessity. The rigid ascetic and ritualist was very different from the bright happy man he was afterwards in England. He was an ascetic of the sternest type, exacting much from himself and others, and was soon quite unpopular. He made sundry excursions on foot and once went by Fort Argyle, by way of Darien, to Frederica. Oddly enough, the famous work of Macchiavelli fell into the hands of the stern rector on this journey and he read it in the Georgia woods. He tells in his journal of the first suicide in Georgia, a poor Welsh saddler, named David Jones, who blew his brains out with a fowling piece. He also tells of the first house-burning in Savannah—the little cottage of Robert Howe.

His parish was small but his rights were large; and, when one of the South Carolina rectors married some of his flock irregularly, he went to Mr. Garden, the Commissary in Charleston to complain and was promised protection thereafter.

Alas! for the young rector's peace, there was a fair maiden in Savannah who had fascinated him because of her loveliness and piety. It is needless here to tell the oft told story. He loved her. There was no doubt of that. But there was a break in their relations and she, who had been the light of his eyes married another man three days after this break. Savannah was a gossipping village and whispering tongues told the faithful pastor of the wretched inconsistency of Miss Sophy, now Mrs. Williamson. It resulted in his passing her by at the communion table and his being prosecuted for libel and for clerical malfeasance in the little apology for a court. The court was composed of the young wife's uncle and two other men—uneducated laymen all of them. Mr. Wesley wanted a trial and demanded it time and again, but the ridiculous cour, refused it and he finally posted notice that he would leave on a certain day. Against the protest of Miss Sophy's husband, he took the boat at high tide and went to Purysburg, whence he made his way through the swamps to Charleston, and thence to England.

He gives in his journal a very satisfactory account of the Georgia he saw. He had but a poor opinion of it. He had never gone fifty miles from the coast and only saw the most unattractive country. The pine woods he saw would produce in one year about four bushels of corn and four bushels of peas to the acre, but the productiveness would steadily decline until it would produce nothing in the fourth year. Potatoes grew well, so did butter beans and watermelons. Oak lands would yield ten bushels of corn to the acre. The swamps and marshes were worthless. Savannah was on a bluff, the soil was white sand. St. Simon's was a hundred miles from Savannah. Here the soldiers were stationed. At Darien were the Scotch Highlanders with their pastor, Mr. McLeod, Augusta had just been settled, but when he left no house had been built. Old Ebenezer, now Marlow, was in the pine barrens, New Ebenezer was on the Savannah river where the Germans were. There was a little settlement where Mary Musgrove, now Mrs. Matthews, was living, some eight miles from Savannah. On the river Sir Francis Bathurst had a plantation; South of Savannah was Highgate where some Frenchmen lived; and Southeast of Savannah was Thunderbolt which still bears the name. Twelve miles South of Savannah, Sir Patrick Houstoun had a plantation. The lowest settlement was Fort St. Andrew.

He had a very low opinion of the Indians. They were drunkards, thieves and liars. The men were worthless and the women were as bad.

After his return to England, he met, in London, Peter Bohler and became connected with the Moravians in social meetings. While less strict than formerly, he was happier and began his work as an evangelist which knew no interruption for over fifty years. He swept annually through England, Ireland, and Scotland and preached from three to five times a day. He founded societies, wrote and published books, edited a religious journal, established a school, sent out missionaries, raised money for the poor, and abounded in every good word and work. At the ripe old age of eighty-eight, he passed triumphantly beyond.

England honors him by putting his statue in Westminster Abbey, and his name has honorable mention in all her histories. He married but had no children.

The Methodists have erected in Savannah a handsome church as a memorial to him to which contributions came from both England and America. Methodism as he preached it in England came into Savannah through his disciple, George Whitefield, whom he induced to come to America and whose warm, zealous, joyous preaching was in quite a contrast with that of his predecessor. GEORGE G. SMITH.

John White.

THIS gentleman was an Englishman by birth, of Irish parentage, and was at one time a surgeon in the British navy. On leaving the naval service, he embarked with his family for America; and purchased a suitable residence near Philadelphia. When the Revolution commenced and all aliens were ordered to quit the country or take the oath of allegiance, he preferred the latter, saying, "that he had fought for the King as long as he ate his bread, but that now America was his home and for America he would fight."

He entered the American army as a captain and was promoted to the rank of colonel. His regiment (4th Georgia Battalion) was ordered to Savannah. His exposure and fatigue brought on a pulmonary disease of which he died in Virginia.

Colonel White effected, during the siege of Savannah, one of the most extraordinary captures that the annals of warfare ever recorded. When General Prevost called in his detachments, he ordered the Commandant at Sunbury, on the Georgia coast, upon evacuating that port, to put the invalids on board of the small armed vessels and to send them by the inland navigation to Savannah, under the care of Captain French of the British regulars. In consequence of headwinds, Captain French and his command were detained until some of D'Estaing's fleet were in possession of the pass, and he was induced to sail up the Ogeechee river, until he reached a point about twenty-five miles from the city of Savannah. Having arrived here, he learned that the passage overland was also blocked up by the allied force, and he therefore made a descent upon the shore, and finally took post with his party about fifteen or twenty miles from Savannah. Colonel White having ascertained that Captain French's force consisted of 111 soldiers, possessing 130 stand of arms, and that he also had under his charge in the river Ogeechee adjacent to his camp five vessels, four of them fully armed, and one of them mounting fourteen guns and manned by forty seamen, formed the resolution of capturing the detachment. He disclosed his plan to those who were with him. McCall in his History of Georgia says that the party consisted of Colonel White, Captains George Melvin and A. E. Elholm, a sergeant, and three privates, seven in all. Other historians make no mention of Captain Melvin or of a sergeant, but give the whole praise to Colonel White, Elholm and three soldiers, reducing the number to five. White built many watch fires around the camp, placing them in such a position and at such intervals as to induce Captain French and his soldiers to believe that he was absolutely surrounded by a large force. The deception was kept up through the night by White and his companions, marching from fire to fire with the measured tread and the loud challenge of sentinels now hailing from the East of the British camp, and then shifting rapidly their position and challenging from the extreme West. Nor was this the only stratagem. Each mounted a horse and rode in haste in divers directions, imitating the manner of the staff and giving orders with a loud voice. The delusion was complete. Captain French suffered himself to be completely trapped. White carried his daring plan forward by dashing boldly and alone to the camp of the British and demanding a conference with French. "I am the commander, Sir," he said, "of the American soldiers in your vicinity. If you will surrender at once to my force, I will see to it that no injury is done to you or your command. If you decline to do this, I must candidly inform

23

you that the feelings of my troops are highly incensed against you, and I can, by no means, be responsible for any consequences that may ensue." French thanked him for his humanity and said despondingly, that it was useless to contend with fate or with the large force that he saw was around him, and announced his willingness to surrender his vessels, his arms, his men and himself to Colonel White. At this instant, Captain Elholm came suddenly dashing up at full speed and, saluting White, inquired of him where he should place the artillery. "Keep, them back, keep them back, Sir," answered White, "the British have surrendered. Move your men off and send me three guides to conduct them to the American post at Sunbury." The three guides arrived. The five vessels were burned and the British urged by White to keep clear of his men, and to hasten their departure from the enraged and formidable Americans, pushed on with great celerity whilst White returned with one or two of his associates, stating that he would go to his troops in the rear and restrain them. He now employed himself in collecting the neighborhood militia, with which he overtook his guides and conducted them in safety to the Sunbury post.

Lee, in his account of this affair, says, "The extraordinary address of White was contrasted with the extraordinary folly of French, and both were necessary to produce this wonderful issue. The affair approaches too near the marvellous to have been admitted in these Memoirs had it not been uniformly asserted and as uniformly accredited and never contradicted." Captain Elholm was one of the officers of Pulaski's Legion. Captain Melvin, it is believed, lived and died in Savannah.

WHITE'S HISTORICAL COLLECTION.

George Whitefield.

GEORGE WHITEFIELD, a companion, beloved friend and co-worker of the Wesleys, from whom he differed on some doctrinal points, being a Calvinist, while they were Arminian, was born in Gloucester, England, December 16th, 1714. After attending the grammar school of St. Mary de Crypt at Gloucester, he entered Pembroke College, Oxford, at the age of eighteen as servitor. Here he became acquainted with the Wesleys and along with them was connected with the small society, styled by their fellow students, "Methodists." He was offered ordination by Dr. Benson, Bishop of Gloucester, at the age of twenty-one, and a year later was, by that prelate, ordained deacon. His first sermon was one of such power that complaint was made to the Bishop that Whitefield had driven several people mad, upon which the reverend gentleman replied that he hoped the madness would not be forgotten before the next Sunday. From letters of the Wesleys in Georgia, he was induced to go to their assistance and arrived at the new town of Savannah in May, 1737. Following out a suggestion of Charles Wesley, he planned an orphanage near Savannah and returning to England to raise funds for the benevolent enterprise, reached the home country in safety in the beginning of 1739. Notwithstanding the opposition of many of the clergy, Bishop Benson conferred upon him priest's orders. The churches in which he preached could not hold the crowds which flocked to hear him. He often preached in the open air at Kingswood, near Bristol, exerting wonderful influence for good among the colliers. He also preached in the open air in Bristol, in Moorfields, Kensington, and other places near London, vast crowds flocking to hear him. In August, 1739, he again embarked for America and traveled through several of the colonies. His preaching had a wonderful effect, a vivid account of which has been preserved by Benjamin Franklin in his autobiography. In January, 1740, he arrived at Savannah, and with the contributions raised by him in England and America, established the Orphan House at Bethesda, a name chosen by him with the hope that it would prove indeed a "house of mercy to many souls." He continued his untiring labors for this enterprise, in addition to the wonderful revival services that he conducted in England, Scotland and Wales. In 1741, he married in Wales and, three years later, returned again to America. He continued to give much time to the Orphan House, of which he wrote an interesting sketch in 1746. Although his preaching met with much opposition in New England, and Harvard College put forth a "testimony" against him, great crowds continued to attend upon his ministry, whether in the eastern or the middle colonies or in Georgia. Returning to England in 1748, he was introduced to the Countess of Huntington, who made him one of her chaplains. He next visited Ireland and made two more voyages to America. After many years of unremitting labor in the Old and the New World, he died at Newburyport, Massachusetts, September 30th, 1770. He preached at Exeter, New Hampshire, and also at Newburyport the day before his death. His body sleeps beneath the pulpit of the Federal Street Church at Newburyport.

In Georgia, the Empire State of the South, he has a noble and enduring monument in the Orphan House at Bethesda. His name is further honored in the State by being given to one of the counties of North Georgia. His works were published in 1771-'72, shortly after his death. Jos. T. DERRY.

Francis Willis.

FRANCIS WILLIS, Congressman from Georgia during its second and third sessions, was born in Frederick county, Virginia, in 1745. He was the son of John Willis and Mildred (Smith) Willis and was given a liberal education for the times. In 1769, he married Elizabeth Edwards of St. Andrew's parish, Brunswick county, Virginia. They lived a short time in that county and then moved to Berkly, afterwards Jefferson county, which was laid off in 1772 by his kinsman Robert Carter Willis, where they lived at Shannon Hall on the Shenandoah River.

In the struggle for American Independence, he early took his stand with his native State. In the fall of 1776, General Washington called upon Virginia for sixteen regiments of volunteers more than he already had in the field. When organized these men were in the command of Colonel Grayson, immediately under General Washington himself. They were known as "Grayson's Additional Virginia Dragoons." They received the title "Additional" from the fact that these men were called out in addition to the many thousands of Virginians already in Washington's army. Captain Francis Willis was given command of one of the sixteen regiments. In this capacity he served with distinction from January, 1777, till May, 1778, when he was promoted to a colonelcy. For faithful service during this time, Captain Willis received the personal compliments of General Washington.

In 1784, the family moved to Wilkes county, Georgia, where Colonel Willis soon became quite a prominent man. He was elected by the Legislature to the United States Congress February 4, 1791, and served two years.

About 1820, he removed from Georgia to Maury county, Tennessee, where he died in 1828. He had one son, Thomas Willis, who married Elizabeth Worsham. They had one son, Dr. Francis T. Willis of Richmond, Virginia.

R. J. MASSEY.

Joseph Wood.

H
E is said to have been a Pennsylvanian by birth. In 1774, he was a resident of the town of Sunbury, in the Parish of St. John and State of Georgia. Repudiating the conclusions of the Provincial meeting of the 10th of August, 1774, which, although patriotic in their character, did not culminate in placing Georgia in full affiliation with her twelve sisters and in commissioning Delegates to the Continental Congress, the inhabitants of the Parish of St. John resolved to act independently and in advance of the rest of the Colony. On the 9th of February, Joseph Wood, Daniel Roberts, and Samuel Stevens—members of the Parish committee—were deputed with a carefully prepared letter to repair to Charlestown and request of the Committee of Correspondence their "permission to form an alliance with them, and to conduct trade and commerce according to the act of non-importation to which they had already acceded."

Reaching Charlestown on the 23d of February, Messrs. Wood, Roberts, and Stevens waited upon the General Committee and earnestly endeavored to accomplish their mission. While admiring the patriotism of the Parish, and entreating its citizens to persevere in their laudable exertions, the Carolinians, deeming it "a violation of the Continental Association to remove the prohibition in favor of any *part* of a Province," declined the application.

Nothing daunted, the inhabitants of St. John's Parish "resolved to prosecute their claims to an equality with the Confederated Colonies," and commissioned Dr. Lyman Hall to represent them in the Continental Congress. Returning to Pennsylvania during the early portion of the Revolutionary War, Mr. Wood entered the Continental service with the Second Pennsylvania Regiment. His promotion was rapid. He was advanced to a Majority on the 4th of January, 1776, to a Lieutenant-Colonelcy on the 29th of July in the same year, and to a full Colonelcy on the 7th of September, 1776.

Toward the close of that year, Colonel Wood was again in Georgia, where he was cordially welcomed. In January, 1777, he was elected a Delegate from Georgia to the Continental Congress, and this compliment was repeated in February of the following year.

His plantation was on North New Port River, not far from the village of Riceboro, in Liberty county (formerly St. John's Parish). The tradition of Colonel Wood's unblemished life and manly virtues still lingers in the community. Joseph Wood departed this life at his plantation in Liberty county, Georgia, in 1791. His will was probated on the 2d of October in that year. His widow, Catholina, two sons, John and Jacob, and two daughters, Hester and Elizabeth, are therein named as legatees and devisees. C. C. JONES, JR.

James Wright.

S IR JAMES WRIGHT was a son of Robert Wright, a
native of Sedgefield in Durham, England. Receiving the
appointment of Chief Justice of South Carolina, he removed to that colony and married a widow Pitts at Charleston.
It was here that James Wright was born about 1714. He was
educated in the mother country, after which he practiced law in
Charleston. Later he was made agent of the province of South
Carolina in Great Britain.

On the 13th of May, 1760, he was made Governor of Georgia
by royal appointment and arrived in Savannah early the following October. He found the province in a languishing condition and, with characteristic promptness and energy, set about
correcting the abuses which had grown up with the colony.
Writs were issued for the election of members of an Assembly,
which met in Savannah, and, at the suggestion of the Governor,
adopted numerous regulations, the wisdom of which was soon
reflected in the progress made in agriculture and commerce.
Every precaution was taken to maintain friendly relations with
the Indians.

In 1763, Governor Boone of South Carolina granted to some
of his friends several thousand acres of land south of the Altamaha river. Governor Wright resented this as being an un-
warranted encroachment on the rights of the colony over which
he presided. An agent was sent to Charleston to protest against
these usurpations on the part of Governor Boone. No attention
was paid to the protest and Governor Wright was compelled to
refer the matter to the Commissioners of Trade and Plantations, who ordered Boone's grants discontinued.

During Governor Wright's administration, Parliament passed the Stamp Act. Like most of the other colonies, Georgia took a bold and decided stand against this usurpation on the part of the mother country. William Knox, Georgia's agent in London, undertook to defend the Stamp Act in a letter to an American friend. As a result, the next general assembly, November 15th, 1765, "resolved to give instruction to the Committee of Correspondence to acquaint Mr. Knox, agent of this province, that the province has no further occasion for his services." Charles Garth was nominated to succeed Mr. Knox. This displeased the Governor and his Council declined to make an appropriation for the new agent's expenses; whereupon the assembly appointed him on the 26th of March, 1767. Greatly incensed at this proceeding, Governor Wright wrote Secretary Conway, "The nomination of a provincial agent by the assembly alone, is a thing, I believe, never before attempted in any province on the continent of America, unless very lately, when they have been seized with their strange enthusiastic ideas of liberty and power." Later he wrote, "That a large proportion of the people of Georgia are 'Sons of Liberty,' and that the same spirit of sedition which first appeared in Boston had reached Georgia." His arguments, protests and even official proclamations were disregarded by the people in their opposition to the Stamp Act. It was a time of stress and storm. Effigies were burnt in the streets of Savannah and incendiary letters were written. An association was formed to prevent the distribution of the stamped paper, which was brought to Savannah on his majesty's ship, Speedwell, December 5th, 1766. The paper was landed and lodged with the Commissary; and despite the assurance given the Governor that no attempt to seize or destroy it would be made, he soon realized that there was much discontent among the people. Accordingly, when on the 2nd of January, 1767, he was advised that about two hundred of the "Liberty Boys" were in town for the avowed purpose of destroying the stamped paper, he did not hesitate to order his officers to collect their men for action. On the following day, Mr. Angus, the stamp distributor, arrived in the river and was brought ashore on a scout boat protected by an officer and a party of men. He was guarded to the governor's house where he remained two weeks and then took refuge in the country.

Later six hundred men assembled and indulged in numerous threats in case the governor did not promise to issue no more stamps; but he fearlessly had the papers removed to Fort George on Cockspur Island, where, they were protected by the King's soldiers. The courts were closed and all judicial business was suspended, though the use of enough stamps was permitted to clear the harbor of vessels whose clearance papers were illegal without the stamps. On this account Georgia was severely criticised by South Carolina and accused of having sold her birthright for a mess of pottage.

There was great rejoicing on the repeal of the Stamp Act, but it was followed by others quite as oppressive. In 1767, the governor informed the assembly that application had been made for barracks to accommodate a company of British soldiers. The members of that body replied, "That they humbly conceive their complying with the requisition would be a violation of the trust reposed in them by their constituents and founding a precedent they, by no means, think themselves justified in introducing."

In 1768, Georgia having entered into correspondence with her sister colonies to the north of her, Governor Wright dissolved the assembly and informed the members that, "If America is to become independent of the mother country, from that day you may date the foundation of your ruin and misery."

On April 23rd, 1771, the House of Assembly met at Savannah and the following day elected Noble W. Jones speaker. The governor disapproved, and the House elected Archibald Bulloch, who opened the session with a speech. The House made it clear to the governor that it considered his action in rejecting their choice for speaker a high breach of the privilege of the House, which tended to subvert the most valuable rights of the people and protested that their action in selecting another speaker should not be considered a precedent. On the following day, April 26th, the governor prorogued the session in a set speech which is still extant.

The breach between the people and their governor continued to widen. In 1774, numerous meetings were held, in which they expressed themselves in no uncertain terms. On July 24th of that year, the governor issued a proclamation declaring one of these meetings unlawful.

On the 11th of the following May, a party of patriots, headed by Joseph Habersham, seized the powder in the magazine. Governor Wright promptly offered a reward for the offenders, but even this inducement failed to produce them. In June, 1775, Governor Wright applied to his government for troops and was referred to General Gage and Admiral Graves, who had been placed at his disposal. His dispatches to those officers, requesting assistance, were intercepted at Charleston and dispatches, reporting Georgia quiet and without the need of troops, substituted for them. The forgery was not discovered till years afterwards.

On the 17th of June, 1775, several English men of war appeared off Tybee. The governor was seized by Joseph Habersham to prevent his communicating with the vessels, and paroled to his own house, with a sentinel at the door. He escaped, however, and was conveyed by a small boat to the English vessels.

Towards the close of the Revolution, when Savannah fell into the hands of the British, he was sent back to Georgia and Savannah's stubborn defense has been credited to his spirit and energy.

After the Revolution, he returned to England, and in 1783, was at the head of the Board of Agents of American Loyalists whose property had been confiscated by the American government. Governor Wright had owned large property in Georgia for which he was reimbursed. He was made a Baronet in 1772. He died November 20th, 1785.

Compiled from *White's Collections.*

John Joachim Zubly.

A NATIVE of St. Gall, Switzerland, where he was born on the 27th of August, 1724, Mr. Zubly was engaged in the discharge of clerical duties at Wando Neck, in the Province of South Carolina, when, on the 25th of April, 1758, he received and accepted a call to a large and influential Presbyterian congregation in Savannah, Georgia. It was not, however, until 1760, that he entered fully upon his pastoral charge of that Independent Presbyterian Church. He was a clergyman of marked ability, eloquence, and learning; preaching with equal ease and power in the German, French, and English languages. A rigid disciple of Calvin, he was tireless in the discharge of his professional labors. Under his guidance, his congregation became the most numerous and popular within the limits of Georgia. In 1770, he was complimented by Princeton College with the degree of Doctor of Divinity.

By an act of the Colonial Legislature, approved on the 17th of March, 1758, Georgia was divided into Parishes, and the patronage of the Crown was specially extended in aid of churches professing the Episcopal faith. While not favored by exclusive recognition, the purpose appeared to be to accord to that denomination, within the limits of Georgia, a prestige akin to that which the Church of England enjoyed within the realm; to create certain offices and provide emoluments for the encouragement of that religious persuasion, and the extension of the gospel in accordance with its forms of worship and mode of government; and to prescribe a method by which faithful registers of births, marriages, christenings, and deaths might be kept and perpetuated. Numerous were the Dissenters then in the Province. They were represented by Presbyterians, Lutherans, Congregationalists, Methodists, a few Baptists, and some Hebrews. To all sects save Papists was free toleration accorded; and whenever a Dissenting congregation organized and applied for a grant of land whereon to build a church, the petition did not pass unheeded. There can be no doubt, however, that it was the intention of the Government, both Royal and Colonial, to engraft the Church of England upon the Province, and, within certain limits, to advance its prosperity and insure its permanency. At the same time an adherence to its rubrics was in no wise made a condition precedent to political preferment.

Despite the advantage thus enjoyed by the Episcopal Church, so popular was Mr. Zubly as a preacher, and so acceptable were his ministrations, that he soon attracted many of the leading citizens of Savannah. So catholic were his views, so pronounced was the interest which he exhibited in public affairs, and so manifest were his sympathies with the protestants against the arbitrary acts of Parliament that his influence as a citizen and a lover of liberty was felt beyond the limits of his pulpit and congregation. As a compliment to the man, and to the position which he then occupied, he was elected a Delegate to the Provincial Congress which assembled in Savannah on the 4th of July, 1775. Before and at the opening of that Congress, he delivered a sermon on American affairs, entitled "The Law of Liberty," which may be accepted as a fair specimen of the composition and manly thought of this eloquent and accomplished divine. When printed by Henry Miller, of Philadelphia, it was prefaced by a forcible and conclusive plea for the liberties of America, embodied in a communication addressed by Mr. Zubly to the Right Honorable and Earl of Dartmouth.

By this Congress Dr. Zubly, in association with John Houstoun, Archibald Bulloch, Noble W. Jones, and Dr. Lyman Hall, was chosen to represent the Province of Georgia in the Continental Congress. Upon a suggestion from him that he was greatly surprised at being selected as a Delegate, and that he could not accept the honor without the consent of his congregation, Messrs. Noble W. Jones and John Houstoun were appointed a committee to interview the members of Dr. Zubly's church and request their permission that he absent himself from his charge for a season, in order that he might perform the important duties devolved upon him by the Congress. Four days afterwards those gentlemen reported that they had conferred with the congregation, and that the members expressed a willingness "to spare their minister for a time for the good of the common cause." Dr. Zubly thereupon declared his acceptance of the appointment, and thanked the Congress for this mark of honor and confidence.

By this Congress the Reverend Doctor Zubly was placed upon four important committees,—one to prepare a petition to the King "upon the present unhappy situation of affairs;" another to address a letter to the President of the Continental Congress, acquainting him fully with the proceedings of this Provincial Congress; a third to frame an address to His Excellency Governor Wright; and a fourth to constitute a Committee of Intelligence.

From the addresses then prepared we reproduce the following:

"To the Inhabitants of the Province of Georgia:

"Fellow-Countrymen,—We are directed to transmit to you an account of the present state of American affairs, as well as the proceedings of the late Provincial Congress.

"It is with great sorrow we are to acquaint you that what our fears suggested, but our reason thought impossible, is actually come to pass.

"A civil war in America is begun. Several engagements have already happened. The friends and foes of America have been equally disappointed. The friends of America were in hopes British troops could never be induced to slay their brethren. It is, however, done, and the circumstances are such as must be an everlasting blot on their character for humanity and generosity. An unfeeling commander has found means to inspire his troops with the same evil spirit that possesseth himself. After the starving, helpless, innocent inhabitants of Boston delivered up their arms and received his promise that they might leave that virtuous, devoted town, he is said to have broken his word; and the wretched inhabitants are still kept to fall a prey to disease, famine, and confinement. If there are powers which abhor injustice and oppression, it may be hoped such perfidy can not go long unpunished.

"But the enemies of America have been no less disappointed. Nothing was so contemptible in their eyes as the rabble of an American militia; nothing more improbable than that they would dare to look regulars in the face, or stand a single fire. By this time they must have felt how much they were mistaken. In every engagement the Americans appeared with a bravery worthy of men that fight for the liberties of their oppressed country. Their success has been remarkable; the number of the slain and wounded on every occasion vastly exceeded theirs; and the advantages they gained are the more honorable because, with a patience that scarce has an example, they bore every act of injustice and insult till their lives were attacked, and then gave the fullest proof that the man of calmness and moderation in counsel is usually the most intrepid and courageous in battle.

"You will doubtless lament with us the hundreds that died in their country's cause; but does it not call for greater sorrow that thousands of British soldiers sought and found their deaths when they were active to enslave their brethren and their country? However irritating all these proceedings, yet so unnatural is this quarrel that every good man must wish and pray that it may soon cease; that the injured rights of America may be vindicated by milder means; and that no.more blood may be shed, unless it be of those who fomented, and mean to take an advantage of, these unhappy divisions.

"From the proceedings of the Congress, a copy of which accompanies the present, you will be convinced that a reconciliation on honorable principles is an object which your Delegates never lost sight of. We have sent an humble and manly petition to his Majesty; addressed his representative, our Governor; provided, as far as in our power, for internal quiet and safety; and Delegates will soon attend the General Congress to assist and co-operate in any measure that shall be thought necessary for the saving of America.

"His Excellency, at our request, having appointed the 19th inst. as a Day of Humiliation, and news being afterwards received that the Continental Congress had recommended the 20th inst. to be observed as such, both days have been observed with a becoming solemnity; and we humbly hope many earnest prayers have been presented to the Father of Mercies on that day through this extensive continent, and that He has heard the cries of the destitute, and will not despise their prayers.

"You will permit us most earnestly to recommend to you a steady perseverance in the cause of Liberty, and that you will use all possible caution not to say or do anything unworthy of so glorious a cause; to promote frugality, peace, and good order; and, in the practice of every social and religious duty, patiently to wait the return of that happy day when we may quietly sit under our vine and fig-tree, and no man make us afraid."

We make no apology for presenting this address *in extenso*, because with its composition the pen of Dr. Zubly is credited, and because it shows how earnestly, at this epoch in his career, his sympathies were enlisted in behalf of American freedom.

Of the five Delegates thus selected by the Provincial Congress to represent Georgia in the Continental Congress, Messrs. Zubly, Bulloch, and Houstoun repaired to Philadelphia, and participated in the deliberations of that body, at an adjourned session held in September. Dr. Lyman Hall, who had been present at a previous meeting as a Delegate commissioned by the Parish of St. Paul, was now absent; and Dr. Noble W. Jones, than whom the "Sons of Liberty" claimed none more competent, courageous, and accomplished,—in deference to the entreaties of his aged father, Colonel Noble Jones, a faithful servant of the Crown, who, trembling upon the verge of the grave, bespoke the companionship of his distinguished and devoted son,—postponed for the while his service to the Province in this prominent capacity, that he might respond to his filial obligations.

Georgia was ably represented. From the inception of the disagreements between Great Britain and her American Colonies, Archibald Bulloch had been a firm friend to the liberties of America. No one stood higher in the respect and affection of his fellow-citizens, and for him the most pronounced honors were in store. John Houstoun, too, was among the most zealous advocates of the rights of the Colonies. Of honorable descent and liberal education, of admitted bravery and commanding influence, his memory is associated with some of the best traditions of the epoch, and of the community in which he dwelt.

Of the early labors of the Reverend Dr. Zubly in the cause of freedom, education, and religion, we may not speak except in praise. His course in the first Continental Congress which he attended was consistent and patriotic. The acceptable pastor of a large Presbyterian congregation in Savannah,—scholarly, gifted in speech, public-spirited, and of marked ability,—his voice and pen had been freely employed in the vindication of the rights of the Colonies against the encroachments of Parliament. Discussing the suggestions made in England to arm the slaves in order to reduce their masters to obedience to British rule, he wrote to the Earl of Dartmouth as follows: "Proposals publicly made by ministerial writers relative to American domestics laid the Southern Provinces under the necessity of arming themselves. A proposal to put it in the power of domestics to cut the throats of their masters can only serve to cover the proposers and abettors with everlasting infamy. The Americans have been called 'a rope of sand," but *blood* and *sand* will make a firm cementation; and enough American blood has been already shed to cement them together into a threefold cord not easily to be broken." In the deliberations and utterances of the Provincial Congress in Savannah no member had borne a more prominent part.

When, however, at a subsequent session of the Continental Congress, he found himself confronted with a determination on the part of its members to sever the ties binding the American Colonies to the Mother Country, and to erect on these shores a separate, independent, and republican confederation, his heart failed him, and, opening a correspondence with Sir James Wright, he revealed to him the plans of Congress, and warned him of the impending rupture. His conduct and language exciting suspicion, he was watched, and one of his treasonable letters was seized. This fact was brought to the notice of Congress by Mr. Chase, of Maryland. So alarmed became Dr. Zubly that, precipitately abandoning his seat, he returned to Georgia, taking sides against the liberty people, he became so obnoxious that, in 1777, he was banished from Savannah, with the loss of half his estate. Taking refuge in South Carolina, he there remained until the Royal government was, in 1779, re-established in Southern Georgia. Then, returning to Savannah, he resumed his ministerial labors, and there abode until his death, which occurred on the 23rd of July, 1781. Broken in heart and fortune, the latest years of his life involved a ceaseless struggle with misfortune. "His political defection," says Dr. Stevens, "while it did no harm to Georgia or the Colonies, brought misery upon himself and family, and tarnished a name which shone among the earlier patriots of Georgia with peculiar brightness. Savannah still bears the record of this learned man in the names of two of its streets, 'Joachim' and 'Zubly,' and one of the hamlets of the city is called 'St. Gall,' in honor of his birthplace in Switzerland."

His declaration, in his place in the Continental Congress, that " a republic was little better than a government of devils," and his subsequent desertion of his post to seek shelter under the authority of the Crown, were but the prelude to unhappiness, disgrace, and an early grave.

There was an oil portrait of this member of the Old Congress, but unfortunately, many years ago, it was accidentally destroyed by fire.   C. C. JONES, JR.

Appendix,

Political and Judicial Divisions of Georgia.

EARLIEST DIVISION.

"Deeming it conducive to the convenience of the inhabitants and promotive of good government, the trustees, on the 15th of April, 1741, divided the province of Georgia into two counties—Savannah and Frederica. The former included all settlements upon the Savannah river and upon both banks of the Great Ogeechee river, and such additional territory south of the latter stream as should be designated when a proper map of the country could be prepared. Within the latter were embraced Darien, Frederica, and the entire region lying south of the Altamaha river."

PARISHES.

One of the most interesting acts passed by the legislature during the administration of Henry Ellis, the second Royal Governor of Georgia, was that dividing the several districts of the province into parishes, providing for the establishment of religious worship according to the rites and ceremonies of the Church of England and for other purposes. This act was approved on the 15th of March, 1758, and by it the province of Georgia was erected into eight parishes, which were as follows:

THE PARISH OF CHRIST CHURCH included the "town and district of Savannah, extending up the river Savannah, including the islands therein, as far as the southeast boundary of Goshen, from thence in a southwest line to the river Great Ogeechee; and from the town of Savannah eastward as far as the mouth of the river Savannah, including the sea islands to the mouth of the river Great Ogeechee, and all the settlements on the north side of the said river to the western boundaries thereof."

THE PARISH OF ST. MATTHEW embraced the district of Abercorn and Goshen and the district of Ebenezer, "extending from the northwest boundaries of the parish of Christ Church up the river Savannah as far as the Beaver Dam, and southwest as far as the mouth of Horse creek on the river Great Ogeechee."

THE PARISH OF ST. GEORGE was erected from the district of Halifax, extending from the northwest boundaries of St. Matthew's Parish up the

Savannah river from the mouth of McBean's swamp to the head thereof, and from thence to the head of Lambol's creek and to the Great Ogeechee river.

THE PARISH OF ST. PAUL comprised "the district of Augusta, extending from the northwest boundary of the parish of St. George and southwest as far as the river Ogeechee, and northwest up the river Savannah as far as Broad river."

THE PARISH OF ST. PHILIP was composed of "the town of Hardwick, and district of Ogeechee, on the south side of the river Great Ogeechee, extending northwest up the said river as far as the Lower Indian Trading Path leading from Mount Pleasant, and southward from the town of Hardwick as far as the swamp of James Dunham, including the settlements on the north side of the north branches of the river Midway, with the island of Ossabaw, and from the head of the said Dunham's swamp in a northwest line."

THE PARISH OF ST. JOHN was made to include Sunbury, in the district of Midway and Newport and all the territory, "from the southern bounds of the parish of St. Philip, extending southward as far as the north line of Samuel Hastings, and from thence southeast to the south branch of Newport, including the islands of St. Catharine and Bermuda, and from the north line of the said Samuel Hastings northwest."

THE PARISH OF ST. ANDREW had within its limits "the town and district of Darien, extending from the south boundary of the parish of St. John to the river Altamaha, including the islands of Sapelo and Eastwood, and the sea islands to the north of Egg Island and northwest up the river Altamaha to the forks of the said river."

THE PARISH OF ST. JAMES was formed from "the town and district of Frederica, including the islands of Great and Little St. Simon and the adjacent islands."

In accordance with the provisions of an act of March 25, 1765, the territory lying between the rivers Altamaha and St. Mary, which had a little before been annexed to the province of Georgia, was divided into four parishes.

THE PARISH OF ST. DAVID was to include, "all that space or tract of land lying and being between the river Altamaha and the north branch of Turtle river, and from the head of the said last mentioned river in a northwest line."

THE PARISH OF ST. PATRICK extended "from the north branch of Turtle river to the southern branch of the river Little Satilla, and from the head of the said river Little Satilla in a northwest line."

THE PARISH OF ST. THOMAS stretched "from the southern branch of the river Little Satilla to the southern branch of the river Great Satilla."

THE PARISH OF ST. MARY spread "from the southern branch of the river Great Satilla to the southern branch of the river St. Mary in a due west line, including all the islands within the said boundary."

COUNTIES.

Georgia at present consists of one hundred and forty-six counties. The dates which follow refer to the acts creating the counties and the names indicate the persons in whose honor the counties were called.

APPLING.—December 15, 1818.
> Colonel Daniel Appling, of Columbia county, who distinguished himself in the war of 1812.

BAKER.—December 12, 1825.
> Colonel John Baker, of Liberty county, and of Revolutionary memory.

BALDWIN.—May 11, 1803.
> Hon. Abraham Baldwin, of Columbia county, a signer from Georgia of the Federal Constitution of 1787, and U. S. Senator.

BANKS.—December 11, 1858.
> Dr. Richard Banks, for many years a leading man in northeastern Georgia, who resided at Gainesville.

BARTOW.—December 6, 1861.
> General Francis S. Bartow, of Chatham county, who fell at the first battle of Manassas.

BEN HILL.—1906.
> Ben. Hill, of Troup county, U. S. Senator.

BERRIEN.—February 25, 1856.
> Hon. John McPherson Berrien, of Savannah, Judge, U. S. Senator from Georgia, Attorney-General of the United States.

BIBB.—December 9, 1822.
> Dr. William W. Bibb, of Elbert county, member of Congress, U. S. Senator from Georgia and Territorial Governor of Alabama.

BROOKS.—December 11, 1858.
> Hon. Preston S. Brooks, member of Congress, etc.

BRYAN.—December 19, 1793.
> Jonathan Bryan, of Chatham county, a patriot.

BULLOCH.—February 8, 1796.
> Hon. Archibald Bulloch, President and Commander-in-Chief of Georgia in 1776.

BURKE.—Sec. IV., Constitution of Georgia of 1777.
> Edmund Burke, of England, the great champion of American liberty.

BUTTS.—December 24, 1825.

Captain Samuel Butts, who lost his life in the battle of Chalibbee, January 27, 1814.

CALHOUN.—February 20, 1854.   ....

Hon. John C. Calhoun, of South Carolina.

CAMDEN.—Sec. IV., Constitution of Georgia of 1777.

Earl of Camden, of England, a defender of colonial rights.

CAMPBELL.—December 20, 1828.

Hon. Duncan G. Campbell, one of the two commissioners appointed by President Monroe in 1824 to treat with the Creek Indians for the sale of their lands.

CARROLL.—December 11, 1826.

Hon Charles Carroll, of Carrollton, a signer from Maryland of the Declaration of Independence.

CATOOSA.—December 5, 1853.   Indian name.

CHARLTON.—February 18, 1854.

Hon. Robert M. Charlton, Judge, U. S. Senator from Georgia, etc.

CHATHAM.—Sec. IV., Constitution of Georgia of 1777.

Earl of Chatham, of England.

CHATTAHOOCHEE.—February 13, 1854.   Indian name.

CHATTOOGA.—December 28, 1838.   Indian name.

CHEROKEE.—December 26, 1831.   Indian name.

CLARKE.—December 5, 1801.

General Elijah Clarke, of Revolutionary memory.

CLAY.—February 16, 1854.

Hon. Henry Clay, of Kentucky.

CLAYTON.—November 30, 1858.

Hon. Augustin S. Clayton, Judge, member of Congress, etc.

CLINCH.—February 14, 1850.

General Duncan L. Clinch.

COBB.—December 3, 1832.

Hon. Thomas W. Cobb, Judge, member of Congress, United States Senator from Georgia, etc.

COFFEE.—February 9, 1854.

Hon. John Coffee, of Telfair county, member of Congress, etc.

COLQUITT.—February 25, 1856.

Hon. Walter T. Colquitt, Judge, U. S. Senator from Georgia, etc.

COLUMBIA.—December 10, 1790.

Christopher Columbus, the discoverer of America.

COWETA.—December 11, 1826.   Tribe of Indians.

CRAWFORD.—December 9, 1822.

Hon. William H. Crawford, of Oglethorpe county, one of Georgia's most distinguished citizens.

CRISP.—1905.

Charles F. Crisp, of Sumter county, Speaker of the national House of Representatives.

DADE.—December 25, 1837.

Major Francis Langhorne Dade, U. S. A., who was killed by the Indians in Florida, in December, 1835.

DAWSON.—December 3, 1857.

Hon. William C. Dawson, U. S. Senator from Georgia, etc.

DECATUR.—December 8, 1823.

Commodore Stephen Decatur, U. S. N.

DEKALB.—December 9, 1822.

Baron DeKalb, who fell in defence of American freedom at the battle of Camden, S. C., August 19, 1780.

DODGE.—October 26, 1870.

Hon. William E. Dodge, of New York.

DOOLY.—May 15, 1821.

Colonel John Dooly, who was murdered by the Tories in 1780.

DOUGHERTY.—December 15, 1853.

Hon. Charles Dougherty, of Clarke county, Judge, etc.

DOUGLAS.—October 17, 1870.

Hon. Stephen A. Douglas, of Illinois.

EARLY.—December 15, 1818.

Hon. Peter Early, Governor of Georgia, etc.

ECHOLS.—December 13, 1858.

Hon. Robert M. Echols, of Walton county.

EFFINGHAM.—Sec. IV., Constitution of Georgia of 1777.

Earl of Effingham, of England, an ardent supporter of colonial rights.

ELBERT.—December 10, 1790.

Governor Samuel Elbert, of Georgia, general in the Continental army, etc.

EMANUEL.—December 10, 1812.

Hon. David Emanuel, Governor of Georgia, etc.

FANNIN.—January 21, 1854.

Colonel J. W. Fannin, who was killed by the Mexicans at Goliad, in March, 1836.

FAYETTE.—May 15, 1821.

Marquis de LaFayette, of France.

FLOYD.—December 3, 1832.

General John Floyd, member of Congress, etc.

FORSYTH.—December 3, 1832.

Hon. John Forsyth, Governor of Georgia, Secretary of State under President Jackson, and U. S. Senator.

FRANKLIN.—February 25, 1784.

Benjamin Franklin, of Pennsylvania.

FULTON.—December 20, 1853.

Robert Fulton, who invented the steamboat.

GILMER.—December 3, 1832.

Hon. George R. Gilmer, of Oglethorpe county, Governor of Georgia, etc.

GLASCOCK.—December 19, 1857.

General Thomas Glascock, of Richmond county.

GLYNN.—Sec. IV., Constitution of Georgia, 1777.

John Glynn, Esq., distinguished for his unwavering support of the colonies.

GORDON.—February 13, 1850.

William W. Gordon, of Savannah, "the pioneer of works of internal improvement in his native state, and first President of the Central. Railroad and Banking Company of Georgia."

GRADY.—1905.

Henry Grady, one of the South's most brilliant orators.

GREENE.—February 3, 1786.

Major-General Nathanael Greene, of Revolutionary fame.

GWINNETT.—December 15, 1818.

Button Gwinnett, signer from Georgia of the Declaration of Independence, and President and Commander-in-Chief of Georgia in 1777.

HABERSHAM.—December 15, 1818.

Col. Joseph Habersham, Postmaster-General of U. S., member from Georgia of Continental Congress.

HALL.—December 15, 1818.

Hon. Lyman Hall, signer from Georgia of the Declaration of Independence, Governor of Georgia, etc.

HANCOCK.—December 17, 1793.

John Hancock, President of the Continental Congress, signer from Massachusetts of the Declaration of Independence, etc.

HARALSON.—January 26, 1856.

Hon. Hugh A. Haralson, member of Congress, etc.

HARRIS.—December 14, 1827.

Hon. Charles Harris, of Savannah, Judge, etc.

HART.—December 7, 1853.

Nancy Hart, of Revolutionary memory. The only county in the state named for a woman.

HEARD.—December 22, 1830.

Hon. Stephen Heard, President of the Executive Council, and de facto Governor of Georgia in 1780.

HENRY.—May 15, 1821.

Patrick Henry, of Virginia.

HOUSTOUN.—May 15, 1821.
> Hon. John Houstoun, of Savannah, Governor of Georgia in 1778 and 1784.

IRWIN.—December 15, 1818.
> Gen. Jared Irwin, Governor of Georgia, etc.

JACKSON.—February 11, 1796.
> General James Jackson, Governor of Georgia, U. S. Senator from Georgia, etc.

JASPER.—December 10, 1807.
> Name changed from Randolph to Jasper in honor of Sergeant William Jasper, December 10, 1812.

JEFF DAVIS.—1905.
> Jefferson Davis, President of the Confederacy.

JEFFERSON.—February 20, 1796.
> Thomas Jefferson, of Virginia, who drew the Declaration of Independence.

JENKINS.—1905.
> Hon. Chas. J. Jenkins, Governor of Georgia.

JOHNSON.—December 11, 1858.
> Hon. Herschel V. Johnson, Governor of Georgia, etc.

JONES.—December 10, 1807.
> Hon. James Jones, member of Congress, etc.

LAURENS.—December 10, 1807.
> Colonel John Laurens, who was killed in the Revolutionary War, near Combahee, S. C., August 27, 1782.

LEE.—December 11, 1826.
> Called after Richard Henry Lee, of Virginia, who, on June 7, 1776, moved "that the colonies declare themselves free and independent."

LIBERTY.—Sec. IV., Constitution of Georgia of 1777.
> As a tribute to the early and conspicuous devotion of the citizens of St. John's Parish to the cause of freedom, this county was called Liberty.

LINCOLN.—February 20, 1796.
> Major-General Benjamin Lincoln.

LOWNDES.—December 23, 1825.
> Hon. William J. Lowndes, of South Carolina, member of Congress, etc., whom Henry Clay pronounced to be "the wisest man he had ever known in Congress."

LUMPKIN.—December 3, 1832.
> Hon. Wilson Lumpkin, Governor of Georgia, U. S. Senator from Georgia, etc.

McDUFFIE.—October 18, 1870.
> Hon. George McDuffie, U. S. Senator from South Carolina, etc.

McINTOSH.—December 19, 1793.

Named to commemorate the services of the McIntosh family (Colonel John, General Lachlan McIntosh, etc).

MACON.—December 14, 1837.

Nathaniel Macon, of North Carolina.

MADISON.—December 5, 1811.

James Madison, President of the United States.

MARION.—December 14, 1827.

General Francis Marion, of South Carolina.

MERIWETHER.—December 14, 1827.

General David Meriwether.

MILLER.—February 26, 1856.

Hon. Andrew J. Miller, of Augusta.

MILTON.—December 18, 1857.

Colonel Homer V. Milton, of Jefferson county, Georgia, an officer in the old U. S. army.

MITCHELL.—December 21, 1857.

General Henry Mitchell, a resident and one of the early settlers of Hancock county.

MONROE.—May 15, 1821.

James Monroe, President of the United States.

MONTGOMERY.—December 19, 1793.

General Richard Montgomery, an early martyr to the cause of American liberty.

MORGAN.—December 10, 1807.

General Daniel Morgan, of Revolutionary memory.

MURRAY.—December 3, 1832.

Hon. Thomas W. Murray, of Lincoln county.

MUSCOGEE.—December 11, 1826. Indian name.

NEWTON.—December 24, 1821.

Named in honor of Sergeant John Newton, a Revolutionary celebrity.

OCONEE.—February 25, 1875. Indian name.

OGLETHORPE.—December 19, 1793.

Gen. James Oglethorpe, the founder of the colony of Georgia.

PAULDING.—December 3, 1832.

John Paulding, one of the captors of Major Andre.

PICKENS.—December 5, 1853.

General Andrew Pickens, of South Carolina.

PIERCE.—December 18, 1857.

Franklin Pierce, President of the United States.

PIKE.—December 9, 1822.

General Zebulon M. Pike.

POLK.—December 20, 1851.

James K. Polk, President of the United States.

PULASKI.—December 13, 1808.

Count Casimir Pulaski.

PUTNAM.—December 10, 1807.

Major-General Israel Putnam.

QUITMAN.—December 10, 1858.

General John A. Quitman.

RABUN.—December 21, 1819.

Hon. William Rabun, Governor of Georgia, etc.

RANDOLPH.—December 20, 1828.

John Randolph, of Roanoke.

RICHMOND.—Sec. IV., Constitution of Georgia of 1777.

Duke of Richmond, of England, a warm friend of American liberty.

ROCKDALE.—October 18, 1870.

So called because of the geological characteristics of the locality, and
the underlying granite formation.

SCHLEY.—December 22, 1857.

Hon. William Schley, Governor of Georgia.

SCREVEN.—December 14, 1793.

General James Screven, who fell in the affair near Midway church,
in November, 1778.

SPALDING.—December 20, 1851.

Hon. Thomas Spaulding, member of Congress, etc.

STEPHENS.—1905.

Alexander H. Stephens, Congressman, Vice-President of the Confederacy and Governor of Georgia.

STEWART.—December 23, 1830.

General Daniel Stewart, of Liberty county, an active partisan officer
in the army of the Revolution.

SUMTER.—December 26, 1831.

Major-General Thomas Sumter, of Revolutionary distinction.

TALBOT.—December 14, 1827.

Hon. Matthew Talbot, Governor of Georgia, etc.

TALIAFERRO.—December 24, 1825.

Hon. Benjamin Taliaferro, member of Congress, etc.

TATNALL.—December 5, 1801.

Hon. Josiah Tatnall, Governor of Georgia, etc.

TAYLOR.—January 15, 1852.

General Zachary Taylor, President of the United States.

TELFAIR.—December 10, 1807.

Hon. Edward Telfair, Governor of Georgia, etc.

TERRELL.—February 16, 1856.

Dr. William Terrell, of Hancock county.

THOMAS.—December 23, 1825.

General Jett Thomas, one of the early settlers of Baldwin county.

TIFT.—1905.

Named for Nelson Tift, of Albany.

TOOMBS.—1905.

Robert Toombs, member of Congress.

TOWNS.—March 6, 1856.

Hon. George W. Towns, Governor of Georgia, etc.

TROUP.—December 11, 1826.

Hon. George M. Troup, Governor of Georgia, U. S. Senator from Georgia, etc.

TURNER.—1905.

Hon. Henry G. Turner, of Brooks county, Congressman, Judge Supreme Court.

TWIGGS.—December 14, 1809.

General John Twiggs, of Revolutionary memory.

UNION.—December 3, 1832.

Union because few but Union men resided in it, i. e., Union men in contra-distinction to States' rights men or Nullifiers.

UPSON.—December 15, 1824.

Hon. Stephen Upson, of Oglethorpe county, an eminent lawyer and one of the first men of his day in Georgia.

WALKER.—December 18, 1833.

Major Freeman Walker, of Augusta, U. S. Senator from Georgia, etc.

WALTON.—December 15, 1818.

Hon. George Walton, signer from Georgia of the Declaration of Independence, Governor of Georgia, etc., etc.

WARE.—December 15, 1824.

Hon. Nicholas Ware, U. S. Senator from Georgia.

WARREN.—December 19, 1793.

Major-General Joseph Warren, who fell at the battle of Bunker Hill.

WASHINGTON.—February 25, 1784.

Gen. George Washington.

WAYNE.—May 11, 1803.

Major-General Anthony Wayne.

WEBSTER.—February 21, 1856.

Name changed from Kinchafoonee county, established December 16, 1853, to Webster county, in honor of Daniel Webster.

WHITE.—December 22, 1857.

Col. John White, of Revolutionary memory.

WHITFIELD.—December 30, 1851.

Rev. George Whitfield, the celebrated preacher.

WILCOX.—December 22, 1857.

Captain John Wilcox, one of the early settlers of Telfair county.

WILKES.—Sec. IV., Constitution of Georgia of 1777.

John Wilkes, the great champion of American liberty.

WILKINSON.—May 11, 1803.

General James Wilkinson.

WORTH.—December 20, 1853.

General William J. Worth.

CONGRESSIONAL DISTRICTS.

Under the Federal Constitution of 1787, Georgia's apportionment of representatives in congress was three. On the 8th of December, 1790, the legislature divided the state into three congressional districts. By the first census of the United States the representation of the commonwealh in the lower house of congress was fixed at two members, they being elected on the general ticket. Under the second census Georgia had four representatives; under the third she had six; and under the fourth seven. By act of December 22, 1825, the state was laid off and divided into seven congressional districts. This statute was, however, repealed in the following year, and it was not until 1843 that the congressional district system came again into play, when, by the U. S. Senate act of June 25, 1842, it was declared that in every case where a state was entitled to more than one representative in congress, the members should be elected by districts, each district electing one representative. In pursuance of an act, approved December 23d of that year, Georgia was divided into eight congressional districts. Twenty-eight years later, when an act to lay out and establish congressional districts in this state, in conformity with the last apportionment of representation in the congress of the United States passed the general assembly, the number of districts was increased to nine. Again in 1883, the state was re-districted and, by an act assented to August 28th of that year, the commonwealth of Georgia was divided into ten congressional districts. This was done in pursuance of, and in conformity with an act of congress, approved on February 25th of the preceding year.

By an act to divide the state of Georgia into eleven congressional districts, in conformity to an act of the congress of the United States, approved February 7, 1891, assented to September 26, 1891, the districts were re-arranged as follows:

FIRST DISTRICT.—Chatham, Burke, Screven, Emanuel, Bulloch, Effingham, Bryan, Tatnall, Liberty, McIntosh, Toombs and Jenkins (last two by Act of 1905).

25

SECOND DISTRICT.—Quitman, Clay, Randolph, Terrell, Calhoun, Dougherty, Worth, Early, Baker, Miller, Mitchell, Colquitt, Berrien, Decatur, Thomas, Grady, Turner and Tift (last three by Act of 1905).

THIRD DISTRICT.—Stewart, Webster, Sumter, Lee, Dooly, Wilcox, Schley, Pulaski, Twiggs, Houstoun, Macon, Taylor, Crawford, and Crisp (by act of 1905).

FOURTH DISTRICT.—Muscogee, Marion, Talbot, Harris, Meriwether, Troup, Coweta, Heard, Carroll and Chattahoochee.

FIFTH DISTRICT.—Fulton, Douglas, Campbell, Clayton, DeKalb, Rockdale, Newton and Walton.

SIXTH DISTRICT.—Bibb, Baldwin, Jones, Monroe, Upson, Pike, Spalding, Fayette, Henry and Butts.

SEVENTH DISTRICT.—Haralson, Paulding, Cobb, Polk, Floyd, Bartow, Chattooga, Gordon, Walker, Dade, Catoosa, Whitfield and Murray.

EIGHTH DISTRICT.—Jasper, Putnam, Morgan, Greene, Oconee, Clarke, Oglethorpe, Madison, Elbert, Hart, Franklin and Wilkes.

NINTH DISTRICT.—Fannin, Union, Towns, Rabun, Habersham, White, Lumpkin, Dawson, Gilmer, Pickens, Cherokee, Forsyth, Milton, Gwinnett, Jackson, Hall, Banks and Stephens (Act of 1905).

TENTH DISTRICT.—Richmond, Columbia, Lincoln, Jefferson, Glascock, McDuffie, Warren, Taliaferro, Washington, Wilkinson and Hancock.

ELEVENTH DISTRICT.—Glynn, Johnson, Laurens, Montgomery, Dodge, Telfair, Irwin, Coffee, Appling, Wayne, Pierce, Ware, Clinch, Echols, Lowndes, Brooks, Charlton, Camden, Jeff Davis (Act of 1905), and Ben Hill (Act of 1906).

STATE SENATORIAL DISTRICTS.

Senatorial districts were first established in Georgia by constitutional amendment in 1843. Section II. of an act approved December 23d of that year declared that the state should be divided into forty-seven senatorial districts. All of those districts, with the exception of the first or Chatham county, were to consist each of two counties. From every one of them a State Senator was to be chosen.

By paragraph I., section II., article II. of the Constitution of Georgia, as amended by the State Convention which assembled at Savannah in 1861, provision was made for the establishment of forty-four senatorial districts instead of forty-seven as theretofore. Each district was to be composed of three contiguous counties and was entitled to one Senator. This order of affairs, in the main, still obtains, and paragraph I., section II., article III. of the Constitution of Georgia of 1877, declares the forty-four state senatorial districts shall be composed as follows:

FIRST DISTRICT.—Chatham, Bryan and Effingham.

SECOND DISTRICT.—Liberty, Tatnall, McIntosh and Toombs.

THIRD DISTRICT.—Wayne, Pierce, Appling and Jeff Davis.

FOURTH DISTRICT.—Glynn, Camden and Charlton.

FIFTH DISTRICT.—Coffee, Ware and Clinch.

SIXTH DISTRICT.—Echols, Lowndes, Berrien and Tift.

SEVENTH DISTRICT.—Brooks, Thomas, Colquitt and Grady.

EIGHTH DISTRICT.—Decatur, Mitchell and Miller.

NINTH DISTRICT.—Early, Calhoun and Baker.

TENTH DISTRICT.—Dougherty, Lee and Worth.

ELEVENTH DISTRICT.—Clay, Randolph and Terrell.

TWELFTH DISTRICT.—Stewart, Webster and Quitman.

THIRTEENTH DISTRICT.—Sumter, Schley and Macon.

FOURTEENTH DISTRICT.—Dooly, Crisp, Wilcox and Pulaski.

FIFTEENTH DISTRICT.—Montgomery, Telfair, Dodge and Irwin.

SIXTEENTH DISTRICT.—Laurens, Emanuel and Johnson.

SEVENTEENTH DISTRICT.—Screven, Bulloch, Jenkins and Burke.

EIGHTEENTH DISTRICT.—Richmond, Glascock and Jefferson.

NINETEENTH DISTRICT.—Taliaferro, Greene and Warren.

TWENTIETH DISTRICT.—Baldwin, Hancock and Washington.

TWENTY-FIRST DISTRICT.—Twiggs, Wilkinson and Jones.

TWENTY-SECOND DISTRICT.—Bibb, Monroe and Pike.

TWENTY-THIRD DISTRICT.—Houstoun, Crawford and Taylor.

TWENTY-FOURTH DISTRICT.—Muscogee, Marion and Chattahoochee.

TWENTY-FIFTH DISTRICT.—Harris, Upson and Talbot.

TWENTY-SIXTH DISTRICT.—Spalding, Butts and Fayette.

TWENTY-SEVENTH DISTRICT.—Newton, Walton, Oconee and Rockdale.

TWENTY-EIGHTH DISTRICT.—Jasper, Putnam and Morgan.

TWENTY-NINTH DISTRICT.—Wilkes, Columbia, Lincoln and McDuffie.

THIRTIETH DISTRICT.—Oglethorpe, Madison, Elbert and Clarke.

THIRTY-FIRST DISTRICT.—Hart, Habersham, Franklin and Stephens.

THIRTY-SECOND DISTRICT.—White, Dawson and Lumpkin.

THIRTY-THIRD DISTRICT.—Hall, Banks and Jackson.

THIRTY-FOURTH DISTRICT.—Gwinnett, DeKalb and Henry.

THIRTY-FIFTH DISTRICT.—Clayton, Cobb and Fulton.

THIRTY-SIXTH DISTRICT.—Campbell, Coweta, Meriwether and Douglas.

THIRTY-SEVENTH DISTRICT.—Carroll, Heard and Troup.

THIRTY-EIGHTH DISTRICT.—Haralson, Polk and Paulding.

THIRTY-NINTH DISTRICT.—Milton, Cherokee and Forsyth.

FORTIETH DISTRICT.—Union, Towns and Rabun.

FORTY-FIRST DISTRICT.—Pickens, Fannin and Gilmer.

FORTY-SECOND DISTRICT.—Bartow, Floyd and Chattooga.

FORTY-THIRD DISTRICT.—Murray, Gordon and Whitfield.

FORTY-FOURTH DISTRICT.—Walker, Dade and Catoosa.

JUDICIAL CIRCUITS.

In connection with the judicial circuits, it may be mentioned that under the act organizing the Supreme Court of Georgia, approved December 10, 1845, provision was made for the laying out and establishing of five judicial districts. These districts were formed with reference to the sessions of the Supreme Court and were as follows:

The First District was composed of the Eastern and Southern Judicial Circuits; the Second comprised the Southwestern and Chattahoochee Judicial Circuits. The Third District consisted of the Coweta and Flint Judicial Circuits; the Fourth comprised the Western and Cherokee Judicial Circuits, while the Fifth District was composed of the Middle, Northern and Ocumulgee Judicial Circuits.

The Supreme Court continued to hold its sessions at the several points designated within these districts until 1868. By the Constitution then framed it was declared that the ambulatory character of that tribunal must terminate, and that henceforth its place of meeting should be the seat of government of the commonwealth. Since December, 1868, the Supreme Court has been permanently established at the state capitol, Atlanta, Georgia.

According to the Code the entire state constitutes one Supreme Judicial District. It is divided into twenty-five judicial circuits in reference to the jurisdiction and sessions of the superior courts, which circuits are as follows:

ALBANY CIRCUIT.—Organized by Act of October 17, 1870. It now comprises Baker, Calhoun, Decatur, Dougherty, Mitchell, Turner, and Worth counties.

ATLANTA CIRCUIT.—Erected by Act of February 21, 1869, changing the name of Coweta Judicial Circuit (organized by Act of December 16, 1833) to Atlanta Circuit. Fulton county now composes it.

ATLANTIC CIRCUIT.—First organized. Now composed of Bryan, Effingham, Liberty, and McIntosh counties.

AUGUSTA CIRCUIT.—Organized by Act of October 24, 1870. It now consists of Burke, Columbia, McDuffie, and Richmond counties.

BLUE RIDGE CIRCUIT.—Organized by Act of November 24, 1851. Now composed of Cherokee, Cobb, Fannin Forsythe, Gilmer, Milton, and Pickens counties.

BRUNSWICK CIRCUIT.—Organized by Act of February 8, 1856. It now comprises Appling, Camden, Charlton, Clinch Coffee, Glynn, Jeff Davis, Pierce, Ware, and Wayne counties.

CHATTAHOOCHEE CIRCUIT.—Organized by Act of December 22, 1826. Now composed of Chattahooche, Harris, Marion, Muscogee, Talbot, and Taylor counties.

CHEROKEE CIRCUIT.—Organized by Act of December 3, 1832. Now composed of Bartow, Catoosa, Dade, Gordon, Murray, and Whitfield counties.

CORDELE CIRCUIT.—Organized by Act of August 6, 1906. Composed of Ben Hill, Crisp, Dooly, Irwin, and Wilcox counties.

COWETA CIRCUIT.—See Act of February 28, 1874, changing the name of Tallapoosa Circuit (organized by Act of February 28, 1856) to that of Coweta Circuit. Now composed of Carroll, Coweta, Heard, Meriwether, and Troup counties.

EASTERN CIRCUIT.—First organized by Act of February 9, 1797. Reorganized by Act of December 19, 1818. It now comprises only Chatham county.

FLINT CIRCUIT.—Organized by Act of December 24, 1821, and now composed of Butts, Fayette, Henry, Monroe, Pike, Spalding, and Upson counties.

MACON CIRCUIT.—Organized by Act of November 24, 1851. It now consists of Crawford, Houstoun, and Bibb counties.

MIDDLE CIRCUIT.—First organized by Act of February 9, 1797. Reorganized by Act of December 19, 1818. Now composed of Bulloch, Emanuel, Jefferson, Jenkins, Johnson, Screven, Tatnall, Toombs, and Washington counties.

NORTHEASTERN CIRCUIT.—Created by Act of August 8, 1881. It now consists of Dawson, Hall, Habersham, Rabun, Towns, White, Stephens, Lumpkin, and Union counties.

NORTHERN CIRCUIT.—Organized by Act of December 19, 1818, and now comprising Elbert, Glascock, Hancock, Hart, Lincoln, Madison, Oglethorpe, Taliaferro, Warren, and Wilkes counties.

OCUMULGEE CIRCUIT.—First organized by Act of December 10, 1807, and reorganized by Act of December 19, 1818. It now consists of Baldwin, Greene, Laurens, Jasper, Jones, Morgan, Putnam, and Wilkinson counties.

26

OCONEE CIRCUIT.—Organized by Act of December 12, 1871. Now composed of Dodge, Montgomery, Pulaski, Telfair, and Twiggs counties.

PAUTAULA CIRCUIT.—Created by Act of February 8, 1856. It now comprises the counties of Clay, Early, Miller, Quitmàn, Randolph, and Terrell.

ROME CIRCUIT.—Organized by Act of February 21, 1869. At present it consists of the counties of Floyd, Chattooga, and Walker.

SOUTHERN CIRCUIT.—Organized by Act of December 19, 1818. It now comprises Berrien, Brooks, Colquitt, Echols, Grady, Lowndes, Thomas, and Tift counties.

SOUTHWESTERN CIRCUIT.—Organized by Act of December 10, 1840. It is now composed of Webster, Schley, Stewart, Lee, Macon, and Sumter counties.

STONE MOUNTAIN CIRCUIT.—Created by Act of September 8, 1885, and now consisting of Campbell, Clayton, DeKalb, Rockdale, and Newton counties.

TALLAPOOSA CIRCUIT.—Created by Act of November 26, 1890, and now consisting of the counties of Polk, Paulding, Haralson, and Douglas.

WESTERN CIRCUIT.—First organized by Act of February 9, 1797. Reorganized by Act of December 19, 1818. At present composed of the counties of Banks, Clarke, Oconee, Franklin, Gwinnett, Jackson, and Walton.

CONGRESSMEN FROM GEORGIA.

THE CONTINENTAL CONGRESS.

Place and Time of Sessions.

Philadelphia from Sept. 5, 1774, to Oct. 26, 1774; from May 10, 1775, to Dec. 12, 1776. Baltimore from Dec. 20, 1776, to March 4, 1777. Philadelphia from March 4, 1777, to Sept. 18, 1777. Lancaster from Sept. 27, 1777, to Sept. 27, 1777. York from Sept. 30, 1777, to June 27, 1778. Philadelphia from July 2, 1778, to June 21, 1783. Princeton from June 30, 1783, to Nov. 4, 1783. Annapolis from Nov. 26, 1783, to June 3, 1784. Trenton from Nov. 1, 1784, to Dec. 24, 1784. New York from Jan. 11, 1785, to Nov. 4, 1785; from Nov. 7, 1785, to Nov. 3, 1786; from Nov. 6, 1786, to Oct. 30, 1787; from Nov. 5, 1787, to Oct. 21, 1788.

DELEGATES FROM GEORGIA.

Abraham Baldwin, 1785-1788; Nathan Brownson, 1776-1778; Archibald Bulloch, 1775-1776; Joseph Clay, 1778-1780; William Few, 1780-1782; William Few, 1785-1788; William Gibbons, 1784-1786; Button Gwinnett, 1776-1777; John Habersham, 1785-1786; Lyman Hall, 1775-1779; John Houston, 1775-1777; William Houston, 1784-1787; Richard Howley, 1780-1781; Noble

Wimberly Jones, 1775-1776; Noble Wimberly Jones, 1781-1783; Edward Langworthy, 1777-1779; William Pierce, 1786-1787; Edward Telfair, 1777-1779; Edward Telfair, 1780-1783; George Walton, 1776-1779; George Walton, 1780-1781; Joseph Wood, 1777-1779; John J. Zubly, 1775-1776.

FIRST CONGRESS.—First session from March 4, 1789, to Sept. 29, 1789; second, from Jan. 4, 1790, to Aug. 12, 1790; third, from Dec. 6, 1790, to March 3, 1791.

Senators.—William Few, Augusta; James Gunn, Savannah.

Representatives.—Abraham Baldwin, Appling (took his seat April 20, 1789); James Jackson, Savannah; George Matthews, Oglethorpe county, (took his seat June 17, 1789).

SECOND CONGRESS.—First session from Oct. 24, 1791, to May 8, 1792; second, from Nov. 5, 1792, to March 2, 1793.

Senators.—William Few, James Gunn.

Representatives.—Abraham Baldwin; John Milledge, Savannah (elected in place of Anthony Wayne) took his seat Nov. 22, 1792; Anthony Wayne (election contested by James Jackson and seat declared by the House to be vacant March 21, 1792); Francis Willis, Savannah.

THIRD CONGRESS.—First session from Dec. 2, 1793, to June 9, 1794; second, from Nov. 3, 1794, to March 3, 1795.

Senators.—James Gunn; James Jackson, Savannah.

Representatives.—Abraham Baldwin; Thomas P. Carnes, Augusta.

FOURTH CONGRESS.—First session from Dec. 7, 1795, to June 1, 1796; second from Dec. 5, 1796, to March 3, 1797.

Senators.—James Gunn; James Jackson (resigned in 1795); Josiah Tatnall, Savannah (elected in place of James Jackson, resigned; took his seat April 12, 1796); George Walton, Augusta (appointed in place of James Jackson, resigned; took his seat Dec. 18, 1795).

Representatives.—Abraham Baldwin; John Milledge.

FIFTH CONGRESS.—First session from May 15, 1797, to July 10, 1797; second, from Nov. 13, 1797, to July 16, 1798; third, from Dec. 3, 1798, to March 3, 1799.

Senators.—James Gunn; Josiah Tatnall.

Representatives.—Abraham Baldwin; John Milledge.

SIXTH CONGRESS.—First session from Dec. 2, 1799, to May 14, 1800; second, from Nov. 17, 1800, to March 3, 1801.

Senators.—Abraham Baldwin; James Gunn.

Representatives.—James Jones, Savannah (died Jan. 13, 1801); Benjamin Taliaferro, Wilkes county.

SEVENTH CONGRESS.—First session from Dec. 7, 1801, to May 3, 1802; second, from Dec. 6, 1802, to March 3, 1803.

Senators.—Abraham Baldwin (elected President pro tempore Dec. 7, 1801, and April 17, 1802); James Jackson.

Representatives.—Peter Early, Madison county (elected in place of John Milledge, resigned; took his seat Jan. 10, 1803) ; David Meriwether, Wilkes county (elected in place of Benjamin Taliaferro, resigned; took his seat Dec. 6, 1802) ; John Milledge (resigned in 1802) ; Benjamin Taliaferro (resigned in 1802).

EIGHTH CONGRESS.—First session from Oct. 17, 1803, to March 27, 1804; second, from Nov. 5, 1804, to March 3, 1805.

Senators.—Abraham Baldwin; James Jackson.

Representatives.—Joseph Bryan, Savannah; Peter Early; Samuel Hammond, Savannah (seat declared vacant Feb. 2, 1805) ; David Meriwether.

NINTH CONGRESS.—First session from Dec. 2, 1805, to April 21, 1806; second, from Dec. 1, 1806, to March 3, 1807.

Senators.—Abraham Baldwin; James Jackson (died March 18, 1806) ; John Milledge (elected in place of James Jackson, deceased; took his seat Dec. 11, 1806).

Representatives.—William W. Bibb, Elbert county (elected in place of Thomas Spalding, resigned; took his seat Jan. 26, 1807) ; Joseph Bryan (resigned in 1806) ; Peter Early; Cowles Mead (election successfully contested by Thomas Spalding) ; David Meriwether; Dennis Smelt (elected in place of Joseph Bryan, resigned; took his seat Dec. 26, 1806) ; Thomas Spalding, Liberty county (successfully contested the election of Cowles Mead; took his seat Dec. 25, 1805; resigned in 1806).

TENTH CONGRESS.—First session from Oct. 26, 1807, to April 25, 1808; second, from Nov. 7, 1808, to March 3, 1809.

Senators.—William H. Crawford, Oglethorpe county (elected in place of Abraham Baldwin, deceased, in 1807, George Jones having been appointed pro tempore; took his seat Dec. 9, 1807) ; George Jones, Chatham county (appointed in place of Abraham Baldwin, deceased in 1807; took his seat Oct. 26, 1807) ; John Milledge (elected President pro tempore, Jan. 30, 1809).

Representatives.—William W. Bibb; Howell Cobb; Dennis Smelt; George M. Troup.

ELEVENTH CONGRESS.—First session from May 22, 1809, to June 28, 1809; second, from Nov. 27, 1809, to May 1, 1810; third, from Dec. 3, 1810, to March 3, 1811.

Senators.—William H. Crawford; John Milledge (resigned in 1809; Charles Tait (elected in place of John Milledge, resigned; took his seat Dec. 28, 1809).

Representatives.—William W. Bibb; Howell Cobb; Dennis Smelt; George M. Troup.

TWELFTH CONGRESS.—First session from Nov. 4, 1811, to July 6, 1812; second, from Nov. 2, 1812, to March 3, 1813.

Senators.—William H. Crawford (elected President pro tempore, March 24, 1812); Charles Tait.

Representatives.—William Barnett (elected in place of Howell Cobb, resigned; took his seat Nov. 27, 1812); William W. Bibb; Howell Cobb (resigned in 1812); Bolling Hall; George M. Troup.

THIRTEENTH CONGRESS.—First session from May 24, 1813, to Aug. 2, 1813; second, from Dec. 6, 1813, to April 18, 1814; third, from Sept. 19, 1814, to March 2, 1815.

Senators.—William Wyatt Bibb (elected Senator in place of William H. Crawford, resigned in 1813, William B. Bullock having been appointed pro tempore; took his seat Dec. 6, 1813); William B. Bullock, Savannah (appointed in place of William H. Crawford, resigned in 1813; took his seat May 24, 1813); Charles Tait; William H. Crawford (resigned, 1813).

Representatives.—William Barnett; William W. Bibb (elected Senator in place of William H. Crawford, resigned in 1813); Alfred Cuthbert, Monticello (elected in place of William W. Bibb, appointed Senator; took his seat Feb. 7, 1814); John Forsyth, Augusta; Bolling Hall; Thomas Telfair, Savannah; George M. Troup.

FOURTEENTH CONGRESS.—First session from Dec. 4, 1815, to April 30, 1816; second, from Dec. 2, 1816, to March 3, 1817.

Senators.—William W. Bibb (resigned in 1816); Charles Tait; George M. Troup (elected in place of William W. Bibb, resigned; took his seat Dec. 12, 1816).

Representatives.—Zadock Cook (elected in place of Alfred Cuthbert, resigned; took his seat Jan. 23, 1817); Alfred Cuthbert (resigned in 1816); John Forsyth; Bolling Hall; Wilson Lumpkin, Athens; Thomas Telfair; Richard Henry Wilde, Augusta.

FIFTEENTH CONGRESS.—First session from Dec. 1, 1817, to April 20, 1818; second, from Nov. 16, 1818, to March 3, 1819.

Senators.—John Forsyth (elected Senator in place of George M. Troup, resigned; took his seat Nov. 23, 1818; resigned Feb., 1819); Charles Tait; George M. Troup (resigned in 1818).

Representatives.—Joel Abbot, Washington; Thomas W. Cobb, Greensboro; Zadock Cook; Joel Crawford, Milledgeville; John Forsyth (elected Senator in place of George M. Troup, resigned; took his seat Nov. 23, 1818; resigned Feb., 1819); Robert Raymond Reid, Augusta (elected in place of John Forsyth, elected Senator; took his seat Feb. 18, 1819); William Terrell, Sparta.

SIXTEENTH CONGRESS.—First session from Dec. 6, 1819, to May 15, 1820; second, from Nov. 13, 1820, to March 3, 1821.

Senators.—John Elliott, Sunbury; Freeman Walker, Augusta (elected in place of John Forsyth, resigned Feb., 1819; took his seat Dec. 15, 1819).

Representatives.—Joel Abbot; Thomas W. Cobb, Lexington; Joel Crawford; John A. Cuthbert, Eatonton; Robert R. Reid; William Terrell.

SEVENTEENTH CONGRESS.—First session from Dec. 3, 1821, to May 8, 1822; second, from Dec. 2, 1822, to March 3, 1823.

Senators.—John Elliott; Nicholas Ware, Richmond (elected in place of Freeman Walker, resigned in 1821; took his seat Dec. 11, 1821).

Representatives.—Joel Abbott; Alfred Cuthbert; George R. Gilmer, Lexington; Robert R. Reid; Edward F. Tatnall, Savannah; Wiley Thompson, Elberton.

EIGHTEENTH CONGRESS.—First session from Dec. 1, 1823, to May 27, 1824; second, from Dec. 6, 1824, to March 3, 1825.

Senators.—Thomas W. Cobb (elected in place of Nicholas Ware, deceased; took his seat Dec. 6, 1824); John Elliott; Nicholas Ware (took his seat Jan. 19, 1824; died Sept. 7, 1824).

Representatives.—Joel Abbot; George Carey, Appling; Thomas W. Cobb (died Oct. 8, 1823); Alfred Cuthbert; John Forsyth; Edward F. Tatnall (took his seat March 27, 1824); Wiley Thompson; Richard Henry Wilde, Augusta (elected in place of Thomas W. Cobb, elected Senator; took his seat Feb. 7, 1825.

NINETEENTH CONGRESS.—First session from Dec. 5, 1825, to May 22, 1826; second, from Dec. 4, 1826, to March 3, 1827.

Senators.—John MacPherson Berrien, Savannah; Thomas W. Cobb.

Representatives.—George Cary; Alfred Cuthbert; John Forsyth; Charles E. Haynes, Sparta; James Meriwether, Athens; Edward F. Tatnall; Wiley Thompson.

TWENTIETH CONGRESS.—First session from Dec. 3, 1827, to May 26, 1828; second, from Dec. 1, 1828, to March 3, 1829.

Senators.—John MacPherson Berrien; Thomas W. Cobb (resigned in 1828); Oliver H. Prince, Macon (elected in place of Thomas W. Cobb, resigned; took his seat Dec. 1, 1828).

Representatives.—John Floyd, Jefferson; Tomlinson Fort, Milledgeville; George R. Gilmer; Charles E. Haynes; Wilson Lumpkin; Wiley Thompson; Richard H. Wilde.

TWENTY-FIRST CONGRESS.—First session from Dec. 7, 1829, to May 31, 1830; second, from Dec. 6, 1830, to March 3, 1831.

Senators.—John MacPherson Berrien (resigned March 9, 1829); John Forsyth (elected in place of John MacPherson Berrien, resigned; took his seat Dec. 8, 1829); George M. Troup, Dublin.

Representatives.—Thomas F. Foster, Greensboro; Charles E. Haynes; Henry G. Lamar, Macon; Wilson Lumpkin; Wiley Thompson; James M. Wayne, Savannah; Richard H. Wilde.

TWENTY-SECOND CONGRESS.—First session from Dec. 5, 1831, to July 16, 1832; second, from Dec. 3, 1832, to March 2, 1833.

Senators.—John Forsyth; George M. Troup.

Representatives.—Augustin Smith Clayton, Athens; Thomas F. Foster, Henry G. Lamar; Daniel Newman McDonough; Wiley Thompson; James M. Wayne; Richard H. Wilde.

TWENTY-THIRD CONGRESS.—First session from Dec. 2, 1833, to June 30, 1834; second, from Dec. 1, 1834, to March 3, 1835.

Senators.—Alfred Cuthbert (elected in place of John Forsyth, resigned; took his seat Jan. 12, 1835; John Forsyth (resigned June 27, 1834, having been appointed Secretary of State); John P. King, Augusta.

Representatives.—Augustin S. Clayton; John Coffee, Jacksonville; Thomas F. Foster; R. L. Gamble, Louisville; G. R. Gilmer; Seaborn Jones, Columbus; William Schley, Augusta; James M. Wayne (resigned Jan. 13, 1835); Richard H. Wilde.

TWENTY-FOURTH CONGRESS.—First session from Dec. 7, 1835, to July 4, 1836; second, Dec. 5, 1836, to March 3, 1837.

Senators.—Alfred Cuthbert; John P. King.

Representatives.—Julius C. Alford, La Grange (elected in place of George W. Towns, resigned; took his seat Jan. 31, 1837); Jesse F. Cleveland, Decatur; John Coffee (died in 1836); William C. Dawson, Greensboro (elected in place of John Coffee, deceased; took his seat Dec. 26, 1836); Thomas Glascock, Augusta; Seaton Grantland, Milledgeville; Charles E. Haynes; Hopkins Holsey, Hamilton; Jabez Jackson, Clarkesville; George W. Owens, Savannah; George W. Towns, Talbotton (resigned in 1836).

TWENTY-FIFTH CONGRESS.—First session from Sept. 4, 1837, to Oct. 16, 1837; second, from Dec. 4, 1837, to July 9, 1838; third, from Dec. 3, 1838, to March 3, 1839.

Senators.—Alfred Cuthbert; John P. King (resigned Nov. 1, 1837); Wilson Lumpkin (elected in place of John P. King, resigned; took his seat Dec. 13, 1837).

Representatives.—Jesse F. Cleveland; Wm. C. Dawson; Thomas Glascock; Seaton Grantland; Charles E. Haynes; Hopkins Holsey; Jabez Jackson; George W. Owens; George W. Towns.

TWENTY-SIXTH CONGRESS.—First session from Dec. 2, 1839, to July 21, 1840; second, from Dec. 7, 1840, to March 3, 1841.

Senators.—Alfred Cuthbert; Wilson Lumpkin.

Representatives.—Julius C. Alford; Edward J. Black, Jacksonboro; Walter T. Colquitt, Columbus(resigned in 1840); Mark A. Cooper, Columbus; Wm. C. Dawson; Richard W. Habersham, Clarkesville; Hines Holt, Columbus (elected in place of Walter T. Colquitt, resigned; took his seat Feb. 1, 1841); Thomas Butler King, Waynesville; Eugenius A. Nisbet, Macon; Lott Warren, Palmyra.

TWENTY-SEVENTH CONGRESS.—First session from May 31, 1841, to Sept.

13, 1841; second, from Dec. 6, 1841, to Aug. 31, 1842; third, from Dec. 5, 1842, to March 3, 1843.

Senators.—John M. Berrien; Alfred Cuthbert.

Representatives.—Julius C. Alford; Edward J. Black (took his seat March 2, 1842); Walter T. Colquitt (took his seat Feb. 1, 1842); Mark A. Cooper (took his seat Feb. 1, 1842); George W. Crawford, Augusta (elected in place of Richard W. Habersham, deceased; took his seat Feb. 1, 1843); William C. Dawson; Thomas F. Foster, Columbus; Roger L. Gamble; Richard W. Habersham (died Dec. 2, 1842); Thomas Butler King; James A. Meriwether, Edenton; Eugenius A. Nisbet; Lott Warren.

TWENTY-EIGHTH CONGRESS.—First session from Dec. 4, 1843, to June 17, 1844; second, from Dec. 2, 1844, to March 3, 1845.

Senators.—John M. Berrien; Walter T. Colquitt.

Representatives.—Edward J. Black; Absalom H. Chappell, Macon; Duncan L. Clinch, St. Marys (elected in place of John Millen, deceased; took his seat Feb. 15, 1844); Howell Cobb, Athens; Hugh A. Haralson, La Grange; John H. Lumpkin, Rome; John Millen, Savannah (died Oct. 15, 1843); A. H. Stephens, Crawfordville; William H. Stiles, Cassville.

TWENTY-NINTH CONGRESS.—First session from Dec. 1, 1845, to Aug. 10, 1846; second, from Dec. 7, 1846, to March 3, 1847.

Senators.—John M. Berrien; Walter T. Colquitt.

Representatives.—Howell Cobb; Hugh A. Haralson; Seaborn Jones; Thomas Butler King, Frederica; John H. Lumpkin; Washington Poe (resigned in 1845, having never taken his seat); A. H. Stephens; Robert Toombs, Washington; George W. Towns (elected in place of Washington Poe, resigned; took his seat Jan. 27, 1846).

THIRTIETH CONGRESS.—First session from Dec. 6, 1847, to Aug. 14, 1848; second, from Dec. 4, 1848, to March 3, 1849.

Senators.—John M. Berrien; Walter T. Colquitt (resigned in 1848); Herschell V. Johnson, Milledgeville (appointed in place of Walter T. Colquitt, resigned; took his seat Feb. 14, 1848).

Representatives.—Howell Cobb; Hugh A. Haralson; Alfred Iverson, Columbus; John W. Jones, Griffin; Thomas Butler King; John H. Lumpkin; A. H. Stephens; Robert Toombs.

THIRTY-FIRST CONGRESS.—First session from Dec. 3, 1849, to Sept. 30, 1850; second, from Dec. 2, 1850, to March 3, 1851.

Senators.—John M. Berrien; William C. Dawson, Greensboro.

Representatives.—Howell Cobb (elected Speaker Dec. 21, 1849); Thomas C. Hackett, Rome; Hugh A. Haralson; Joseph W. Jackson, Savannah (elected in place of Thomas Butler King, resigned in 1849; took his seat March 4, 1850); Allen F. Owen, Talbotton; A. H. Stephens; Robert Toombs; Marshall J. Wellborn, Columbus.

THIRTY-SECOND CONGRESS.—First session from Dec. 1, 1851, to Aug. 31, 1852; second, from Dec. 6, 1852, to March 3, 1853.

Senators.—John M. Berrien (resigned May 28, 1852); Robert M. Charlton, Savannah (appointed in place of John MacPherson Berrein, resigned; took his seat June 11, 1852); William C. Dawson.

Representatives.—David J. Bailey, Jackson; E. W. Chastain, Toccoa; Junius Hillyer, Monroe; Joseph W. Jackson; James Johnson, Columbus; Charles Murphy, Decatur; Alex. H. Stephens; Robert Toombs.

THIRTY-THIRD CONGRESS.—First session from Dec. 5, 1853, to Aug. 7, 1854; second, from Dec. 4, 1854, to March 3, 1855.

Senators.—William C. Dawson, Greensboro; Robert Toombs (took his seat March 4, 1853).

Representatives.—David J. Bailey; E. W. Chastain; Alfred H. Colquitt, Newton; William B. W. Dent, Newnan; Junius Hillyer, Monroe; David A. Reese, Monticello; James L. Seward, Thomasville; A. H. Stephens.

THIRTY-FOURTH CONGRESS.—First session from Dec. 3, 1855, to Aug. 18, 1856; second, from Aug. 21, 1856, to Aug. 30, 1856; third, from Dec. 1, 1856, to March 3, 1857.

Senators.—Alfred Iverson, Columbus; Robert Toombs.

Representatives.—Howell Cobb; Martin J. Crawford, Columbus; Nathaniel G. Foster, Madison; John H. Lumpkin; James L. Seward, Thomasville; Alex H. Stephens; Robert P. Trippe, Forsyth; Hiram Warner, Greenville.

THIRTY-FIFTH CONGRESS.—First session from Dec. 7, 1857, to June 14, 1858; second, from Dec. 6, 1858, to March 3, 1859.

Senators.—Alfred Iverson; Robert Toombs.

Representatives.—Martin J. Crawford; Lucius J. Gartrell, Atlanta; Joshua Hill, Madison; James Jackson, Athens; James L. Seward; Alex H. Stephens; Robert P. Trippe; Augustus R. Wright, Rome.

THIRTY-SIXTH CONGRESS.—First session from Dec. 5, 1859, to June 25, 1860; second, from Dec. 3, 1860, to March 3, 1861.

Senators.—Alfred Iverson, Columbus (retired from the Senate Jan. 28, 1861); Robert Toombs (seat declared vacant March 14, 1861).

Representatives.—Martin J. Crawford; Lucius J. Gartrell; Thomas Hardeman, Jr., Macon; Joshua Hill; James Jackson; John J. Jones, Waynesboro; Peter E. Love, Thomasville; John W. H. Underwood, Rome. (The Georgia delegation retired from the House Jan. 23, 1861.)

THIRTY-SEVENTH CONGRESS.—First session from July 4, 1861, to Aug. 6, 1861; second, from Dec. 2, 1861, to July 17, 1862; third, from Dec. 1, 1862, to March 3, 1863.

Senators.—(Vacant).

Representatives.—(Vacant).

THIRTY-EIGHTH CONGRESS.—First session from Dec. 7, 1863, to July 4, 1864; second, from Dec. 5, 1864, to March 3, 1865.

Senators.—(Vacant).

Representatives.—(Vacant).

THIRTY-NINTH CONGRESS.—First session from Dec. 4, 1865, to July 28, 1866; second, from Dec. 3, 1866, to March 3, 1867.

Senators.—(Vacant).

Representatives.—(Vacant).

FORTIETH CONGRESS.—First session from March 4, 1867, to March 30, 1867; July 3, 1867, to July 20, 1867; Nov. 21, 1867, to Dec. 2, 1867; second, from Dec. 2, 1867, to July 27, 1868; Sept. 21, 1868, to Sept. 21, 1868; Oct. 16, 1868, to Oct. 16, 1868; Nov. 10, 1868, to Nov. 10, 1868; third, from Dec. 7, 1868, to March 3, 1869.

Senators.—(Vacant).

Representatives.—Joseph W. Clift, Savannah (took his seat July 25, 1868); W. P. Edwards, Butler (took his seat July 25, 1868); Samuel F. Gove, Griswoldville (took his seat July 25, 1868); Charles H. Prince, Augusta (took his seat July 25, 1868); Nelson Tift, Albany (took his seat July 25, 1868); P. M. B. Young, Cartersville (took his seat July 25, 1868).

FORTY-FIRST CONGRESS.—First session from March 4, 1869, to April 10, 1869; second, from Dec. 6, 1869, to July 15, 1870; third, from Dec. 5, 1870, to March 3, 1871.

Senators.—Joshua Hill, Madison (took his seat Feb. 1, 1871); H. V. M. Miller (took his seat Feb. 24, 1871).

Representatives.—Marion Bethune, Talbotton (took his seat Jan. 16, 1871); Stephen A. Corker, Waynesboro (election unsuccessfully contested by Thomas P. Beard; took his seat Jan. 24, 1871); Jefferson F. Long, Macon (took his seat Jan. 24, 1871); William W. Paine, Savannah (took his seat Jan. 23, 1871); William P. Price, Dahlonega (took his seat Feb. 24, 1871); Richard H. Whiteley, Bainbridge (election unsuccessfully contested by Nelson Taft; took his seat Feb. 9, 1871); P. M. B. Young (took his seat Feb. 24, 1871).

FORTY-SECOND CONGRESS.—First session from March 4, 1871, to April 20, 1871; second, from Dec. 4, 1871, to June 10, 1872; third, from Dec. 2, 1872, to March 3, 1873.

Senators.—Joshua Hill; Thomas Manson Norwood, Savannah (election unsuccessfully contested by Foster Blodgett; took his seat Dec. 19, 1871).

Representatives.—Erasmus W. Beck, Griffin (elected in place of Thomas J. Speer, deceased; took his seat Dec. 2, 1872); John Summerfield Bigby, Newnan; Dudley M. DuBoise, Washington (election unsuccessfully contested by J. S. Fannin); A. T. McIntyre, Thomasville (election unsuccessfully contested by Virgil Hillyer); William P. Price; Thomas J. Speer,

Barnesville (died Aug. 18, 1872); Richard H. Whiteley (election unsuccessful contested by Nelson Tift); P. M. B. Young.

FORTY-THIRD CONGRESS.—First session from Dec. 1, 1873, to June 23, 1874; second, from Dec. 7, 1874, to March 3, 1875.

Senators.—John B. Gordon, Atlanta; Thomas Manson Norwood.

Representatives.—Hiram P. Bell, Cumming; James H. Blount, Macon; Phillip Cook, Americus; James C. Freeman Griffin; Henry R. Harris, Greenville (election unsuccessfully contested by M. Bethune); Morgan Rawls, Guyton (election successfully contested by Andrew Sloan); Andrew Sloan, Savannah (successfully contested the election of Morgan Rawls; took his seat March 24, 1874); Alex H. Stephens; Richard H. Whiteley; P. M. B. Young.

FORTY-FOURTH CONGRESS.—First session from Dec. 6, 1875, to Aug. 15, 1876; second, from Dec. 4, 1876, to March 3, 1877.

Senators.—John B. Gordon; Thomas Manson Norwood.

Representatives.—James H. Blount; Milton A. Candler, Atlanta; Philip Cook; William H. Felton, Cartersville; Henry R. Harris; Julian Hartridge, Savannah; Benjamin H. Hill, Atlanta (elected in place of Garnet McMillan, deceased, in 1875; took his seat Dec. 6, 1875); William E. Smith, Albany; A. H. Stephens.

FORTY-FIFTH CONGRESS.—First session from Oct. 15, 1877, to Dec. 3, 1877; second, from Dec. 3, 1877, to June 20, 1878; third, from Dec. 2, 1878, to March 3, 1879.

Senators.—John B. Gordon; Benjamin H. Hill, Atlanta.

Representatives.—Hiram P. Bell; James H. Blount; Milton A. Candler; Philip Cook; William H. Felton; Henry R. Harris; Julian Hartridge (died Jan. 8, 1879); William E. Smith; Alex H. Stephens.

FORTY-SIXTH CONGRESS.—First session from March 18, 1879, to July 1, 1879; second, from Dec. 1, 1879, to June 16, 1880; third, from Dec. 6, 1880, to March 3, 1881.

Senators.—Benjamin H. Hill (took his seat Jan. 22, 1881); Joseph E. Brown, Atlanta (unseated Jan. 22, 1881, by H. Bisbee).

Representatives.—John C. Nicholls, Blackshear; Phillip Cook; N. J. Hammond, Atlanta; William H. Felton; Emory Speer, Athens; William E. Smith, Albany; Henry Persons, Geneva; James H. Blount, Macon; Alex H. Stephens.

FORTY-SEVENTH CONGRESS.—First session from Dec. 5, 1881, to Aug. 8, 1882; second, from Dec. 4, 1882, to March 3, 1883; special session of the Senate from Oct. 10, 1881, to Oct. 29, 1881.

Senators.—Joseph E. Brown; Pope Barrow, Athens (took his seat Dec. 5, 1882, to fill vacancy caused by death of B. H. Hill.

Representatives.—George R. Black, Sylvania; Phillip Cook; N. J. Hammond; J. C. Clements, LaFayette; Emory Speer; Henry G. Turner, Quit-

Forty-eighth Congress.—First session from Dec. 3, 1883, to July 7, 1884; second, from Dec. 1, 1884, to March 3, 1885.

Senators.—Joseph E. Brown; Alfred H. Colquitt, Atlanta.

Representatives.—Thomas Hardeman, Macon; Henry G. Turner; H. Buchanan; James H. Blount; Seaborn Reese; John C. Nicholls; Charles F. Crisp, Americus; N. J. Hammond; J. C. Clements; Allen D. Candler, Gainesville.

Forty-ninth Congress.—First session from Dec. 7, 1885, to Aug. 5, 1886; second; from December 6, 1886, to March 3, 1887; special session of Senate from March 4, 1885, to April 2, 1885.

Senators.—Joseph E. Brown; Alfred H. Colquitt.

Representatives.—Thomas M. Norwood, Savannah; Charles F. Crisp; Nathaniel J. Hammond; Judson C. Clements; A. D. Candler; Henry G. Turner; Henry R. Harris; James H. Blount; Seaborn Reese; G. T. Barnes, Augusta.

Fiftieth Congress.—First session from Dec. 5, 1887, to Oct. 20, 1888; second from Dec. 3, 1888, to March 3, 1889.

Senators.—Joseph E. Brown; A. H. Colquitt.

Representatives.—Thomas M. Norwood; Charles F. Crisp; John D. Stewart, Griffin; Judson C. Clements, Rome; Allen D. Chandler; Henry G. Turner; Thomas W. Grimes, Columbus; James H. Blount; Henry H. Carlton, Athens; George T. Barnes.

Fifty-first Congress.—First session from Dec. 2, 1889, to Oct. 1, 1890; second, from Dec. 1, 1890, to March 2, 1891.

Senators.—Joseph E. Brown; A. H. Colquitt.

Representatives.—Rufus E. Lester, Savannah; Charles F. Crisp; John D. Stewart; Judson C. Clements; Allen D. Candler; Henry G. Turner; Thomas W. Grimes; James H. Blount; Henry H. Carlton; George T. Barnes.

Fifty-second Congress.—First session from Dec. 7, 1891, to Aug. 5, 1892; second, from Dec. 5, 1892, to March 3, 1893.

Senators.—A. H. Colquitt; John B. Gordon.

Representatives.—Rufus E. Lester; Charles F. Crisp; L. F. Livingston, Covington; Robert W. Everett, Fish; Thomas E. Winn, Gwinnett county; Henry G. Turner; Charles L. Moses, Turin; James H. Blount; Thomas G. Lawson, Eatonton; Thomas E. Watson, Thomson.

Fifty-third Congress.—First session from Aug. 7, 1893, to Nov. 3, 1893; second, from Dec. 4, 1893, to Aug. 28, 1894; third, from Dec. 3, 1894, to March 3, 1895.

Senators.—A. H. Colquitt (died March 26, 1894); Patrick Walsh, Augusta (took his seat April 9, 1894, having been appointed to fill the vacancy caused by the death of A. H. Colquitt); John B. Gordon.

Representatives.—Rufus E. Lester; Charles F. Crisp; Leonidas F. Liv-

man; H. Buchanan, Newman; James H. Blount; S. Reese, Sparta (filled the vacancy caused by resignation of A. H. Stephens, and took his seat Dec. 4, 1882); A. H. Stephens (resigned in 1882).

ingston; John W. Maddox, Rome; F. C. Tate, Jasper; Henry G. Turner; Benjamin E. Russell, Bainbridge; Charles L. Moses; Thomas B. Cabaniss, Forsyth; Thomas G. Lawson; James C. C. Black, Augusta.

FIFTY-FOURTH CONGRESS.—First session from Dec. 2, 1895, to June 11, 1896; second, from Dec. 7, 1896, to March 2, 1897.

Senators.—John B. Gordon; A. O. Bacon, Macon.

Representatives.—Rufus E. Lester; C. F. Crisp (died Oct. 26, 1896); L. F. Livingston; John W. Maddox; Farish C. Tate; Henry G. Turner; B. E. Russell; C. L. Moses; C. L. Bartlett, Macon; Thomas G. Lawson; J. C. C. Black; C. R. Crisp, Americus (elected to succeed his father, C. F. Crisp, deceased; took his seat Dec. 19, 1896).

FIFTY-FIFTH CONGRESS.—First session from March 15, 1897, to July 24, 1897; second, from Dec. 6, 1897, to July 8, 1898; third, from Dec. 5, 1898, to March 3, 1899.

Senators.—Augustus O. Bacon; Alexander S. Clay, Marietta.

Representatives.—Rufus E. Lester; Elijah B. Lewis, Montezuma; L. F. Livingston; John W. Maddox; Farish C. Tate; William G. Brantley, Brunswick; James M. Griggs, Dawson; William C. Adamson, Carrollton; C. L. Bartlett; William M. Howard, Lexington; William H. Fleming, Augusta.

FIFTY-SIXTH CONGRESS.—First session from Dec. 4, 1899, to June 7, 1900; second, from Dec. 3, 1900, to March 4, 1901.

Senators.—Augustus O. Bacon; A. S. Clay.

Representatives.—Rufus E. Lester; Elijah B. Lewis; Leonidas F. Livingston; John W. Maddox; Farish C. Tate; William G. Brantley; James M. Griggs; William C. Adamson; Charles L. Bartlett; William M. Howard; William H. Fleming.

FIFTY-SEVENTH CONGRESS.—First session from Dec. 2, 1901, to July 1, 1902; second, from Dec. 1, 1902, to March 4, 1903.

Senators.—Augustus O. Bacon; Alexander S. Clay.

Representatives.—Rufus E. Lester; James M. Griggs; Elijah B. Lewis; William C. Adamson; Leonidas F. Livingston; Charles L. Bartlett; John W. Maddox; William M. Howard; Farish C. Tate; William H. Fleming; William G. Brantley.

FIFTY-EIGHTH CONGRESS.—First session from Nov. 9, 1903, to Dec. 7, 1903; second, from Dec. 7, 1903, to April 28, 1904; third, from Dec. 5, 1904, to March 3, 1905

Senators.—Augustus O. Bacon; Alexander S. Clay.

Representatives.—Rufus E. Lester; James M. Griggs; Elijah B. Lewis;

William C. Adamson; Leonidas F. Livingston; Charles L. Bartlett; John W. Maddox; William M. Howard; F. Carter Tate; Thomas W. Hardwick, Washington; William G. Brantley.

FIFTY-NINTH CONGRESS.—First session from Dec. 4, 1905, to June 30, 1906; second, from Dec. 4, 1906, to March 3, 1907.

Senators.—Augustus O. Bacon; Alexander S. Clay.

Representatives.—Rufus E. Lester (died June 16, 1906, and was succeeded by J. W. Overstreet; James M. Griggs; Elijah B. Lewis; William C. Adamson; Leonidas F. Livingston; Charles L. Bartlett; Gordon Lee; William M. Howard; Thomas M. Bell, Gainesville; Thomas W. Hardwick; William G. Brantley.

Governors of Georgia.

COLONIAL:

GEN. JAMES E. OGLETHORPE..1732
WILLIAM STEPHENS (Acting) 1743
HENRY PARKER (Acting)....1751

PROVINCIAL:

JOHN REYNOLDS...........1754
HENRY ELLIS.............1757
JAMES WRIGHT...........1760

PROVISIONAL:

ARCHIBALD BULLOCK, President...................1776
BUTTON GWINNETT, President...................1777

STATE:

JOHN A. TREUTLEN........1777
JOHN HOUSTOUN..........1778
JOHN WEREAT............1778
GEORGE WALTON..........1779
RICHARD HOWLEY.........1780
STEPHEN HEARD..........1781
NATHAN BROWNSON........1781
JOHN MARTIN............1782
LYMAN HALL.............1783
JOHN HOUSTOUN..........1784
SAMUEL ELBERT..........1785
EDWARD TELFAIR.........1786
GEORGE MATTHEWS........1787
GEORGE HANDLY..........1788
GEORGE WALTON..........1789
EDWARD TELFAIR.........1790
GEORGE MATTHEWS........1793
JARED IRWIN............1796
JAMES JACKSON..........1798
DAVID EMANUEL..........1801
JOSIAH TATNALL.........1801
JOHN MILLEDGE..........1802

JARED IRWIN............1806
DAVID B. MITCHELL......1809
PETER EARLY............1813
DAVID B. MITCHELL......1815
WILLIAM RABUN..........1817
MATTHEW TALBOT, President of Senate...........1819
JOHN CLARK.............1819
GEORGE M. TROUP........1823
JOHN FORSYTH...........1827
GEORGE R. GILMER.......1829
WILSON LUMPKIN.........1831
WILLIAM SCHLEY.........1833
GEORGE R. GILMER.......1837
CHARLES J. MCDONALD....1839
GEORGE W. CRAWFORD.....1843
GEORGE W. TOWNS........1847
HOWELL COBB............1851
HERSCHEL V. JOHNSON....1853
JOSEPH E. BROWN........1857
JAMES JOHNSON, Provisional Governor...............1865
CHARLES J. JENKINS.....1865
GEN. T. H. RUGER, U.S.A.,
Military Governor........1868
RUFUS B. BULLOCK.......1868
BENJAMIN CONLEY, President of Senate...........1871
JAMES M. SMITH.........1872
ALFRED H. COLQUITT.....1876
ALEXANDER H. STEPHENS..1882
JAMES S. BOYNTON, President of Senate...........1883
HENRY D. MCDANIEL......1883
JOHN B. GORDON.........1886
WILLIAM J. NORTHEN.....1890
WILLIAM Y. ATKINSON....1894
ALLEN D. CANDLER.......1898
JOSEPH M. TERRELL......1902

Consolidated Index

Prepared by: Staff, Special Collections,
University of Georgia Libraries, Athens.

www.ingramcontent.com/pod-product-compliance
Lightning Source LLC
Chambersburg PA
CBHW031115020426
42333CB00012B/95